Administrative Ethics
in the Twenty-first Century

TEACHING TEXTS IN LAW AND POLITICS

David A. Schultz
General Editor

Vol. 28

PETER LANG
New York • Washington, D.C./Baltimore • Bern
Frankfurt am Main • Berlin • Brussels • Vienna • Oxford

J. MICHAEL MARTINEZ
& WILLIAM D. RICHARDSON

Administrative Ethics
in the Twenty-first Century

PETER LANG
New York • Washington, D.C./Baltimore • Bern
Frankfurt am Main • Berlin • Brussels • Vienna • Oxford

Library of Congress Cataloging-in-Publication Data

Martinez, J. Michael (James Michael)
Administrative ethics in the twenty-first century / J. Michael Martinez,
William D. Richardson.
p. cm. — (Teaching texts in law and politics; vol. 28)
Includes bibliographical references and index.
1. Public administration—Moral and ethical aspects. 2. Political ethics.
3. Law and ethics. I. Richardson, William D. (William Donald) II. Title.
JF1525.E8M37   172'.2—dc22   2006101866
ISBN 978-0-8204-6120-5
ISSN 1083-3447

Bibliographic information published by **Die Deutsche Bibliothek.**
Die Deutsche Bibliothek lists this publication in the "Deutsche
Nationalbibliografie"; detailed bibliographic data is available
on the Internet at http://dnb.ddb.de/.

Cover design by Joni Holst

The paper in this book meets the guidelines for permanence and durability
of the Committee on Production Guidelines for Book Longevity
of the Council of Library Resources.

© 2008 Peter Lang Publishing, Inc., New York
29 Broadway, 18th floor, New York, NY 10006
www.peterlang.com

Printed in the United States of America

To all of our students who, throughout the years, have struggled with the concepts of right conduct, legitimacy, and the principles and practices of public administration.

Contents

Introduction

It is almost always interesting—sometimes even unsettling—to note the ways in which generations are linked across the seeming chasms of time and distance. Our parents and grandparents can still experience visceral and passionate reactions to the mere mention of a now-infamous date, December 7th. Most of them find that it is one of perhaps a handful of key memory markers, a date that is figuratively frozen in time to such an extent that they can tell their listeners exactly what they were doing, wearing, and even thinking when they first heard the events of that day. The remembered facts of the date seldom vary: a slumbering democracy preparing to greet its traditional day of worship was viciously attacked by the massed forces of a totalitarian regime that gave neither warning nor quarter. The details of the devastating world war that America entered thereafter may be colored by the extent of the speaker's participation, sacrifice and personal loss, but the reason for engaging in it are remarkably consistent regardless of who is speaking and the amount of time that has since passed: the beleaguered democracies (America, Britain, France) were forced to defend their "ways of life" against the brutal imperial ambitions of totalitarian regimes (Germany, Japan, Italy) intent on ruling the world. (The alliance of another brutal totalitarian regime, Russia, with the besieged democracies is usually passed over in silence. The basic story doesn't need undue complexity.) The speakers may even be adept at detailing how these democracies, victorious but crippled by the horrendous war, subsequently rebuilt the vanquished dictatorships into the vibrant democracies that we today proudly hail as allies.

When the current generation of American democrats, comfortably enjoying the numerous national and international benefits that accompanied their predecessors' sacrifices of nearly sixty-six years ago, experienced its own infamous attack, the dates of "9/11" and "December 7th" were destined to become thoroughly intertwined. To be sure, 9/11 was distinguished by a number of factors—it involved religiously inspired terrorists rather than a totalitarian nation; the targeting primarily of civilians rather than military forces—but the reaction to it was strikingly similar in several critical ways. Battered but only slightly reeling, the nation's leaders sought ways both to channel and react to the outrage and passion of ordinary Americans. That they subsequently launched a reprisal attack on the Afghanistan Taliban regime that facilitated the attacks is not surprising. The expansion of the "War on Terrorism" to Iraq was certainly less obvious and more controversial, but the rationale for it would have struck the December 7th generations as very familiar: the former "Arsenal of Democracy" was going to conquer its totalitarian foes and transform not just one nation, but, hopefully, a whole region by installing democracy and its benefits to oppressed peoples who had known nothing but self-serving dictatorships and intractable conflicts for generations.

That these goals would resonate with American democrats, who would see them as noble, generous and honorable, is difficult to deny. That they would prove to be so elusive, requiring a commitment of so much blood, treasure, and sacrifice, may be an unwelcome surprise to some current and former architects of the American policies. However, had they been appropriately consulted, neither the December 7th generations nor the philosophical fathers of America would have given encouragement to policy-makers who seemed to think that having right and might on the same side practically assured transformational political change. Instead of enjoying the democratic benefits of greater equality, rights, the rule of law, and legitimate rulers, the peoples of Iraq and, to a lesser extent, Afghanistan, exist in a near-Hobbesian state of nature in which everyday life is "nasty, poor, brutish, and short." Independent of (but in no way isolated from) the fundamental requirement that people first and foremost must be secure in their persons and possessions before other cherished rights can be properly secured, the authors of American policies in Afghanistan and Iraq seemingly failed to understand fully some of the fragile ingredients that make democratic regimes flourish or fail.

Perhaps the current generation of leaders and policy-makers can be excused for such inattention to the critical ingredients for the successful founding of a democracy (especially one to be founded on the ashes of a decidedly non-democratic nation), for the political, cultural, and social successes of America's regime really owe an incalculable debt to the enduring contributions of lamented "greatest generation[s]" which long ago entrusted the maintenance of the nation to their successors. The true original of these "greatest generations" was unquestionably that of the Founders, whose regime-building efforts were premised on a clear-eyed understanding of the character or "ethos" of the citizens and leaders who could reliably be expected to inhabit the new nation. Perhaps we are all too accustomed to the habits, mores and traditions of our own democracy to fully appreciate that their secure possession was not assured at the founding and cannot be assumed for the future. For a democracy to thrive, both rulers and ruled must have a respect—ideally, a deep and abiding reverence—for the supremacy of laws over the transitory whims of men (no matter how powerful or popular such men may appear to be at any given moment). For a regime to long endure, their "law-abidingness" must be suitably reinforced not just by the visible processes and methods of democracy (most of which revolve around the fundamental concept of equality of political rights), but, even more importantly, by far less visible (but perhaps even more vital) "traits" or "qualities" such as tolerance and its tamed companions, moderate passions, that steadfastly resist provocation by differences among strongly contending persons, opinions, and beliefs. Without the wide spread presence of these and other widely held "regime values," contemporary democratic political arrangements cannot credibly accommodate the critical Aristotelian principle of "rule and be ruled in turn." In other words, as policy-makers have learned all too belatedly in nation-building experiments in Iraq and elsewhere, successful democracies require that contending factions accept electoral defeat with resignation (sighs of unhappiness may be permitted, though) and a promise of "Next time." In order for this tolerant attitude to prevail, contenders and their supporters may have a long and difficult journey to reach a point where they believe in nothing too strongly, that is, where they are no longer too passionately attached to the contending persons, beliefs and opinions that are so fearsomely roiling the political, cultural and social battlegrounds of some of our fragile experiments in nation-building.

The contemporary use of sterile terms such as "traits" or "qualities" or "characteristics" to identify certain sine qua nons that enable tolerance to flourish may rightfully strike some observers as awkward or even inaccurate. In many ways, that awkwardness was deliberate, for it is merely the latest manifestation of a fascinating "war of ideas" that can be traced back to a once little-known political philosopher living in an Italian city-state that all too regularly found itself roiled by ambitiously contending persons, beliefs and opinions. Niccolo Machiavelli was a very bold man, and so would appreciate being linked to a bold and even audacious statement: Machiavelli set out to alter the way in which we thought about the ends of politics and, equally important, the means we would be willing to employ to achieve those goals.[1] For our purposes, the ultimate success of his endeavor is partially but most significantly indicated by the way in which public discussion—even mention—of "virtues" and "vices" all but vanished from contemporary American discourse. In their place, a variant of his "virtu"—a term he used to obfuscate the accepted distinctions between "virtue" and "vice"—became the dominant substitute because it was suitably vague. As intended, "values" minimized if not erased the ethical distinctions that, even in a tolerant democracy such as ours, form the essence of a regime. In so doing, it severely undermined a fundamental purpose of politics, namely, the educative role of *public* discussion, debate, and, ultimately, decisions about what actions, words and even thoughts should be praised and blamed. The moral haze that "values" spread over the landscape was but the latest advance in Machiavelli's determined project to promote "relevance" (or, more accurately, "irrelevance") so that there would be no enduring set of elevated, difficult to obtain, absolute standards diverting mankind from confronting earthly life as it really is, rather than as we might fervently wish it to be. The pursuit of this objective was not intended by Machiavelli to end with mankind's choices being seen as little more than mutually equivalent preferences, but such sea changes in "values" are more than capable of sweeping all manner of impediments before them.

The above is not to contend, of course, that all discussion of "virtues" and "vices" disappeared; in a sense, it simply became less visibly a part of public life. Indeed, any regime that could once unapologetically convene an official government body called "The House Un-American Activities Committee" (imagine, if you can, a comparable "Un-French" or "Un-Mexican" or "Un-Spanish" body) probably has a fairly resilient but intuitive understanding of its basic core "values." Unfortunately, recognizing the importance of such values to one's regime is far different from understanding how to transmit them (which, in turn, ignores the more troubling questions of when and even if they should be so transmitted) to a distant people who are markedly different from you in history, culture, traditions, beliefs and mores. For a people to be united into a nation—and for that nation to long endure—it must possess and nurture a particular ethos or character. (It is possible to modify a nation's character—after all, isn't that what the democracies deliberately set out to do when they undertook to transform Germany and Japan from totalitarian to democratic regimes?—but, as we are rediscovering to our sorrow in the Middle East, it is a project requiring extensive external assistance, a sizeable long-term physical presence, and a commitment of decades, not just years.) It is precisely the various combinations of "virtues" and "vices" possessed by a people that collectively distinguish the character of one regime from that of another—and, to a lesser extent, the citizens of the same regime from each other (as Americans are fond of noting when they compare the inhabitants of some regions of the country with their counterparts in others). To the extent that these virtues and vices are deeply ingrained, they constitute important barometers that reveal potentially significant strengths and weaknesses of different regimes.[2] If a regime is united and well governed, the character of its citizens will likely embody the ends for which it was established. A sage observer of our own early years took careful note of this connection between character and ends:

> What do you expect from society and its government? We must be clear about that....[I]f you think it profitable to turn man's intellectual and moral activity toward the necessities of physical life and use them to produce well-being, if you think that reason is more use to men than genius, if your object is not to create heroic virtues but rather tranquil habits, if you would rather contemplate vices than crimes and prefer fewer transgressions at the cost of fewer splendid deeds, if in place of a brilliant society you are content to live in one that is prosperous, and finally, if in your view the main object of government is not to achieve the greatest strength or glory for the nation as a whole but to provide for every individual therein the utmost well-being, protecting him as far as possible from all afflictions, then it is good to make conditions equal and to establish a democratic government.[3]

In comparison to the bold ends of some regimes that are known to us through history (for example, Athens and, to a lesser extent, Sparta), the ends of a contemporary democratic regime appear lower, more probable of being attained, and one more indication that Machiavelli's project of earthly realism has largely succeeded. Precisely because those ends are, so to speak, more visible and attainable in the eyes of the citizenry, the degree to which the latter's character is compatible with them is more apparent. At the same time, the citizenry's character is in some ways more easily affected—positively and negatively—by the extent to which the actions and, yes, the words of the regime's leaders advance or retard movement toward the low-hanging ends. In a nation famously premised on a foundation that nurtures an "equality of conditions," the citizenry is proud of its attendant individualism—one aspect of which is a solid attachment to one's private affairs and a concomitant distaste for those of the public sector.[4] When that public sector inevitably encroaches on the private sphere as the regime experiences steady growth in population and wealth—and the government becomes correspondingly large and complex—opportunities multiply for the citizenry to question both the substance and the process by which that public sector attempts to impose its will. In the words of Herbert Storing, these occasions invariably give rise to a critical implicit or explicit question by the democratic citizens, to wit, "Who says?"[5] Who says I have to obey you? In this equality-of-conditions nation where the leaders make a conspicuous show of their citizen origins, who gave *you* the authority to tell me what to do? The question is understandable, for it is really about the very legitimacy of the political power that some wield over others.

At the time of America's founding, there was only one principal way (or perhaps one direct and one indirect way) in which rulers justified their possession of enormous political powers. Divine Right famously contended that the ruler was either selected by God or descended from the loins of someone so selected. Even if you were so bold as to challenge such a ruler, how would you meet the claim that God had anointed him?[6] The American founders, the intellectual descendants of a this-world orientation that stretched from Machiavelli through Hobbes to Locke, deliberately grounded the claim to rule in a highly visible principle: majoritarian election. Understanding that "man as he was" meant that the members of the new regime could reliably be counted on to pursue their own base self interests if the opportunity presented itself, the Founders divided and separated the political powers into different levels of government, each with their own respective branches that might not always be inclined to cooperate with their counterparts. The portion of that power wielded by most of the rulers most of the time was derived from the innate executive, legislative and judicial powers that each and every member of the regime would have exercised in a theoretical "state of nature" prior to the decision to seek the greater predictability and benefits of a civil society. Such rulers are chosen not by God but elected by the majority of its members for defined terms of office. It is this election that conveys legitimacy to the rulers' use of whatever political powers attend their offices, that is, the latent or dormant executive, legislative or judicial powers of the citizens are temporarily conveyed to the elected rulers with the fundamental caveat that those powers are to be used for the benefit of the ruled, not the rulers. The elected officials may occasionally err in how or why they use those powers, but there is no mistaking where such powers came from, namely, directly from the citizens via an election. If the citizens consider the powers to have been poorly used for their benefit, the remedy is also close at hand: choose someone more qualified to wield them at the next regular election.

The visible means by which these democratic rulers receive the political powers entrusted to them and the origin of such powers in each and every member of the regime make for a mighty solid foundation of legitimacy. If elected officials were then responsible for formulating, executing, and judging the application of every law and regulation, the answer to the challenge of "Who says I have to obey you?" would be crystal-clear: You do. But, alas, the burden of ruling a 220 year-old democratic republic with 301,139,947 current members means that ministering to the regime's multitude of complex domestic and international problems has necessitated the development of a correspondingly large body of executive branch "assistants."[7] These executive branch employees, who far and away outnumber the elected rulers, provide the critical expertise that permits the ever more numerous citizens to enjoy the benefits of the regime to which they gave up the exercise of their innate political powers. Indeed, the complexity of both the citizens' problems and the government entities tasked with resolving them is so great that no law or regulation can realistically be expected to encompass every combination of circumstances that the citizenry would face. Accordingly, in order to make the glove of the law fit the hand of the citizenry, the unelected executive branch assistants must exercise a portion of political power that is delegated to them by both elected legislators and executives. We refer to this delegated political power as "discretion," but do so in less than bold voices, for we recognize that those who wield it have but a halting and barely audible answer to the question of "Who says...?" Under these circumstances, the character or "ethics" of the assistants who wield this discretionary political power is of vital importance, for it can provide one means of reassuring the citizenry that such powers are being used in appropriate ways. Because this is a democratic republic, special attention is focused on those traits, values or, more precisely, "virtues" that are most compatible with such a regime. The current text is intended to address the ways in which ethics, understood as those virtues that make one's character distinctive, affect the vital work that these assistants—who will henceforth be more precisely identified as "public administrators" or "bureaucrats"—perform in the service of this nation. In its intended role as a supplement to introductory texts on public administration, this work asks readers to think through the implications of the concepts discussed by contemplating a series of questions and case studies at the end of each chapter.

Accordingly, Chapter 1 provides a general overview of the origins and place of ethics within the Western philosophical tradition. The journey takes us from Plato and Aristotle, through Aquinas and the ever-bold Machiavelli, to John Rawls via Hobbes, Locke, Hume, Kant and Mill. The intent is not to make the readers expertly versed in any one of these leading theorists, but to invite them to join the conversation between and among these authors in so far as it pertains to the subject of ethics in a democratic republic. This conversation flows almost seamlessly into the subject matter of Chapter 2, which addresses the development of the administrative state in the twentieth century and the resultant search for plausible explanations as to why public administrators should be entrusted with the political powers inherent in the use of discretion to implement laws and regulation. As discussed above, the critical concept is that of "legitimacy," that is, how secure and appropriate are these delegated powers in a nation that essentially recognizes only one answer to the "Who says?" question: majority approval through elections?

The treatment of discretion readily takes us to the topic of Chapter 3, which explores more fulsomely some of the political powers that attend the use of administrative discretion, the ways in which they are used to benefit the diverse circumstances of the nation's citizens, and the internal and external constraints on misusing them. Chapter 4 addresses some of the models of decision-making that can assist an ethical public administrator—and the citizens affected by an agency's actions—in assessing whether an exercise of discretion is appropriate or not. Particular attention is given to the rational-comprehensive, incremental, and flow-of-work models of decision-making, after which we discuss the external restraints imposed on such decisions by law and the internal ones posed by ethical considerations.

The decisions made by an administrator are still further influenced by the peculiar dynamics imposed by the large organizations that have come to characterize the contemporary administrative state. Appropriately, Chapter 5 treats the ways in which various organizational structures affect behavior—especially in regards to ethical conduct. The survey stops at some familiar way stations— Wilson, Weber, Taylor, Goodnow, White, Gulick—as it explains the theoretical debts owed to the various schools of thought that have periodically dominated the ways in which we have looked at organizational behavior and how such schools in turn have accommodated the political, economic, psychological, sociological, and ethical pressures influencing decision-making by public administrators.

As if we needed reminding, Chapter 6 emphasizes that decision-making by public administrators in this complex democratic republic also occurs within the constraining embrace of law. Constitutional provisions, statutes seeking to delegate broad legislative or executive political powers to the discretion of administrators who will be implementing a given law, regulations promulgated as a result of such delegations, and, most visibly, the actions taken by public administrators as they apply a broad law to a specific citizen can all find themselves scrutinized by one or more parts of the judiciary. Such scrutiny is intended to be an external check on the exercise of administrative discretion and, as such, understanding its applicable decisions should be a fundamental part of the preparations an ethical public administrator makes for properly carrying out his or her responsibilities.

The subdued response of public administrators to the fundamental "Who says?" challenge to their exercise of discretion has consequences for the very stability of public service itself. Chapter 7 examines how the issue of legitimacy has affected the theories and practices of public personnel management over time. The survey ranges from the Founders' view of public service as an obligatory noblesse oblige for those who had been blessed with many advantages, through the Jacksonian emphasis on patronage (which answered the "Who says?" question in a deep baritone voice, saying "My boss, whom you elected"), to the contemporary reliance on the seemingly demonstrable intellectual superiority of the early merit system, and on to the unraveling of support for PACE, and finally on to the growing presence of collective bargaining in public employment.

The distribution of benefits that public administrators are supposed to facilitate is the subject of Chapter 8, which explores the fundamental problem of how scarce resources can be more equitably and efficiently distributed. The discussion traces the various ways in which the government historically has attempted to raise revenues, differing theories about how public expenditures affect the domestic economy (along with the issues as to whether they should or can be so used), the ways in which public budgets have been devised, some recent attempts to control them, and the role the ethical public administrator should play when using budgetary discretion.

While the fit between the individual ethics of any given bureaucrat and the general mission of his or her agency may be less than perfect, it is fair to say that a great many career administrators are attracted to public service because they agree with what their particular agencies are attempting to accomplish. An individual may spend a whole career in a state Family and Children Services agency because of a concern—maybe even a passionate one—about helping troubled youngsters to become productive citizens.

Similarly, a career in the Parks Service may have begun because of one's dedication to preserving the unique natural beauty of our federal parks. Chapter 9 takes a careful look at the formulation and implementation of public policies that may inspire such dedication to an agency. To a greater or lesser extent, a public policy comes into being through a process that must respond to political, economic, and oftentimes ideological pressures that ultimately affect how efficiently it uses public expenditures and how equitably it distributes any benefits. If a policy has been formulated and implemented in accord with an agency's mission and goals, the ethical public administrator has the difficult task of accurately determining if the policy is not only attaining its stated goals, but that its success is not the result of chance or some other unidentified variable. After grappling with issues of causation, the ethical public administrator is undoubtedly ready for the retrospective review of how the practice of ethics came to this focus on public policies. In providing that, Chapter 10 contends that the contemporary dilemma has to do with how effectively an administrator is able to link the responsibilities imposed by his individual character with the demands of the organizational model in which he must operate. Both that character and the organization exert pressures on the decision-making process, and the ethical public administrator must conscientiously strive to see how his actions in the service of this democratic republic are a reflection of those influences.

* * *

The authors gratefully acknowledge the assistance provided by two excellent University of South Dakota MPA students, Dan Palmer and Svien Senne, who dutifully undertook the tedious but vitally important task of verifying the accuracy of quotations and citations. Research assistance in the early stages of the manuscript was also ably provided by Siri Buller and Drake Olson. Sandi Harper was invaluable in coordinating the various tasks associated with having authors working a thousand miles apart. We also wish to express our appreciation to the editor of this series, David Schultz of the Hamline University Graduate School of Management, and Sophie Appel, our Production Supervisor at Peter Lang USA, whose enormous individual and collective patience with the plodding pace of our writing would surely qualify them for "Moral Exemplar" awards if only the authors could ever get around to writing the nominations.

Notes

[1]   Even a truncated discussion of Machiavelli's project is considerably beyond the scope of this book. Interested readers could profitably commence their attempt to understand it by attending to Niccolo Machiavelli, *The Prince*, ed. L. S. P. Alvarez (Prospect Heights, Ill.: Waveland Press, 1989), and Leo Strauss, "Niccolo Machiavelli," in *History of Political Philosophy*, 2 ed., ed. Leo Strauss and Joseph Cropsey (Chicago, Ill.: The University of Chicago Press, 1981), 271-292. Carolina Academic Press granted permission for the authors to use a small revised segment of their earlier introductory section on Machiavelli that appeared in William D. Richardson, J. Michael Martinez, and Kerry R. Stewart, Eds., *Ethics and Character: The Pursuit of Democratic Virtues* (Durham, N.C.: Carolina Academic Press, 1998).

[2]   During a recent visit to the Parliamentary Monarchy of Spain—which replaced the rigid authoritarian regime of Franco in 1978—one of the authors was struck by the concerted efforts to eradicate the much beloved afternoon "siesta" to improve the population's work ethic and assist the efforts to be more productive within the new marketplace of the EU. Needless to say, these efforts severely affected everything from the working hours of commercial establishments to the traditional late-night life-styles of the urban citizens.

[3]   Alexis de Tocqueville, *Democracy in America*, ed. J. P. Mayer (Garden City, N.Y.: Anchor Books, 1969), 243.

[4]   Alexis de Tocqueville, *Democracy in America*, 503-27.

[5]   Herbert J. Storing, "American Statesmanship: Old and New," in *Bureaucrats, Policy Analysts, Statesmen: Who Leads?* Robert A. Goldwin, ed. (Washington, D.C.: The American Enterprise Institute, 1980), 88-113.

[6]   In recent memory, the Ayatollah Khomeini rode to power in Iran on the claim that he was the anointed spokesman for Allah and so destined to rule. Cf. George W. Braswell, Jr., "Iran and Islam," *Theology Today* 36 (January 1980): 532.

According to 2006 and 2005 Census estimates, there are a minimum of 16,135,699 state and local government employees in addition to the 2,720,462 civilian employees of the federal government.

PART ONE:
BACKGROUND

Chapter One
Ethical Theory in the Western Intellectual Tradition

Ethics, or "right conduct," is a topic of enormous significance for persons faced with making choices where clear-cut answers do not exist. In the public sector, the effect of making ethical choices assumes special significance owing to the large-scale consequences of decisions affecting the populace. Yet the topic of "ethics" is broad and diverse, even when limited to the field of public administration. Indeed, to understand the evolution of public administration ethics, one must first understand the broader concept of "ethics" as a field of study.

Virtually everyone professes support for ethical behavior, but defining ethics and applying the definition in concrete situations is challenging. The concept itself is open to conflicting interpretations. Moreover, even when the meaning of ethics is more or less uncontested, applying ethical precepts to day-to-day behavior remains problematic because of the many different circumstances and nuances that individuals face in their daily lives. To understand how public administrators can behave in an ethical manner, therefore, it is necessary to begin with a discussion of ethics as the concept has developed over time in the western intellectual tradition.

Law versus Ethics

The search for standards of "right conduct" has been an integral part of the western intellectual tradition for more than twenty-five centuries. "Law" is a concept developed by governments to ensure that citizens engage in "right conduct" as that term is defined by the nation-state. Legal standards are enforced through the coercive power of the nation-state backed with sanctions for violations of known and knowable rules of behavior. Thus, contract law focuses on the minimum requirements for developing a legally-enforceable agreement among individual parties living within a regime. Tort law is designed to spell out which party among multiple ones is liable for damages occasioned by acts deemed negligent or intentional. Criminal law is premised on the need for prohibitions to ensure that one citizen does not harm another one on pain of punishment set forth in a series of clearly defined sanctions. In short, the western legal system is grounded on public rules, known and knowable beforehand, governing the manner in which persons within a regime act in conducting public transactions.[1]

Law is universal; it applies to everyone within the regime equally, at least in theory if not always in practice. As the great jurist William Blackstone wrote, law is the result of society's contractual obligation to citizens "in exchange for which every individual has resigned a part of his natural liberty."[2] Thomas Hobbes defined law as a creature of the "sovereign"—his term for the nation-state—"to every subject those rules which the commonwealth has commanded him, by word, writing, or other sufficient sign of the will, to make use of for the distinction of right and wrong...."[3] Hobbes's philosophical successor, John Locke, contended that law is formed "in Assemblies empowered to act by positive Laws, where no number is set by that positive Law which empowers them, the act of the Majority passes for the act of the whole...."[4]

In each of these definitions of "law" as a measure of right conduct, the public nature of the rules is an essential ingredient. The great virtue of legal rules promulgated by authoritative governmental entities—the essential element in "positivist" law—is their well-defined, explicated characteristics. If the search for measures of right conduct were to end there, the law would have to suffice as the full measure of correct human behavior; no further inquiries would be necessary or desirable. Yet human beings have always insisted that matters existing outside the public realm require a separate concept of "right conduct." The concept of "ethics" as involving purely private concerns distinguishes an individual's *particular* code of conduct from a nation-state's *universal* and enforceable rules of right conduct.

In a 1981 article, commentator Mark Lilla characterized ethics as something more than merely "an abstract justification for actions or a series of propositions that can be applied with legal precision to fact situations that arise. A system of ethics—an ethos—is something that is lived and practiced." According to Lilla, an individual's sense of ethics is "anthropological...a way of learning virtue which is time-tested and subtly complex," developed through a life-long association with families, churches, peers, and schools.[5] In contrast to the clearly-defined characteristics of positivist law designed to cover analogous factual situations, a system of ethics envisions the particular, context-specific problems that confront individuals in their daily lives outside of the public realm. Another commentator has observed that, while "moral decisions are value-based decisions that are content- and context-specific, legal decisions are just the opposite: procedure-based decisions that are dependent upon historical precedent." In other words, law seeks to resolve a specific issue and provide a more-or-less universal guideline for how similar issues should be resolved in the future. "Generally, a law is born as a response to a peculiar (atypical) behavior that exceeds the bounds of social acceptability, even where those bounds might not be representative of the society as a whole. Thus, the specific exception gives rise to the general rule, which thereafter provides the basis for countering comparable exceptions." The law seeks to codify an acceptable standard of behavior; in the meantime, an ethical system provides tools for analyzing a dilemma and leaves it to the discretion of the individual to grapple with a specific issue.[6]

The table below summarizes the differences between law and ethics. Notice that this conception of ethics depends on a distinction between principles and rules. The former are general ideas about how humans should behave. Homilies such as "human life is precious" and "a person should honor his promises" are the principles by which many societies profess to live. As general mission statements, they hold value, but as tools for resolving particular disputes they are vague. Human life may be precious, but upon occasion an individual may be called to self-defense. The principle does little to assist in plotting an appropriate course of action in specific situations. A legal rule stating the requirements of self-defense and outlining the consequences thereof provides the specificity necessary to act in accordance with accepted norms of behavior within the community and the nation-state.

Distinguishing Law and Ethics

Law	Ethics
Positivist Law— right conduct based on established rules	Ethical System— right conduct based on principles
Rules known and knowable beforehand; codified	Heuristic; not necessarily codified
Authoritative institutions resolve practical issues	Individuals use conscience to resolve dilemmas
Coercive; state sanctions enforce rules	Coercion and sanctions optional

The distinction between law and ethics is relatively clear when the two concepts are examined side-by-side, but such comparisons explain few of the reasons why ethical theory has been so important to western thinkers and why ethics developed as a field of study apart from the law. The ancient Greeks began the search for ethical standards by positing a framework where "right" and "wrong" were meaningful, absolute distinctions that could be identified and adhered to by persons who possessed the requisite character leading to virtue. Enlightenment and post-Enlightenment philosophers such as Hobbes, Locke, Hume, Kant, and the English Utilitarians—all of whom are the quintessential ethical theorists of the western tradition—modified the Greek understanding, thereby affecting societal behavior in the modern world. Recent claims that philosophy is dead and few, if any, absolute standards exist have not moved beyond the field of ethics; they are an interpretation of ethics. Thus, even twentieth-century postmodern thinkers, despite inconsistencies arising from limitations inherent in their relativism, have embraced implicit assumptions about what constitutes right conduct.

Ethical Theory in Historical Context

For the ancient Greeks, character was the cornerstone of ethics. The term "character" generally referred to the combination of qualities and attributes that comprise the personality of an individual. A person exhibited good character when he or she acted in ways that reflected virtue (excellence), that is, when an individual tried to become a fully actualized human being by engaging in right conduct in accordance with absolute, recognizable standards.[7] Because the western understanding of what constitutes virtue and what makes someone an individual of good character has varied throughout history, this definition falls short when one moves beyond the ancient Greek perspective.

Plato is the starting point for understanding the ancient Greeks.[8] He observed the Sophists, a group of wandering teachers who instructed students in a variety of popular subjects, and expressed concern over their conception of virtue, which they argued was little more than mastering techniques of oratory and debating skills. The time-honored qualities of courage, wisdom, loyalty, personal honor, moderation, and justice were not important.[9] The Sophists' perspectives were well-suited to a democratic political system where pluralism was a prized value, but Plato was disturbed by their relativism. If acting virtuously involved little more than mastering and applying a series of techniques that caused a person to appear to be "good," the concept of virtue was not an immutable characteristic. It depended on the time and place in which it was practiced. Sophistry was a base education, a chimera, a false front that constantly changed as tastes and appetites changed.[10]

Plato opposed the Sophists by developing a theory of "forms," or blueprints for the world of appearance. The "forms" were a series of unseen, nonphysical, nonspatial, and nontemporal "urstuff" that served as the foundation for all matter.[11] Plato viewed the forms as the unchanging, eternal, objective blueprints that underlay everything. Without the generality allowed by the existence of an underlying, invisible urstuff, the particularity of the world encountered by mankind through his senses could not exist.[12]

More to the point, without the forms, the universe would not be an orderly, coherent place. With the forms, a universal construct existed for the particularity of the world, whether the thing was concrete and physical, like a horse, or an abstract concept such as justice, love, or ethics. A key feature of the forms was that virtue was grounded as an absolute value. The form of the "good" was an unchanging concept that applied to all human beings any time, any place, anywhere. An absolute value of the "good" allowed a person to say with conviction that one act was superior to another act. This was far removed from the ethics of the Sophists, who taught that concepts such as "good," "bad," "right," or "wrong" depended on the time, place, and circumstances of the act. The nineteenth-century philosopher Friedrich Nietzsche would later criticize Plato, the "great dogmatist," for conjuring up a theoretical construct and positing it as real, but the forms provided the basis for undermining the relativism of the Sophists.[13]

The existence of immutable qualities allowed for the possibility of absolute or formal knowledge, which was valuable in grounding ethics in a universal standard of conduct. Although it could never be fully attained, a person could come as close as possible to acquiring absolute knowledge by relying on experiential knowledge acquired through day-to-day living coupled with reflection and a proper education. The quest to attain absolute knowledge (the "good") was the goal of all men of good character—or "well-ordered souls," in Plato's parlance—and it was the goal of the well-ordered regime. A man of good character led an orderly life with other well-educated, like-minded individuals in a community that reflected the characteristics of its citizens. Plato was a prolific writer, and in his major works he repeatedly explored the form of the good as well as the connection between virtue and character.[14]

Many attributes contribute to the good life, depending on the abilities and interests of the people seeking the good. According to Plato, the attributes include courage,[15] friendship,[16] honor,[17] justice,[18] and wisdom.[19] Persons who naturally possess greater abilities must assist the less fortunate in realizing virtues such as responsibility, self-discipline, and courage. In this philosophy, only persons with superior abilities—"souls of gold"—were fit to be rulers (philosopher-kings), while other persons who lacked abilities to govern themselves without assistance from a philosopher-king were either auxiliaries (souls of silver) or workers (souls of bronze).[20]

Plato's dialogue "Gorgias" argues that a person must first rule himself before he is fit to rule a polis or city-state.[21] Using the analogy of a leaking vessel, he writes that some persons have souls, like sieves, that will never be filled because such persons are intemperate and undisciplined with insatiable appetites. The philosopher-king has developed the self-discipline necessary to control his appetite and discern what is good for himself as an individual and what is good for the polis. In short, the philosopher-king possesses an ordered soul that is just and temperate. He can live a virtuous life without being enslaved by his appetites, which makes him exactly the ruler to assist those who do not exhibit a similar measure of self-control. This recognition is the first step in developing a system of ethics for the individual and a political hierarchy for the polis. The most virtuous, disciplined, temperate man in the polis is the ethical man. Owing to his ability to live a good life, he can legitimately lead others. Plato's republic, a "city in speech," can therefore be characterized as a meritocracy where the most virtuous persons rule because they possess superior abilities and wisdom; a man of good character is also a man of good intellect. Ethics and polis are inextricably intertwined.[22]

As compelling as the theory of forms was as an explanation for the immutable qualities of right and wrong, the nature of the concept was never clear. Plato's most famous student, Aristotle, shouldered the burden of further explicating ethical concepts in his most influential work on ethical theory, *The Nicomachean Ethics*.[23] Some scholars contend that *The Nicomachean Ethics* "is the greatest work ever written on practical philosophy."[24] Unlike Plato, Aristotle argued that ethical standards are not purely questions of interiority. He established a tradition of seeking the intermediate position, that is, the mean between two extremes.[25] Moderation is the core concept required to practice right conduct.[26]

The Nicomachean Ethics discounted Plato's theory of forms.[27] At the outset, Aristotle contends that the notion of a "Good" is plural, not singular. Moreover, "Goods" are valuable because they create the conditions for man's happiness (*eudaimonia*), as opposed to an overarching "Good" that is intrinsically valuable, as Plato had argued.[28] Always the scientist, Aristotle categorizes happiness according to the types of people who seek to be happy. The masses link happiness to sensual pleasure while men of affairs identify happiness with honor. A person interested in commerce views wealth as a source of happiness. Whatever its source, happiness does not exist absent the virtues. Any study of the behavior of men must be rooted in an understanding of the virtues and their relationship to happiness.[29] Aristotle suggests that virtues, or qualities of excellence, are divided into two categories. The "ethical" virtues occupy one category, while the "intellectual" virtues occupy the second. Much of *The Nicomachean Ethics* is devoted to discussing the ethical virtues as the mid-point—the mean—between extreme qualities.[30]

The Nicomachean Ethics goes far beyond Plato's work to explain how ethical precepts can become part of human life on a daily basis. By eschewing Plato's emphasis on the other-worldly, ethereal character of ethics, Aristotle makes ethics "real-world," a practical approach to problem-solving.[31] Yet even he cannot fully explain how ethical and intellectual virtues are related. He suggests that man's will is rationally guided by desire and controlled through a proper education in ethical virtues. The question of whether, or to what extent, man exercises free will or is driven by his nature to act in certain ways was left for later philosophers to consider. This lack of precision makes Aristotle's understanding of character difficult to grasp, albeit a few general conclusions can be drawn.

Aristotle argues that all human beings possess an *ergon*, or a characteristic "work." A person of good character is someone who performs his work well, in accordance with the excellences befitting the work. Over time, patterns of work develop into habits, which then lead to excellence. Eventually, as workers grow to maturity, their habits become solidified as character traits. Good character traits ensure that adults will strive to do the best work possible. For Aristotle, a well-ordered life where people always strive for excellence in their endeavors leads to happiness. Good character leads to a good, happy, fulfilling life.[32]

After Aristotle died in 322 BCE, a variety of philosophical systems arose—Skepticism, Stoicism, Epicureanism, and Neoplatonism—but none offered the same detailed, richly nuanced perspective on ethics found in ancient Greek thought. For more than a thousand years, as religion and mysticism became intertwined with philosophy, western philosophers and theologians, who often were one and the same, rarely distinguished between philosophy and theology in their works. Ethical precepts were a part of these systems, but they did not garner attention as separate areas of inquiry.[33]

Christian thought was important in the history of western ethics because it presented an alternative to the anthropocentric focus of Athenian philosophy. The ancient Greek philosophy established the standards for applying a rational approach to problems and Christianity shifted the focus to God and His perfection. Faith became a paramount concern for the Christian, while reason was the most important tool for Athens. Christian thinkers struggled to find a way for man to return to the transcendent creator who had created the universe.[34]

The chasm between the rationality of Greece and the faith of Christianity was perhaps best illustrated by Tertullian, a second-century jurist-turned-theologian who wrote, "What indeed has Athens to do with Jerusalem? Away with all attempts to produce a Stoic, Platonic, and dialectical Christianity."[35] Tertullian and other early Christians believed that the Athenian philosophical tradition represented a threat to religious faith. They contended that theology was superior to philosophy not despite its logical inconsistencies, but precisely *because* of them. Reflecting on Christ's resurrection, for example, Tertullian is reputed to have insisted that "the fact is certain, because it is impossible."[36]

During the Medieval period, the faith-reason debate only grew in power and intensity. Peter Abelard, a twelfth-century thinker, and, later, St. Thomas Aquinas wrestled with this chasm. Both men insisted that, Tertullian notwithstanding, rationality need not be divorced from a Christian life. Aquinas was especially interested in reconciling the tradition of Athens (reason) with the tradition of Jerusalem (faith) in his great works, *Summa Theologica* and *Summa Contra Gentiles.*[37]

Aquinas argued that Aristotle had correctly surmised that happiness is the ultimate goal for human beings, but the ancient Greek philosopher failed to appreciate that man has a higher purpose than his life on earth. The "natural" ethical virtues of self-actualization are supplemented by "theological" virtues. Natural virtues can be attained through proper training and practical reason, but theological virtues such as faith, hope, and love require divine grace. Eternal beatitude can be achieved only through the church and its sacraments. In articulating a philosophy that allowed for the coexistence of both religion and natural science, Aquinas became the towering figure of medieval philosophy, serving as a bridge between the Hellenistic and Roman ethics of the ancient world and the ethics of the Enlightenment.[38]

The Medieval period ended in the sixteenth and seventeenth centuries with the evolution of feudalism and the decline of the church as a religious, ethical and political power after the Reformation, the Copernican and Galilean revolutions in science, and the ascent of secular governments. Rapid social transformations triggered a crisis in philosophy. If the old rules of living no longer applied and "science" would solve mankind's problems, what did it mean to live an "ethical" life?[39] The Italian thinker Niccolo Machiavelli especially marks a turning point with *The Prince*, a work that focuses on the practical questions necessary to sustain a ruler. Machiavelli views society as an artificial construction allowing individuals to satisfy their base desires with minimal civil strife. He believes that questions about how people *ought* to behave are secondary to considerations about how people in fact behave. Instead of spending time ruminating on ideal behavior, Machiavelli suggests that philosophers set forth precepts on how men behave in order to achieve their goals. This perspective is far removed from the ancient Greeks' desire to establish rules for ideal behavior or the Christian church's emphasis on pleasing God. The ethical man is the man who understands that expediency is paramount. If it works, do it.[40]

Thomas Hobbes, a seventeenth-century English philosopher, builds on Machiavelli's foundation when he emphasizes practical matters in lieu of esoteric metaphysical theories. Hobbes lived in an age of enormous political instability. Therefore, in his works he rejects the theoretical suppositions of the ancients and focuses on the overarching need for self-preservation. In constructing his argument in favor of a stable political unit, Hobbes conceives of man as material subject to various scientific principles. According to this view, an ethical theory must be based on the scientific, mechanistic principles of nature and a psychology of human behavior.[41]

Mankind invariably strives to create the conditions necessary to preserve peace and social harmony or else aggressively seeks to dominate others to avoid being dominated. In his masterwork, *Leviathan*, Hobbes cites these insights as "fundamental laws of nature."[42] The desire for social harmony applies in a civil society, while the impulse toward aggression occurs in a "state of nature." Man living in a state of nature is crude and animalistic; he is subject to natural conditions of war.[43] Hobbes observes in a famous passage that human life in a state of nature consists of "continual fear and danger of violent death," which means that "the life of man [is] solitary, poor, nasty, brutish, and short."[44] To insulate themselves from the natural condition of war, men voluntarily forfeit a portion of their natural liberty in exchange for a measure of security. They do this by creating a covenant with each other to establish a commonwealth, or a civil government, which enforces the law through the power of a new entity called the "sovereign."[45]

Hobbes's positivist outlook ensures that moral virtue requires obedience to the laws and customs promulgated by the sovereign. He does not distinguish between law and ethics; they are essentially the same concept. "For moral philosophy is nothing else but the science of what is *good* and *evil* in the conversation and society of mankind," he observed.[46]

Hobbes's materialistic view of mankind fails to explain how man can act as a free, rational, independent causal agent if he is only the sum and substance of his materiality. If man's behavior is attributable solely to physical laws, he cannot be held morally responsible for actions he is compelled to undertake owing to his material needs and limitations.

Voluntary motion, Hobbes argues, is "endeavor," which consists of "appetite" or "aversion."[47] Voluntary actions are the result of a mechanical movement toward pleasure and away from displeasure while pleasure is only a physical reaction to stimuli.[48] Hobbes's work creates difficult philosophical problems because it posits that morally neutral mechanical processes are the focus of natural philosophy, and ethical theory is a subjective series of rules created by man to govern behavior. This represents a resurgence of the controversy between the external world (*phusis*) and the internal world (*nomos*) that has plagued philosophy since the days of the ancients.[49]

Hobbes overcomes many of the metaphysical problems presented by earlier philosophers by insisting on rational discourse as the hard currency of philosophical inquiry. He retreats from the increasingly theoretical, anthropomorphic view of man that was prevalent in his era.[50] Moreover, he brings philosophy back to the practical issues facing man.[51]

Building on Hobbes's work, the English philosopher John Locke sets out to demonstrate "moral knowledge is as capable of real certainty as mathematics."[52] Locke argues for the necessity of combining experience (*a posteriori* knowledge) and reflection (*a prior* i knowledge), which leads him to distinguish between "speculative" and "practical" epistemological principles. Speculative knowledge is independent of action, while practical knowledge, including ethics, is useful insofar as it is acted upon in the course of daily life.[53] Locke believes that virtue is necessary if a human being is to be actualized. Moral virtue requires man to conform to custom and law, although Locke breaks from Hobbes by distinguishing between positive law promulgated by an authoritative governmental body and natural law or natural rights. The latter are higher than the former because God grants natural rights to human beings and they precede rights bestowed on individuals by governments.[54]

Unlike Hobbes, Locke views man's natural condition not as a state of constant war or a search for self-preservation, but as an "ill condition" that is difficult for man because the circumstances are so primitive. To escape from this ill condition, people covenant with each other to establish a civil society. A civil society provides an effective mechanism for resolving disputes and allowing human beings to use their reason to overcome the harshness of natural conditions. Ethical behavior requires citizens of the civil society to follow the rules of the society unless, in egregious situations, the rules promulgated by government are oppressive. Hobbes argues that even unjust laws and rules must be obeyed, but Locke allows for disobedience and even revolution as a last resort.[55]

Living half a century after Locke, the Scottish philosopher David Hume has been labeled the "great skeptic" and "a thoroughgoing critic of human reason" for his ruthless materialism and his rejection of metaphysical explanations for experiential phenomena.[56] According to Hume, skepticism is the only logical response for man owing to the "narrow capacity of human understanding" in considering questions that go beyond his sense perception.[57] Because man cannot objectively know metaphysical concepts with any reasonable degree of certainty, Hume argues, he cannot trust those concepts to guide human life. Other than mathematics and "experimental reasoning concerning matter of fact and existence," everything else is "sophistry and illusion" and must be "committed to the flames."[58]

Hume is willing to recognize concepts such as "good" and "bad," "right" and "wrong," but he values them because they serve as the basis for a well-ordered society. "The inner and outer aspects of human life are unified in morality," he observes.[59] He suggests that the rules governing human behavior must be grounded in something other than universal standards of conduct because such standards do not exist. It naturally follows that ethical decisions cannot be understood except insofar as they serve man's purposes: A thing is "good" if it serves man's purposes and "bad" if it does not. Ethical precepts are not absolute rules applicable in the same manner throughout time. Standards change as their utility changes. What might have been useful for the ancient Greeks is not necessarily useful or agreeable for modern man. A code of conduct must be adapted to its time and place.

Base utilitarian calculation alone is necessary, but insufficient, to ground ethics. Feeling, or taste, is necessary because rational knowledge alone cannot allow a person to assign moral blame or approbation. Therefore, utility and feeling together allow people to make ethical judgments.[60] If men were not naturally benevolent—if they did not exhibit sympathy—they would not make ethical judgments because they would have no interest in making such judgments or in behaving ethically. Thus, moral virtue is similar to the artificial quality of justice.[61] Hume's view of ethics can be thought of as a philosophy of "modified self-interest and a confined benevolence."[62]

His refusal to embrace metaphysics does not prevent Hume from identifying qualities that underlie man's natural benevolence and contribute to character development. He identifies four qualities of virtue. First, some qualities, such as justice, generosity, beneficence, and honesty, are useful to everyone. Other qualities, including prudence, frugality, industry, and temperance, are useful primarily to the person who possesses them. A third category of qualities—which includes modesty, wit and decency—are agreeable to other people. Self-esteem, love of glory, and magnanimity are agreeable to the person possessing those qualities.[63]

Hume's philosophy of ethics contains the same deficiencies that all utilitarian-based ethical systems face. If the utility of the philosophy determines its value, the standards are not absolute. It is difficult to establish guidelines for behavior because the standards constantly change over time. One commentator highlights the shortcomings of this approach:

> With all respect to David Hume, the fact that a trait is generally useful and agreeable to the possessor and to others is not sufficient to make it a virtue. Amiability, cleanliness, and wit are beneficial in these ways, but these traits do not tend to make one a good person. In order for a trait to be a virtue, it must tend to foster good human life in extensive and fundamental ways. It must be the perfection of a tendency or capacity that connects

and interlocks with a variety of human goods in such a way that its removal from our lives would endanger the whole structure.[64]

Immanuel Kant recognizes this inherent difficulty in Hume when he seeks to reconcile Christian religious beliefs with the intellectual state of western culture. In arguing that human beings are obligated to develop their natural capacity for rational thought and translate it into rational, autonomous and moral action, Kant sets the stage for nineteenth-century ethics and philosophy.[65] He writes that he was awakened from his "dogmatic slumbers" by Hume's skepticism. Kant is disturbed by Hume's characterization of morals as a matter of opinion. The logical implications of Hume's "hypothetical imperative," in Kant's view, are to reduce standards of conduct to merely a hypothetical discussion of the behavior expected to bring about happiness. Hume's ethical theory seems to be a moral sophistry that allows individuals to rationalize their behavior according to the situation.

In Kant's view, this relativism cannot stand. If man is to be free to act as a rational, moral agent, he must have immutable rules of conduct to guide him. In a world where a hypothetical imperative exists, anyone can avoid moral responsibility for his actions by asserting that he acted in accordance with the exigencies of time and place. Such a utilitarian notion of moral law reduces man to little more than an animal because it posits that men undertake actions to fulfill a basic need without reflection or analysis.[66]

Kant rejects Hume's utilitarian understanding of ethics in *Fundamental Principles of the Metaphysics of Morals.* Instead, he theorizes that a universal moral law exists, which he labels the "categorical imperative." The imperative is a standard of behavior for free, rational, moral agents under all circumstances without respect to space and time.[67] "Act only on that maxim whereby thou canst at the same time will that it should become a universal law," he writes.[68] The categorical imperative is, in essence, the Golden Rule where a person should do unto others as he would have them do unto him. If a person chooses to undertake an action, he must ask himself a question— "would I want to live in a society where everyone acts in this manner?" If the answer is "no," the person must refrain from acting. If the answer is "yes," the person should act. Utilitarian calculations are not a factor because the categorical imperative applies in all instances regardless of intervening factors.[69]

Detractors have argued that the categorical imperative reduces ethics to platitudes that are not useful in resoling ethical dilemmas. Kant's theory of an *a priori* categorical imperative begs the question of whether ethical precepts are immutable. Admonitions such as "always keep your promises" or "tell the truth" may advance the cause of a well-ordered society that desires to produce citizens who can cooperate with each other, but it does not explain how human beings can be persuaded to step beyond utilitarian calculations. Friedrich Nietzsche especially attacked "old Kant's" assertion of absolute truths as dogmatic assertions with no practical foundation.[70]

An alternative to Kant's categorical imperative can be found in the doctrines presented by the nineteenth-century English Utilitarians Jeremy Bentham, James Mill, and John Stuart Mill. These thinkers argued that men make rational decisions according to the principle of utility, which dictates that people will always seek the greatest happiness, that is, the greatest pleasure, from a choice among competing courses of action. Bentham developed this philosophy from Hume's theory of moral sentiments, which posited that human beings have an instinctive understanding of utility, that is, of liking or not liking an act.[71]

John Stuart Mill, Bentham's godson, writing in the mid-nineteenth century, embraced a more pragmatic, positivist understanding of ethical conduct than Kant posited. Mill refused to engage in "armchair reasoning," that is, the Kantian enterprise of seeking objective proof for the principle of utility. Instead, he suggested that it is intuitively obvious that human beings seek pleasure in their day-to-day lives in the real world.[72] Mill relied on the principle of utility as a philosophical justification for maximizing individual freedom in a democratic regime.[73] The wisdom of individual choices is dictated by the character of the people who make the decisions. In some cases, people forgo their own short-term happiness to advance a larger goal, such as their future happiness. A person of good character sometimes chooses a course of action that may not be immediately seen as pleasurable. He chooses "higher" pleasures based on his past experiences with different forms of pleasure and pain[74]

An opponent of utilitarianism might argue that ethics based on maximizing a person's selfish desires is base and presents fundamental problems for a society filled with such appetite-driven human beings. Mill answers this criticism by arguing that a proper utilitarian considers not only his own happiness, but also the happiness of other persons—the greatest amount of happiness in society. Thus, utilitarianism requires persons to calculate happiness based not simply on their own selfish interests and desires, but on an impartial judgment divorced from self-interest. A truly utilitarian calculation may require someone to sacrifice his own happiness for the happiness of the majority. This is the philosophical basis for democratic government and majority rule. Public policy is made by calculating the greatest good for the greatest number of people and acting in accordance with that good.[75]

Utilitarianism has had many critics. Mill's insistence on an ethical empiricism raises problems that go to the core of democratic government. Simply because a person seeks pleasure, this does not mean that a desire is "just" or "right." If a majority of individuals desires something, this could lead to an oppressive policy where the majority tyrannizes a minority. Utilitarianism assumes that ethical choices are a matter of calculating costs and benefits and choosing actions where benefits outweigh costs. Yet this calculation assumes that ethical choices can be identified and quantified so that a common unit of measure exists. It also assumes that choices can and will be made on a rational, orderly basis.[76]

Individuals make decisions based on a variety of factors that may have no rational basis. Understanding the many reasons that an individual decided on a course of action, much less a group of individuals, is extremely problematic. In an ethical and political system based solely on quantitative calculations, it is possible that persons would surrender their liberty on the altar of the greatest good, that is, they would maximize their short-term pleasure with little regard for their long-term interests. Different depths of preferences exist, which means that some people desire a particular good a great deal while others are disinterested. Unfortunately, utility calculations generally afford each person's preferences the same unit value.

One of the more cogent twentieth-century debates on the principle of utility and whether it can serve as the basis for an equitable ethical and political theory is the famous exchange between John Rawls and Robert Nozick, two former Harvard University professors. In a groundbreaking 1971 book, *A Theory of Justice*, Rawls set forward his celebrated understanding of justice as fairness. According to Rawls, one of the reasons that so many people embrace free market principles and reject equity—treating like cases alike—as an ethical precept is because they know their position in society. If I am a well-educated, reasonably well-to-do white male living in the United States, this fact will color my perception of the world. I am inclined to reject equity because, after all, I am near the top of the socio-economic stratum. The question arises whether I would reach this same conclusion if I did not know anything about my original position in society.[77]

Rawls was disturbed by Anatole France's famous observation that the rich and the poor alike are free to sleep under bridges. This maxim of the classical liberal, laissez-faire school of thought—used as a sarcastic criticism by France but accepted as gospel by neoclassical economists—failed to account for government's responsibility to the less fortunate members of society. To circumvent the phenomenon of what Alexis de Tocqueville called "self-interest, properly understood," Rawls proposed a theoretical construct, which he called the "veil of ignorance." If a person had to establish the rules of society while operating under a metaphorical veil of ignorance that would not reveal anything about the person's relative position in society, a rational person would no longer merely seek to maximize his or her gain based on self-interest. The principle of utility would cease to be important because no one could say for certain what was or was not useful. Self-interest would be an unknown variable; consequently, the rational person would choose to construct a state that would provide for the least advantaged—after all, the person making the decision might be one of the least advantaged—as a way of ensuring that no one in the society would be allowed to suffer and fall behind while others benefited. The society would be constructed so that any change in the position of the most advantaged would result in a change for the better of the least advantaged. Rawls argues that people who were hurt by the change and later compensated must be made *better* than they were when they lived in the original position.[78]

Rawls's concept of fairness—that a society must be constructed so that no one is made worse off by the actions of others—received enormous attention after *A Theory of Justice* was published. Robert Nozick's book *Anarchy, State, and Utopia* is arguably the most famous response. Published in 1974, three years after *A Theory of Justice*, Nozick's work attacked Rawls's theoretical construct of societal fairness by focusing instead on individual rights. Nozick argues that either individual rights are inviolable and worthy of legal protections or they are not. People do not make decisions in a vacuum or under a metaphorical veil of ignorance. They make decisions based on their position in society, and they seek to better that position. Their major incentive—to maximize their "good," whether that is private property, knowledge, or pleasure—drives people to take chances in the marketplace. If those people can build a better mousetrap, according to the old adage, they will benefit individually, but society will benefit, too, because now everyone can enjoy a better mousetrap. Eventually, the benefits of better mousetraps will accrue to the less fortunate. This schema depends on the protection of individual rights and the principle of utility maximization.[79]

If people knew that their individual rights would be violated by public policies that sought to redistribute their resources according to government-sanctioned notions of "fairness," they would have fewer incentives to build the better mousetrap. This is always the problem with government intervention into the marketplace, according to Nozick: It creates entitlements among the least advantaged. The least advantaged know that, whatever else happens, they will be supported. As a result, they become dependent on government as a surrogate father that will provide for their needs. Everyone is hurt: Talented individuals have fewer incentives to build a better mousetrap because they know their rights will be infringed whenever it suits government policy-makers to do so, and the least advantaged are sucked into a cycle of dependency because they are constantly seeking government entitlements. If society is to function properly, in Nozick's view, rights must be protected and incentives must be offered so that the least advantaged have an incentive and a means to pursue their own goals instead of waiting for others to step in and do it for them. Right or wrong, this is the philosophical justification for efforts to reform welfare in the 1990s.[80]

The Rawls and Nozick "conversation" highlights the tension between efficiency and equity as ethical concepts. The crucial concern is how people—and, by extension, public policies adopted by government—can use the fewest resources to accomplish their goals while concomitantly ensuring equitable treatment for everyone. This is exactly the problem that Arthur M. Okun confronts in his classic 1975 book, *Equality and Efficiency: The Big Tradeoff*. In that work, Okun examines government programs and finds that most programs, no matter how well-designed, lose some measure of efficiency when they are implemented. By passing through so many hands, taking so much time, and using so much money—for example, in administrative overhead—in the budgetary process, these programs invariably change and lose momentum, leading to a loss of some efficiency. Government policies are similar to a leaky bucket where water sloshes out whenever the bucket is moved. Too much government intervention may hurt everyone, including those who are supposed to be helped by government programs, when an inefficient party such as government is too heavily involved in economic decisions. Yet, at the same time, if government is completely removed from the marketplace, the ruthless efficiency of the marketplace invariably harms a large number of people who cannot compete in free markets. In each of these twentieth-century debates, ethics and politics are seen as interrelated. This perspective is reminiscent of the ancient Greeks' view of ethics as rules governing the behavior of individuals and politics as rules governing the behavior of a collective group of individuals.[81]

For all of the changes since the Enlightenment, the greatest challenge to ethics in recent years has come from the postmodernists, an eclectic group of philosophers who argue that the modern paradigm of knowledge has broken down, to borrow a phrase from Thomas Kuhn.[82] Postmodern thinkers include Michel Foucault,[83] Jacques Derrida,[84] Jean-Francois Lyotard,[85] and Richard Rorty,[86] although occasionally writers such as Jurgen Habermas[87] and Roland Barthes[88] are included. For postmodernists, "totalizing metadiscourses"—that is, grand narratives that explain how human beings live—are meaningless. According to postmodernists, the structure of previous philosophies is restrictive and stifles human creativity. Postmodernists seek to overcome oppressive, dogmatic rules found in traditional metaphysics in favor of what Barthes calls "the death of the author."[89]

Postmodernism holds enormous repercussions for ethics. "Character" is not an objective fact. The only absolute in the relative world of postmodernism is the realization that there are no absolutes. The difficult feature of postmodernism, therefore, is that it destroys the structures of philosophy, yet it offers no alternative structures. As one commentator has recognized, in the wake of postmodernism, "[w]hat political theory most certainly cannot do, it seems, is to fulfill the promise of the Enlightenment. It is unable, among other things, to divine the rational principles necessary to reinvigorate or reestablish a political and ethical culture where certain limited shared values provide a basis for universally respected rights and a rational and humane politics."[90]

Good character for postmodernists is exhibited by someone who does not subscribe to the metanarratives of long-dead dogmatists. In fact, "character" is a meaningless term. A person must decide which values are important and live in a manner that makes sense for that person rather than search for ongoing standards that apply to everyone in every situation. With the rise of postmodernism, the western intellectual tradition has come full circle since the days when Plato attacked the Sophists for their relativistic views. Postmodernism is the ultimate reinvigoration of Sophistry because it allows each person's perspective to take center stage.

Postmodernism suffers from a ruthless tautology. By using philosophical discourse to call for an end to philosophical discourse, the postmodern thinker becomes nonsensical, although they argue that nonsense is not a problem. All theories are nonsense. Postmodernists unintentionally reflect Tertullian's observation that a concept is believable precisely because it is unreasonable. Postmodernism may provide philosophical food for thought, but, as a contribution to western theory, it does not provide a workable alternative basis for grounding ethics. It destroys previous philosophies without providing a new structure.

As the concept of ethics has evolved in the western intellectual tradition, so, too, has the concept of ethics evolved for persons employed in administrative agencies within the United States government. Late in the nineteenth century, with the beginning of the modern American bureaucracy, ethical conduct was fairly simple to understand. A public administrator was supposed to follow orders from superiors without regard to his or her predilections. As public administrators developed a deeper appreciation of the nuances and subtleties inherent in crafting policy inside a public agency, ethical considerations changed. Public administration ethics in the twenty-first century has been influenced in no small measure by the postmodernism of the age. The loss of certainty in the world of the philosopher presaged the loss of certainty in the world of the public administrator. As discussed in coming chapters, however, a loss of certainty does not necessarily prevent the development of public administration ethics.

Exercises and Discussion Questions

1. Why is it difficult to define ethics and how has the concept changed over time? What is the essential distinction between ethics as an absolute standard (for example, with the ancient Greeks or with Kant) and ethics as a relative standard (for example, with Hume or the postmodernists)?

2. An attorney learns that his client will soon be released from prison on bail and intends to attack the witness who testified against him in court. In your opinion, what, if anything, should the attorney do in this situation? Does the answer depend on legal duties versus moral or ethical duties? What is the difference between law and ethics? Can you think of instances when they are at odds with each other?

3. What was the key issue in the debate between faith and reason in medieval philosophy? How does this debate affect the study of ethics?

4. Should wealthy members of a society be compelled to provide assistance to needy people? How would John Rawls analyze the issue? What would Robert Nozick argue in response? In your opinion, which perspective holds more merit? Why?

5. Does postmodernism threaten the traditional understanding of ethics in the western intellectual tradition? Name some positive features of postmodernism and some negative features. In your view, is postmodernism valid? Why or why not?

6. Why has the concept of character been so important in the western intellectual tradition? In your view, are there any problems in determining what constitutes "good" character? Explain.

Notes

[1]   Henry Campbell Black, *Black's Law Dictionary*, 5th ed. (St. Paul, Minn.: West Publishing Company, 1979), 291-94, 1335, 336-37.

[2]   William Blackstone, *Commentaries on the Laws of England*, 4 vols., edited by David Christian (Boston: T.B. Wait and Sons, 1818), Vol. 1, 34.

[3]   Thomas Hobbes, *Leviathan* (Indianapolis: Bobbs-Merrill, 1958), 210.

[4]   John Locke, *Two Treatises of Government*, edited by Thomas I. Cook (New York: Hafner, 1947), 169.

[5]   Mark T. Lilla, "Ethos, 'Ethics,' and Public Service," *The Public Interest* 63 (Spring 1981), 14.

[6]   Gregory D. Foster, "Law, Morality, and the Public Sector," *Public Administration Review* 41 (January/ February 1981), 31.

[7]   One commentator explains the importance of character to the study of ethics: "Traits of character...play an important part in our understanding of human behavior and in our evaluation of individuals and their actions. These ideas are rich and complex. They can be made to yield the most subtle and profound insights about human beings by wise and skilled novelists, historians, and playwrights. A philosophical study of character traits must deal with the most fundamental aspects of human life: value and education—human goodness, merit, and responsibility; practical reason—action, desires, motives, reasons, reasoning, and judgment; and relations among people— community, convention, and shared ideals." James D. Wallace, *Virtues & Vices* (Ithaca, N.Y.: Cornell University Press, 1978), 10.

[8]   W.T. Jones, *The Classical Mind: A History of Western Philosophy*, 2d. ed. (New York: Harcourt Brace Jovanovich, 1970), 108, 215.

[9]   In Greek, "virtue" is *arete*, which also can be translated as "excellence." David E. Cooper, *World Philosophies: An Historical Introduction* (Cambridge, Mass.: Blackwell, 1996), 123.

[10]   Perhaps nowhere is Plato's point about the perils of an improper education better illustrated than in his description of the myth of Gyges in Book II of *The Republic*. The shepherd who finds a ring that can make him invisible understands that he can act un-

justly, while still *appearing* just, and thereby avoiding the negative consequences of his unjust acts. Because he favors appearances over reality, the shepherd represents the educational ethic of the Sophists. Much of Plato's task in *The Republic* is to show, through his teacher and mentor, Socrates, why justice—a virtue—is good in and of itself, not simply for its utilitarian value—its payoff.

[11] In his classic work, *Confessions*, St. Augustine recognized the similarities between the concepts expressed by Neo-Platonism, which was influential at the end of the fourth-century, and the Christian understanding of God. By substituting "Word" for "forms" and describing an active, benevolent God in lieu of the indifferent universe envisioned by Plato, Augustine demonstrated how important Plato's theory of forms was in later religious works: "So you made use of a man, one who was bloated with the most outrageous pride, to procure me some of the books of the Platonists, translated from the Greek into Latin. In them I read—not, of course, word for word, though the sense was the same and it was supported by all kinds of different arguments—that *at the beginning of time the Word already was; and God had the Word abiding with him, and the word was God. It was through him that all things came into being, and without him came nothing that has come to be.*" (Emphasis included in the original.) St. Augustine, *Confessions*, translated by R.S. Pine-Coffin (New York: Penguin Books, 1961), 144.

[12] Jones, *The Classical Mind*, 124-26.

[13] Nietzsche's objection to Plato's philosophy was clear in the preface to *Beyond Good and Evil*: "...[I]t must certainly be conceded that the worst, more durable, and most dangerous of all errors so far was a dogmatist's error—namely, Plato's invention of the pure spirit and the good as such. But now that it is overcome, now that Europe is breathing freely again after the nightmare and at least can enjoy a healthier—sleep, we, *whose task is wakefulness itself*, are the heirs of all that strength which has been fostered by the fight against this error. To be sure, it meant standing truth on her head and denying *perspective*, the basic condition of all life, when one spoke of spirit and the good as Plato did." (Emphasis included in the original.) Friedrich Nietzsche, *Beyond Good and Evil*, translated by Walter Kaufmann (New York: Vintage Books, 1966), 3.

[14] See, for example: Plato, *The Republic of Plato*, translated by Allan Bloom (New York: Basic Books, 1968), 184-92.

[15] Plato, *The Republic*, 52, 58, 74, 81.

[16] Plato, "Gorgias," translated by W.D. Woodhead, in *The Collected Dialogues of Plato*, edited by Edith Hamilton and Huntington Cairns (New York: Pantheon Books, 1961), 290-92. See also Plato, "Laws," translated by A.E. Taylor, in *The Collected Dialogues of Plato*, edited by Edith Hamilton and Huntington Cairns (New York: Pantheon Books, 1961), 1323-24.

[17] Plato, "Laws," 1315-16. See also: Plato, *The Republic*, 598, 807-8.

[18] Plato, "Protagoras," translated by W.K.C. Guthrie, in *The Collected Dialogues of Plato*, edited by Edith Hamilton and Huntington Cairns (New York: Pantheon Books, 1961), 319-20. See also Plato, *The Republic*, 585, 597-98, 601-2, 604; and Plato, "Meno," translated by W.K.C. Guthrie, in *The Collected Dialogues of Plato*, edited by Edith Hamilton and Huntington Cairns (New York: Pantheon Books, 1961), 356.

19   Plato, "Phaedo," translated by Hugh Tredennick, in *The Collected Dialogues of Plato*, edited by Edith Hamilton and Huntington Cairns (New York: Pantheon Books 1961), 50; Plato, "Meno," 373-74; Plato, *The Republic*, 684-85; Plato, "Laws," 1232-33; Plato, "Protagoras," 324-25.

20   Jones, *The Classical Mind*, 168-69.

21   Plato, "Gorgias," 274-75.

22   Plato, "Gorgias," 286-88.

23   Aristotle, *The Nicomachean Ethics*, translated by David Ross (New York: Oxford University Press, 1980).

24   See, for example: Cooper, *World Philosophies*, 122.

25   Aristotle wrote: "By the intermediate in the object I mean that which is equidistant from each of the extremes, which is one and the same for all men; by the intermediate relatively to us that which is neither too much nor too little—and this is not one, nor the same for all." Aristotle, *The Nicomachean Ethics*, 37.

26   For a more detailed discussion of this point, see, for example: Alasdair MacIntyre, *After Virtue: A Study in Moral Theory* (Notre Dame: University of Notre Dame Press, 1982).

27   Aristotle wrote: "Further, since 'good' has as many senses as 'being'...clearly it cannot be something universally present in all cases and single; for then it could not have been predicated in all the categories, but in one only." Aristotle, *The Nicomachean Ethics*, 8.

28   Aristotle, *The Nicomachean Ethics*, 11-12. "Happiness," as the term is used today, often refers to amusements or sensual pleasures. Yet, as Aristotle explained throughout *The Nicomachean Ethics*, his shorthand reference to happiness is not the precise connotation of *eudaimonia*. "The happy life is thought to be virtuous; now a virtuous life requires exertion, and does not consist in amusement," he wrote. "[T]he activity of this in accordance with its proper virtue will be perfect happiness. That this activity is contemplative we have already said." Aristotle, *The Nicomachean Ethics*, 263. Thus, *eudaimonia* more appropriately refers to certain deliberative activities that may lead to the happiness of the contemplative man, for he is less like an animal and more like a thinking, self-actualizing being than is the non-contemplative man. If the contemplative man is happier than the non-contemplative man, happiness is not a psychological state. It is the result of living a life devoted to thinking and reason.

29   Aristotle described the need for examining virtue as follows: "Since happiness is an activity of the soul in accordance with perfect virtue, we must consider the nature of virtue; for perhaps we shall thus see better the nature of happiness.... But clearly the virtue we must study is human virtue; for the good we were seeking was human good and the happiness human happiness." Aristotle, *The Nicomachean Ethics*, 24-25.

30   The term "ethical" should not be confused with "morals." The ancient Greeks did not confuse the two concepts. As referenced earlier, virtue referred to "excellences of character," or the propensity of men to behave in ways that maximize human rationality. Cooper, *World Philosophies*, 124.

31   Aristotle wrote: "Happiness extends, then, just so far as contemplation does, and those to whom contemplation more fully belongs are more truly happy, not as a mere concomitant but in virtue of the contemplation; for this is in itself precious. Happiness, therefore, must be some form of contemplation." Aristotle, *The Nicomachean Ethics*, 268.

32 Aristotle, The Nicomachean Ethics, 138-39.

33 Cooper, *World Philosophies*, 145-54.

34 Cooper, *World Philosophies*, 162-64.

35 Quoted in Terence Irwin, *Classical Thought* (Oxford: Oxford University Press, 1989), 203.

36 Quoted in H.A. Wolfson, *The Philosophy of the Church Fathers* (Cambridge, Mass.: Harvard University Press, 1956), Vol. I, 103. For more detail on the development of medieval philosophy, see also: W.T. Jones, *The Medieval Mind: A History of Western Philosophy* (New York: Harcourt Brace Jovanovich, 1970).

37 Jones, *The Medieval Mind*, 190-286.

38 Jones, *The Medieval Mind*, 257-72. See also: Ernest L. Fortin, "St. Thomas Aquinas," in *History of Political Philosophy*, 2d. ed., edited by Leo Strauss and Joseph Cropsey (Chicago, Ill.: The University of Chicago Press, 1972), 223-50.

39 Cooper, *World Philosophies*, 226-35.

40 Much of *The Prince* was devoted to describing the conditions necessary for a ruler to establish and maintain his power. It was a curious work for a man known to harbor republican tendencies, as evidenced by his work *Discourses on Livy*. Cooper, *World Philosophies*, 232. Machiavelli was able to forgo an extended treatment of virtue in *The Prince* except to say that a virtuous man was effective in achieving his political goals. He defined the central problem of ethics and politics facing a ruler as follows: "We have said above that a Prince must have strong foundations, otherwise his downfall is inevitable. The main foundations of all states, new, old, or mixed, are good laws and good arms; and since there cannot be good laws where there are not good arms and likewise where there are good arms the laws must be good too, I shall omit discussion of laws and speak only of arms." Niccolo Machiavelli, *The Prince*, translated and edited by Thomas G. Bergin (Arlington Heights, IL: AHM Publishing, 1947), 34. This emphasis on the coercive power of the state as the foundation for a legitimate regime would have been anathema to earlier philosophers owing to its "might makes right" ethic.

41 In the opening of Hobbes's most influential work, *Leviathan*, he explained his objections to metaphysics and theology in no uncertain terms: "Nor are we therefore to give that name [truth] to any false conclusions, for he that reasons aright in words he understands can never conclude an error; Nor to that which any man knows by supernatural revelation, because it is not acquired by reasoning; Nor that which is gotten by reasoning from the authority of books, because it is not by reasoning from the cause to the effect nor from the effect to the cause, and is not knowledge, but faith." Hobbes, *Leviathan*, 3-4.

42 Hobbes, *Leviathan*, 110.

43 Hobbes wrote: "Hereby it is manifest that, during the time men live without a common power to keep them all in awe, they are in that condition which is called war, and such a war as is of every man against every man." Hobbes, *Leviathan*, 106.

44 Hobbes, *Leviathan*, 107.

45 Hobbes concluded: "A *commonwealth* is said to be *instituted* when a *multitude* of men do agree and *covenant, every one with every one*, that to whatsoever *man or assembly of men* shall be given by the major part the *right* to *present* the person of them all—that is to say, to be their *representative*—every one, as well he that *voted for it* as he that *voted against it*,

shall *authorize* all the actions and judgments of that man or assembly of men in the same manner as if they were his own, to the end to live peaceably among themselves and be protected against other men." (Emphasis included in the original.) Hobbes, *Leviathan*, 143-44.

[46]   Hobbes, *Leviathan*, 131. (Emphasis included in the original.)

[47]   Hobbes, *Leviathan*, 52-53.

[48]   Hobbes, *Leviathan*, 54.

[49]   David Gauthier, "Thomas Hobbes: Moral Theorist," *The Journal of Philosophy* 76 (1979), 547. See also: David Gauthier, "Morality and Advantage," *Philosophical Review* 76 (1967), 460-75.

[50]   Unlike many philosophers who obscured their heretical views in their work, Hobbes boldly stated his premises in *Leviathan*: "With the introduction of false, we may join also the suppression of true philosophy by such men as neither by lawful authority nor sufficient study are competent judges of the truth…. For whatsoever power ecclesiastics take upon themselves (in any place where they are subject to the state) in their own right, though they call it God's right, is but usurpation." Hobbes, *Leviathan*, 20.

[51]   Daniel M. Farrell, "Hobbes as Moralist," *Philosophical Studies* 48 (1985), 259-60.

[52]   John Locke, *An Essay Concerning Human Understanding*, edited by Peter H. Nidditch (Oxford: Clarendon Press, 1975), 565.

[53]   John Locke, *Some Thoughts Concerning Education and of the Conduct of Understanding*, edited by Ruth W. Grant and Nathan Tarcov (Cambridge: Hackett Publishing Company, 1996).

[54]   Locke, *Two Treatises of Government*, 228-47.

[55]   While both Hobbes and Locke grounded their philosophical writings in analyses of a hypothetical "state of nature," Locke recognized that some principles of natural law take precedence over the laws of the state. Robert A. Goldwin, "John Locke," in *History of Political Philosophy*, 2d. ed, edited by Leo Strauss and Joseph Cropsey (Chicago: Rand McNally & Company, 1972), 459-60.

[56]   Robert S. Hill, "David Hume," in *History of Political Philosophy*, 2d. ed., edited by Leo Strauss and Joseph Cropsey (Chicago: Rand McNally & Company, 1972), 509-31. See also: Gottfried Dietze, *The Federalist: A Classic on Federalism and Free Government* (Westport, Conn.: Greenwood, 1960), 316.

[57]   David Hume, *An Enquiry Concerning Human Understanding* (Indianapolis: Hackett Publishing, 1977), 111-12.

[58]   Hume, *An Enquiry Concerning Human Understanding*, 114.

[59]   Hume, *An Enquiry Concerning Human Understanding*, 4.

[60]   Cooper, *World Philosophies*, 250.

[61]   Justice is artificial because it serves only to protect property rights in a civil society. As is the case with all philosophical abstractions, it does not exhibit characteristics in and of itself "which fit it for the nourishment of a human body." Hume, *An Enquiry Concerning Human Understanding*, 21.

[62]   Knud Haakonssen, "Preface," in David Hume, *Political Essays*, edited by Knud Haakonssen (Cambridge: Cambridge University Press, 1994), xxvi.

[63]   Hill, "David Hume," 518.

64   Wallace, *Virtues & Vices*, 153.

65   Cooper, *World Philosophies*, 295. See also: Pierre Hassner, "Immanuel Kant," in *History of Political Philosophy*, 2d. ed., edited by Leo Strauss and Joseph Cropsey (Chicago: Rand McNally & Company, 1972), 554-93.

66   Cooper, *World Philosophies*, 303. Kant observed: "Each thing in nature works according to laws. Only a rational being has the faculty to act *according to the conception* of laws, that is, according to principles, in other words, has a will." Immanuel Kant, "The Categorical Imperative," in *Combating Corruption/Encouraging Ethics: A Sourcebook for Public Service Ethics*, edited by William L. Richter, Francis Burke, and Jameson W. Doig (Washington, D.C.: The American Society for Public Administration, 1990), 27.

67   Immanuel Kant, *Fundamental Principles of the Metaphysics of Morals*, translated by T. Abbott (New York: Prometheus, 1987).

68   Kant, *Fundamental Principles of the Metaphysics of Morals*, 49.

69   From a twentieth-century perspective, Kant's categorical imperative seems intuitive. Parents all over the world instruct their children on the proper method of fulfilling the categorical imperative on a daily basis. It is an absolute command. For Kant, once moral laws are subject to bargaining, negotiation and rationalization, they lose their moral force. A concomitant formulation of this absolute value is expressed by Kant when he insists that a rational being should be treated never as a means only, but always as an end in itself. Kant, *Fundamental Principles of the Metaphysics of Morals*, 303.

70   Nietzsche wrote: "...[I]t is high time to replace the Kantian question, 'How are synthetic judgments *a priori* possible?' by another question, 'Why is belief in such judgments *necessary*?'—and to comprehend that such judgments must be *believed* to be true, for the sake of the preservation of creatures like ourselves; though they might, of course, be *false* judgments for all that! Or to speak more clearly and coarsely: synthetic judgments *a priori* should not 'be possible' at all; we have no right to them; in our mouths they are nothing but false judgments. Only, of course, the belief in their truth is necessary, as a foreground belief and visual evidence belonging to the perspective optics of life." Nietzsche, *Beyond Good and Evil*, 19.

71   The natural human tendency to engage in tasks that increase pleasure and avoid tasks that decrease pleasure "placed mankind under the governance of two sovereign masters, *pain* and *pleasure*," Bentham observed. (Emphasis included in the original.) Jeremy Bentham, *An Introduction to the Principles of Morals and Legislation* (New York: Hafner, 1948), 1.

72   Cooper, *World Philosophies*, 348-49.

73   In his influential work, *On Liberty*, Mill wrote: "The object of this Essay is to assert one very simple principle, as entitled to govern absolutely the dealings of society with the individual in the way of compulsion and control, whether the means used be physical force in the form of legal penalties, or the moral coercion of public opinion. That principle is, that the sole end for which mankind are warranted, individually or collectively, in interfering with the liberty of action of any of their number, is self-protection. That the only purpose for which power can be rightfully exercised over any member of a civilized community, against his will, is to prevent harm to others." John Stuart Mill, *On Liberty* (Arlington Heights, Ill.: AHM Publishing, 1947), 9.

[74]   Mortimer J. Adler and Seymour Cain, *Ethics: The Study of Moral Values* (Chicago: Encyclopedia Britannica, Inc., 1962), 262.

[75]   Adler and Cain, *Ethics: The Study of Moral Values*, 262-63.

[76]   In his landmark work, *A Theory of Justice*, John Rawls observed: "This means, as Mill remarks, that one person's happiness assumed to be equal in degree to another person's happiness is to be counted exactly the same. The weights in the additive function that represents the utility principle are identical for all individuals, and it is natural to take them as one. The principle of utility, one might say, treats persons both as ends and means. It treats them as ends by assigning the same (positive) weight to the welfare of each; it treats them as means by allowing higher life prospects for some to counterbalance lower life prospects for others who are already less favorably situated." John Rawls, *A Theory of Justice* (Cambridge, Mass.: Belknap Press, 1971), 182-83.

[77]   Ibid., 136-38.

[78]   Ibid., 17-22.

[79]   Robert Nozick, *Anarchy, State, and Utopia* (New York: Basic Books, 1974), 96-101.

[80]   Ibid., 149-82.

[81]   Arthur M. Okun, *Equity and Efficiency: The Big Tradeoff* (Washington, D.C.: The Brookings Institution, 1975), 120.

[82]   Thomas S. Kuhn, *The Structure of Scientific Revolutions*, 2d. ed. (Chicago: University of Chicago Press, 1970).

[83]   See, for example: Michael Foucault, *The Archaeology of Knowledge*, translated by A. Sheridan (New York: Pantheon Books, 1972); and Michel Foucault, *The Order of Things: An Archaeology of the Human Sciences* (London: Tavistock, 1980).

[84]   A famous deconstructionist, Derrida produced a number of important works, including *Of Grammatology*, translated by G. Spivak (Baltimore: Johns Hopkins University Press, 1976); *Writing and Difference*, translated by A. Bass (Chicago: University of Chicago Press, 1978); and *Margins of Philosophy*, translated by A. Bass (Chicago: University of Chicago Press, 1982).

[85]   Lyotard coined the term "postmodernism" in his book *The Postmodern Condition: A Report on Knowledge* (Minneapolis: University of Minnesota Press, 1984).

[86]   The American "neopragmatist" Richard Rorty is noted for several works, including *Consequences of Pragmatism: Essays 1972-1980* (Brighton: Harvester, 1982) and *Contingency, Irony, and Solidarity* (Cambridge: Cambridge University Press, 1989).

[87]   Jurgen Habermas, *The Philosophical Discourse of Modernity* (Cambridge: Polity, 1987).

[88]   See, for example, Roland Barthes, *Mythologies* (New York: Hill and Wang, 1957).

[89]   Cooper, *World Philosophies*, 465-68.

[90]   Lawrence J. Biskowski, "Political Theory in the 1990s: Antifoundationalist Critics and Democratic Prospects," *Southeastern Political Review* 20 (Spring 1992), 62.

Chapter Two
The Rise of the Administrative State and the Quest for Legitimacy

Scholars and political philosophers always have sought to ground the principles of a regime on something other than "might makes right." If the underlying rationale for the existence of a particular government is that its current rulers control the military or forces of oppression, the regime is no better—and may even be a good deal worse—than life in Hobbes's hypothetical state of nature, which is "solitary, poor, nasty, brutish, and short."[1] The point of entering into a social compact and creating an entity called the "sovereign" or the "state" is to improve mankind's position so that he is not subject to the vagaries of nature, what later thinkers called "nature, red in tooth and claw."

It is ironic that too much individual liberty and not enough governmental authority—Hobbes's state of nature—results in a situation where the mightiest overwhelm the meek just as too much governmental authority and not enough individual liberty—a totalitarian state—leads to the principle of might makes right. The paramount task for founders of a regime is to find the proper balance between the freedom of the individual and the authority of the state and then justify that balance. Accordingly, an alternative to a regime where one group wields a disproportionate share of political power is to design a government that legitimizes its authority through a reasoned articulation of its political principles. The quest for legitimacy is not a point of mere semantics; it is an integral feature of a regime.

Legitimizing a regime is an exceedingly difficult enterprise; in a democratic government, for example, democratic and non-democratic elements coexist. In the national government of the United States, members of Congress are elected directly by the electorate while the president is selected by the Electoral College. Judges and justices in the federal judiciary are appointed by the president with the advice and consent of the U.S. Senate and serve for life during good behavior. Given these "mixed elements" of the regime, the question of legitimacy is complicated. The American Founders believed that citizens should elect some of their leaders but, as a check on the potential for the masses to degenerate into a mob, other leaders must be selected through different means. The Electoral College was created on a fiduciary model whereby electors would ratify the wishes of the electorate unless voters had unwittingly cast their ballots for a demagogue, in which case electors would serve as trustees and substitute their judgment for the judgment of the voters. As for the federal judiciary, the people have no influence on the process of selecting judges and justices except by indirectly communicating their desires to their elected officials.[2]

For unelected public administrators in the executive branch, the question of legitimacy is especially problematic. Typically, the top one percent of any federal executive branch agency consists of political appointees whose fealty to the current presidential administration secures their positions. The remaining slots, with some exceptions, are filled through a competitive process protected by civil service laws and regulations. Because the public has no direct input in the selection of public administrators, the quest for their legitimacy is a crucial issue. In a system of government that professes to be accountable to the people, demonstrating that the executive branch is justified in its creation and operation is no small matter.[3]

One method for understanding how public administrators justify their authority is to contrast their role with that of private firms. A private firm in a democratic, capitalist company is devoted to generating a profit for its owners or shareholders. Although private firms are subject to a multitude of federal and state laws and regulations, first and foremost the firms seek to best their competitors and capture as much of the market as possible. Private firms do not have a larger societal obligation to the "public interest," however it might be defined, unless they voluntarily assume such an obligation. The realization that private firms seek to maximize the goods and services enjoyed by private parties is not to suggest that private firms are inherently selfish or opposed to the public good, although sometimes that may be the case. Instead, private firms are left to maximize the private interests of their owners and shareholders. The centrality of private interests and private enterprise was a crucial component of the Founders' view of the classical liberalism of the American state.[4]

Public firms or agencies are distinguished from private firms by the "public" nature of their duties. Public firms are supposed to answer to the general public, a much larger and more amorphous group than the owners and shareholders associated with private firms. Except in cases of inheritance or involuntary transfers such as bankruptcy liquidation and the like, owners and shareholders generally choose to participate, actively or passively, in the firm's dealings. Their participation, or at least their knowing acquiescence in the firm's activities, is assured because they had to take steps to acquire an ownership interest in the firm. The general public, by contrast, "owns" a public firm or agency by virtue of citizenship or, at a minimum, of geographic proximity. Many members of the general public have no interest in, or knowledge of, public administration and management and therefore take little or no part or interest in the activities of public firms.

The issue of public accountability is not obviated by the public's lack of attention to public administration. Indeed, one might argue that the duties of openness and honesty on the part of public sector employees are even greater when the public is inattentive. In the private sector, owners and shareholders often monitor the activities of a firm to protect their ownership interest. Cases of malfeasance are handled expeditiously to ensure that the underlying property interest is not diminished. The managers of private firms can be quickly reprimanded or removed for transgressions and, because private managers who are not under contract or protected through union membership are considered "at will" employees, they can be removed with or even without cause. This authority over personnel and the ability to move with alacrity is too often lacking in the public sector, leading to what is often referred to as the collective action dilemma or, as a related concept, the tragedy of the commons.[5]

Perhaps the most cogent articulation of the dilemma is found in a famous 1968 journal article by Garrett Hardin. In that article, Hardin argued that individual users of a resource that is not privately owned (a "common pool resource," in economists' terms) have an incentive to use as much as they can, even to the point of exhausting the resource, to satisfy their individual desires with little regard for future uses by other parties. Unfortunately, by taking a short-term view of their actions, individuals risk destroying the resource for everyone in the long term. Hardin's article has been influential because it explains why so many public sector decisions fail to resonate with the public. If people do not see tangible evidence of their ownership interest, they do not protect the interest or call for accountability from guardians of the public interest except in cases where a failure to protect the public interest becomes highly visible in the media.[6]

Private firms are a quintessential result of an emphasis on individualism, a philosophical belief in the worth and dignity of persons. Proponents of the individual creed believe that the welfare of individuals is superior to the welfare of the state. In fact, the welfare of the individual *is* the end, and the state is the means by which the end is achieved. For this reason, political scientists often contend that American statism—that is, the desire for a government entity to control many aspects of day-to-day life—is much weaker than its European counterparts. European nations tend to develop strong governments that require massive funding for ambitious public programs to serve the needs of many citizens. National health care and government-protected employment programs are prime examples of such statism. By contrast, American government generally leaves decisions about health care and employment to individuals to handle for themselves. Although in the United States some health care coverage is provided by Medicare and Medicaid and anti-discrimination laws and regulations provide some protections for employees, generally the American system of government allows wider latitude for the private sector to control aspects of human life and the economy than is typically the case in Europe.[7]

The comparison between Europe and the United States is not to suggest that the American system of government has remained static over time. In the decades since the 1930s, the American federal executive branch—the bureaucracy—has grown tremendously. With the growth of government come renewed calls for government to justify its existence, especially when people within it are not elected.

One method for justifying government is to set forth an argument in favor of representative bureaucracy. Some political scientists have observed that often the people elected to public office are elites; in fact, only elites could raise the millions of dollars necessary to run effectively for most elective offices. Successful candidates for Congress, for example, may portray themselves as the "people's representatives," but such a slogan may not be wholly accurate. The idea of representative bureaucracy may prove to be a countervailing value to the concern about elites winning election to powerful positions inside government. Because many positions within a bureaucracy, particularly in the lower levels of state and local agencies, are entry-level positions or do not require specialized training, these positions are filled by middle-class and even lower middle-class Americans who could not be characterized as "elites." In some areas, an agency employs people from the community. Thus, in an African-American community, for example, many of the "street-level bureaucrats" are black, thereby reflecting the demographic characteristics of the community in a manner absent from the pool of elected officials.

Assuming that employees in a bureaucracy resemble the population served by the bureaucracy, one might argue that, despite the lack of regular elections, the bureaucracy actually resembles the client groups more faithfully than the representatives elected to public office. This concept is known as "representative bureaucracy." The concept refers to a sincere desire to "democratize" administrative values. If public administrators can demonstrate that they value democracy as a core foundation of the regime, they will do much to demonstrate the legitimacy of executive branch agencies. The problem, of course, is that the term "democracy" is vague and open to interpretation. When Americans use the term, they generally refer to a set of values rooted in the tradition and history of the American republic.[8]

Historical Influences on American Administrative Values

To understand democratic values and their role in legitimizing a regime, it is necessary to recall the influences on the American Founders. During the seventeenth century, English philosopher John Locke, referenced in Chapter 1, advanced a labor theory of value that helped shape the development of the American republic. In Chapter V of his classic work, "The Second Treatise of Government," Locke contends that man has the right to appropriate private property from the fruits of the earth, which were "given to men [by God] for the support and comfort of their being." Property rights are so important to Locke that they form the basis for legitimate civil government as rational human beings enter into a social compact to protect their rights.[9]

Locke initiates a discussion of property rights to contradict Sir Robert Filmer's notion, expressed in *Patriarcha* (which Locke attacked in the "First Treatise of Government"), that God gave the world to Adam and his heirs and, therefore, a monarch owned all property exclusive of everyone else in society by virtue of his or her lineage extending back to the Garden of Eden. As an alternate theory to justify the concept of private property, Locke writes that, although "nobody has originally a private dominion exclusive of the rest of mankind in any of them [i.e. the fruits of the earth], as they are thus in their natural state," it is impossible for any particular person to enjoy the fruits of the earth without appropriating individual parts of the whole for himself. If the fruits of the earth remain in their natural state, they do not benefit mankind since they are unavailable for consumption. Ironically, because items remaining in their natural state are unused, they may spoil more rapidly than if they are used by man. An apple hanging from a tree eventually rots and falls to the ground if it is not eaten. It is only when the apple is picked that it holds any value for man.[10]

Locke's labor theory of value posits that, since man "has a property in his own person," it is human labor that, when mixed with something taken from the state of nature, creates what modern men call "value." "Whatsoever then he removes out of the state that nature hath provided and left it in, he hath mixed his labour with, and joined to it something that is his own, and thereby makes it his property," Locke explains.[11]

Such a vigorous defense of private property rights leads to Locke's belief in the primacy of individual liberty. Through the use and enjoyment of his property, a person interacts with the world and defines his relationship with others. Property rights establish a zone of protection around an individual. If the property right is abrogated, the individual's liberty is at risk, which explains why so many people react violently when their property is damaged or the value is diminished.[12]

This emphasis on property and liberty was influential to Locke's progeny. The Founders of the American republic agreed with Locke that private property rights were profoundly important and inextricably linked with individual human liberty. To deny property rights was tantamount to limiting liberty. Being good classical liberals, the Founders were loath to create a strong, robust central government for fear that it would grow oppressive and threaten the rights of citizens. Their motto was, "That government is best which governs least."[13]

Apart from its philosophical antecedents, Americans' distrust of a strong, centralized, potentially obdurate government was rooted in the distinctive regional characteristics imparted by the different settlers who came to the New World with a more-or-less blank slate.[14] They were not beholden or subservient to the centuries of tradition that formed a backdrop for the English parliamentary system. With an ocean separating the English-speaking peoples of the new nation from European affairs, Americans were free to develop their system of government, along with many of its new methods of operation, unencumbered by the old ways. While it was true that most American opinion leaders viewed themselves as subjects of the English Crown throughout most of the colonial period and well into the latter half of the eighteenth century, it is equally true that they were quick to take offense at slights from the Mother Country and were sorely tested by Walpole's salutary neglect and the more stringent governance later imposed on them.[15]

Little wonder that when it came time to justify the exercise of power, unelected administrators would be viewed with skepticism by people raised in a grand tradition of skepticism. "Federalist 72," the clearest articulation of the Founders' views of public administration during the Founding period, reports that "all the operations of the body politic," in any branch of the new government, are "limited to executive details, and falls peculiarly within the province of the executive department."[16] As such, the executive department would have to be staffed with people of good character who had been educated in the proper virtues associated with a democratic regime, namely, the primacy of property rights, the protection of individual liberties, the need for periodic elections, the separation of powers into distinctive departments according to function, and the importance of checks and balances to ensure that no branch would eclipse the others.[17]

In the event that people with good character were not to be found staffing executive agencies, the Founders had reason to believe that their system of government would limit the potential for mischief. Separation of powers and federalist principles would all but guarantee that no party could grab too much power for misuse because power had to be shared among a variety of interests, each of which had its own "rival ambition." Public servants employed within the executive branch would be required to comply with all rules regarding the use of executive power; therefore, regime principles that encouraged the correct behavior by elected officials would similarly encourage correct behavior by unelected public servants.[18]

Over time, as the bureaucracy grew, concerns about the legitimacy of unelected officials increased, along with criticism of executive branch performance, which was viewed as ridiculously cumbersome, needlessly time-consuming, and appallingly inefficient. In certain circles within and without the academy, denouncing the "big, fat, bloated, top-heavy federal bureaucracy" became de rigueur. The practice of bureaucrat bashing especially increased during the post-Watergate period when outsider Jimmy Carter campaigned for the presidency by promising to reform the civil service and root out the corruption and inefficiency a scandal-weary public felt must exist. Carter's successor, Ronald Reagan, famously commented that government was not the solution to societal problems; government *was* the problem.[19]

Improving Government Performance as a Means of Legitimizing Bureaucracy

Recognizing that reform, or at least the appearance of reform, was needed to persuade the public that bureaucracy was legitimate, during the past quarter century policy-makers have sought to improve government performance through many strategies and techniques. Reform efforts have traveled under a variety of names. New Zealand and Great Britain have labeled it "New Public Management" while Americans preferred the sobriquet "Reinventing Government." Whatever it is called, the focus has been on ensuring greater productivity with fewer resources so that bureaucracy is a "lean, mean, efficiency-effectiveness machine." Private-sector manufacturing companies speak of "lean manufacturing technologies" and "smart growth," buzzwords for industry's desire to manufacture the same number—or more, if possible—of products using an ever smaller labor force. Proponents of government performance reform argue that the same ideals that apply to the private sector—emphasizing customer service while relying on market mechanisms to increase performance efficiencies and ensure greater accountability—should be applied to the public sector.[20]

In the abstract, improving government performance is a laudable goal, but it remains to be seen whether reform initiatives fulfill early promises to increase efficiency and effectiveness. Two related questions immediately arise. First, is improving government performance genuinely possible or is the much-heralded reform movement merely "old wine in new bottles"? Second, even if it is possible, a deeper question arises—is reform desirable as a means of legitimizing the administrative state?[21]

Insofar as the first question is concerned, focusing on customer service sounds promising, but implementing such a program in executive branch agencies is easier said than done. Practical questions abound: Assuming that an entrepreneurial public administrator is desirable, how can performance incentives be incorporated into public service agencies when the profit motive is not the paramount objective of the public sector? How can customer service be improved without incurring additional expenses or, ironically, generating increased bureaucracy and red tape? Owing to myriad conflicting and overlapping statutory obligations and political considerations—not to mention the multitude of political actors and the fragmented nature of American government—is the development of a customer service initiative feasible?

The Clinton administration decided that it was feasible. As part of the National Performance Review, an effort led by Vice President Al Gore, customer service became a key component in improving the federal government so that it operated more efficiently and at a lower cost. Moreover, in September 1994, the president issued Executive Order 12862, "Setting Customer Service Standards." The order required all federal agencies within a year to identify customers, survey them to determine their needs and expectations, develop and post service standards and measure results against them, and benchmark customer service standards. All agencies complied with the order, although specific standards differed widely among each agency.[22]

For reformers seeking to improve the policy process beyond merely revamping customer service in the federal agencies, the call for privatization became a key strategy. Privatization is when private sector firms supply goods and services previously supplied by government agencies. The rationale is that private firms are subject to competitive market forces that require them to supply goods and services far more efficiently than the government can. The theory is that private firms can supply the same goods and services but better, faster, and cheaper because they cut through red tape and focus on market forces such as customer satisfaction, rewards for stellar performance, and efficiency.[23] In 1993, Congress enacted the Government Performance and Results Act (GPRA), a major initiative designed to shift the federal government's focus from government "inputs" to government "outputs," or the successful implementation and measurement of results. To accomplish this goal, GPRA established long-term policy goals, set out specific annual performance targets, and required annual reporting of actual, as opposed to expected, performance. Managers of federal executive branch programs were held accountable for the failure to meet appropriate goals under the statute.[24]

If the GPRA sounds idealistic and difficult to implement, in many ways that was exactly the problem with the law. Agencies are subject to a variety of requirements—laws and regulations imposed by external forces, difficulties fulfilling agency duties when budgets are reduced, and responsibilities shared with other agencies and institutions—that frequently frustrate their performance. Still, the act pushed policy-makers to develop policies and programs that met specific needs. In this context, policymakers employed a series of management tools in an effort to improve the policy process. Strategies such as Total Quality Management (TQM), Continuous Quality Improvement (CQI), and Customer Service Quality Improvement (CSQI) ideally focus more on the needs of "customers" in policy development than on those of government. Each of these strategies subscribes to core principles: a commitment to meeting customers' needs; empowerment of employees to make decisions, especially at lower levels within an organization; actions based on data, facts, outcome measures, and statistics, when available; a commitment to process change; and organizational changes and teamwork to accomplish goals.[25]

A criticism of TQM, CQI, and CSQI, however, is that the goals stated in these trendy management strategies often are so vague as to be meaningless. A pledge to listen to customer feedback and respond accordingly sounds reasonable, but in practice it is difficult to know how that pledge changes an administrator's response in a specific situation. In addition, many managers profess their adherence to TQM, CQI, and CSQI, but they fail to integrate these strategies with existing management strategies and goals. Breaking down hierarchies and reshaping organizations so that individuals work in teams where no one is above anyone else but everyone shares "ownership" of a job or a problem requires a sea change in thinking as well as constantly reinforced training.[26] As a result, new, innovative, "customer-driven" management strategies frequently are afforded lip service but do not always change management practices. If they do not effect genuine positive change, they are unnecessary diversions from an agency's core function.[27]

In 2005, Carolyn J. Hill and Laurence E. Lynn, Jr. published an article examining whether the traditional hierarchical model of governance was in decline owing to reform movements. In short, has the reform movement actually led to fewer hierarchies, and, hence, a supposed improvement in efficient government performance—assuming *arguendo* that efficiency is the key measure of success? Their conclusion, as one might expect, suggested that reform is evident to a greater or lesser extent across different agencies. The results—improved efficiencies—did not necessarily result from a leveling effect or from privatization. The results depended on a variety of contextual factors. The nature of the agencies, how closely agency goals were tied to service delivery, the nature of contractual and statutory obligations, the degree of discretion exercised by managers, the determination of "productivity" within an agency, and many other factors influenced the outcome. In other words, some reform is possible, but the nature and extent of the reform depends on so many factors that, in the authors' words, "these findings may not generalize to other types of policies, organizations, locations, or times."[28]

The second and more complex question—is reform desirable?—confronts a more profound issue than whether reform is possible; it goes to the core values of the republic. Reformers make a persuasive case that change is possible and desirable. By reducing institutional impediments and making managers more responsive to the public, government performance will cost less and produce more. When public managers are no longer constrained by a complex labyrinth of rules and regulations, they will be more innovative. Proponents of reform argue that this goal is value-neutral because, after all, who would not want to revitalize government performance through improved efficiencies? If a rational maximizer could receive two widgets instead of one by using the same resources, who would balk at such increased productivity? Reformers contend that such a theory of government performance is descriptive, not normative; that is, it offers an explanation of how public sector agencies would work if their design were improved.

Reformers have accepted a vision of public administration that may or may not be accurate. They see public agencies as rule-bound, top-heavy, static institutions mired in customs and bureaucratic norms where people do things a certain way because that is the way things have always been done. To their way of thinking, such a cramped, stifling type of government is a natural offshoot of Max Weber's "ideal type" of bureaucracy, a carryover from a different age. Weber, a German sociologist who influenced the development of public administration early in the twentieth century, developed a series of "ideal types" that would provide clear examples of scientific principles in various institutional structures. In coining the term "bureaucracy," Weber emphasized the need for a strict, rigid hierarchy that determined responsibility for certain duties separate from the corrosive influence of charismatic personalities. In an age before "bureaucracy" took on its negative connotations, he posited that bureaucracy was preferable to the rampant partisanship and cronyism that characterized much of nineteenth-century politics.[29]

In the "ideal type" of bureaucracy, each person would hold a clearly defined job and would know who was above or below him in the chain of command. The personality or discretion of individuals within the hierarchy was irrelevant to the efficient functioning of the bureaucracy. Each employee could be hired, supervised, trained, evaluated, or fired on the basis of firmly established rules and guidelines that were known to everyone beforehand. An ideal type of bureaucracy ensured neutral, equitable treatment because it theoretically removed ambiguous goals, discretion, patronage, and other "non-scientific" considerations from the organizational hierarchy.[30]

Weber's model—and federal executive branch agencies premised on this model—may have been an improvement in its time, but reformers contend that its time has come and gone. Hierarchical bureaucracies are wasteful, inefficient, unproductive, and ultimately dehumanizing. In their famous work *Reinventing Government*, David Osborne and Ted Gaebler championed the need for an "entrepreneurial revolution" led by "entrepreneurial leaders" who understand "the shared visions and goals of a community" and use their position and influence to "rally their communities to their visions." They envisioned the establishment of a government that costs less, performs better, encourages innovation, and moves quickly.[31]

According to professors Linda deLeon and Robert B. Denhardt, the public administration reform movement, whatever it is called and wherever it is heralded, is grounded in a political theory that relies on three basic premises: the market model, an emphasis on customers rather than citizens, and, in their words, the "glorification of entrepreneurial management." The market model suggests that government should be operated as though it were a private business. The model does not apply to policy agencies or regulatory bodies, but it is designed to improve the performance of service agencies. Professors deLeon and Denhardt, among others, question whether markets and competition are appropriately applied to public agencies that must consider factors other than the profit motive. Similarly, focusing on customers or clients ignores the benefits of treating people as citizens, which implies that they have duties and obligations in a democratic society that extend far beyond a customer-supplier relationship.[32]

Finally, pushing public managers to be entrepreneurial may have unintended negative consequences because it stresses potentially risky behavior that may be at odds with accountability. "As a practical matter, in real organizations, entrepreneurial managers pose a difficult and risky problem: they can be innovative and productive, but their single-mindedness, tenacity, and willingness to bend the rules make them very difficult to control," deLeon and Denhardt contend. "They can become loose cannons."[33] Larry D. Terry summarizes the difficulties more succinctly. "The New Public Management is not an 'objective,' *value-free* enterprise, nor is it concerned primarily with explanation and prediction," he observes. Instead, it is grounded in an economic theory that may portend negative things for democratic theory.[34]

The concern about reforming government performance and its conflict with democratic theory is perhaps the most cogent issue raised by critics of the New Public Management and Reinventing Government movements. Should the masses of people be considered "citizens" or "customers"? This is no mere semantics game. "Citizens" are expected to take part in political decision-making. Their participation is a two-way street; they receive government services, but they have obligations in return. This emphasis on citizenship is what John F. Kennedy was referring to in his inaugural address when he said, "ask not what your country can do for you; ask what you can do for your country." The new president was appealing to citizens to shoulder a measure of the burdens imposed on people by a democratic government. "Customers," by contrast, expect their needs to be met by suppliers. The old adage that "the customer is always right" means that customers do not recognize mutual obligations apart from payment for goods and services. Governments can expect to impose obligations on citizens, but not on customers.[35]

The republican form of government in the United States is structurally inefficient, and it was designed that way. The Founders of the American republic deliberately built inefficiencies into the U.S. Constitution as a check on "too much power in two few hands." Owing to the almost universal antipathy toward democracy—a political theory believed by Enlightenment-era theorists to be tantamount to rule by an unruly mob—the Founders attempted to design a government that would transform "the infirmities and depravities of the human character," that is, the acquisitive nature of human beings, from vices into some semblance of virtues. By establishing "good government" through ratification of the U.S. Constitution, citizens could use, if not redeem, their base human nature to advance nobler purposes. They could, in effect, establish a government that would allow them to pursue their material desires while restraining the destructive tendencies of avaricious individuals.[36]

"Good government" would never be created through a direct democracy. The people were incapable of self governance absent institutional controls. These controls mitigated the problem of factions or self-interested groups of people seeking their own ends at the expense of the public interest. Because removing the causes of faction could never be achieved outside of a totalitarian government, the Founders proposed to control its effects by establishing a federal system of government with limited constitutional purposes, institutional checks and balances, and a separation of powers. Such a government—a "republic," in their parlance—is a structured, indirect democracy that "channels" the self-interested behavior driven by human nature. This view of human nature was perhaps best expressed in a famous passage from "Federalist 51":

> If men were angels, no government would be necessary. If angels were to govern men, neither external nor internal controls on government would be necessary. In framing a government which is to be administered by men over men, the great difficulty lies in this: You must first enable government to controul the governed; and in the next place, oblige it to controul itself. A dependence on the people is no doubt the primary controul on the government; but experience has taught mankind the necessity of auxiliary precautions.[37]

For the Founders, "auxiliary precautions" were inefficient, but they ensured a measure of government stability and institutional control. Such precautions protected the principles underlying the new regime and embedded in the Constitution, namely a desire to advance liberty and property interests through government, the need to safeguard minority rights through "mitigated democracy" created and maintained by institutional controls, and the relative sovereignty of citizens who participate in consensual self-government. These principles, many of which directly contradict neoclassical microeconomic theory, served as the foundation of American political thought.[38]

As part of the American republic, legal requirements contained in statutes and regulations often impose requirements on federal agencies that deliberately interfere with efficiency. Throughout our history, due process is said to occur when all parties are afforded an opportunity to be heard. In the case of administrative agencies, due process requires that parties subject to rules and regulations must be allowed an opportunity to contest the application of a particular rule as applied to the specific party challenging the rule. "Due process" is inefficient because it is time-consuming and costly, but it is a necessary component to ensure that the administrative state is viewed as legitimate.[39]

Larry D. Terry has rightly observed that proponents of government performance reform occasionally lose sight of the need for democratic governance. In his view, "the language of economics undoubtedly dominates the conversations regarding global governmental reform." We must take care, however, to ensure that economics does not supplant law and the democratic process. "We must constantly remind champions of the New Public Management that while economy and efficiency are important values, one must not lose sight of the fact that responsiveness, equity, representation and the rule of law are highly prized in the U.S. constitutional democracy."[40] In short, some incremental reforms are possible, and some may be desirable, but they must be implemented with care, and with due concern for the democratic process. The rule of the marketplace must not supercede the rule of law; efficient markets must not supplant democratic governance or the costs of increased efficiency outweigh the benefits.

Conclusion

The quest for legitimacy is as old as the republic itself. Recognizing that "might makes right" is not an ethic that can, or should, ground a modern regime, political scientists and philosophers have sought to find a means for justifying the use of political power by modern governments. This quest is especially pronounced for bureaucracy owing to the controversial nature of unelected officials exercising power in a regime ostensibly founded on democratic principles.

The Founders of the American republic were influenced by their intellectual predecessors, especially John Locke, to establish a system of government that allowed for a robust private sector and laws protecting private property rights. This system of government necessarily embraced laissez faire capitalism and a classical liberal system of government that called for a small, "night watchman" state. Over time, as the executive branch of the American federal government increased, the challenge for public administrators was to justify the growth of government power in a regime founded on principles of limited government administration.

Proponents of a strong system of public administration also have faced the challenge of a public calling for improved government service. Recent trends toward decentralization and privatization have heralded the need for a government that costs less, acts more efficiently, and is user friendly to customers (i.e., citizens). These trends have required defenders of the bureaucracy to explain why the executive branch does not perform as poorly as the public sometimes believes. Moreover, they have stressed the need for a strong executive branch to protect the public interest because the private sector is not designed for such a purpose. That this argument has not been persuasive to a significant number of people says as much or more about the jaded behavior of the public as it does about the failure of public administrators to craft a coherent, sound argument.

The challenge for public administration ethics is to help legitimize the administrative state at a time when the bureaucracy is growing tremendously but public antipathy is rising. One method for assuaging public concern is to set forth the case for representative bureaucracy. Because many agencies, especially at the sub-federal level, more accurately mirror the demographic characteristics of the community than do elected officials, an argument can be made that the bureaucracy represents the needs of constituents better and more accurately than elected officials. Another method of contributing to the legitimization of the administrative state is to suggest that bureaucracy, while imperfect, compares favorably to private administration. The negative public perception of bureaucracy is largely based on myths or isolated cases taken out of context. In any case, bureaucracy is not nearly as flawed or unnecessary as the public believes.

The ethical public administrator is the person who never loses sight of the challenge to administer government services in a fair, equitable, impartial manner while also accounting for the public's desire to have a more accountable and efficient government. Adhering to regulations when they are clear and on point but exercising judgment, discretion, and thinking creatively when ambiguous or unusual situations arise is the preferred method for public servants to perform their duties, but these tasks, of course, are far easier said than done. TQM, CQI, CSQI and similar management techniques may be tools to assist in improving government performance, but no one should forget that the tools are the means, not the ends, of government service. When the public views its servants as part of the solution to life's woes and not part of the problem owing to superior performance, however it is achieved, the case of bureaucratic legitimacy will be considerably less difficult to advance.

Exercises and Discussion Questions

1. Why is it difficult to legitimize government authority, especially for an unelected bureaucracy? Discuss ways in which a bureaucracy can be justified as a "rightful" exercise of authority.

2. How are public and private firms distinguished? What is it about the structure and operation of public firms that creates greater ethical duties than the duties imposed on private firms?

3. Walter Collins, a black man, is the local representative for the U.S. Department of Agriculture. He is not a political appointee, but he gained employment with the federal government through the competitive civil service. He lives in a predominantly rural, black neighborhood where many of his neighbors receive benefits from the Department of Agriculture, including home and equity loans. How might Mr. Collins explain the legitimacy of his position? Discuss the problems, if any, with defending the concept of representative bureaucracy. What, if any, implication does this concept hold for the subject of public administration ethics?

4. Why was John Locke's emphasis on the primacy of property rights so important to the founding of the American republic? Do you agree with Locke that property is a crucial component in legitimizing a democratic government? Why or why not? What would Locke say if the protection of property rights precluded the protection of individual liberty? What are the ethical implications?

5. How does improving government performance legitimize bureaucracy in the eyes of the public? Do you agree that improved performance leads, or should lead, to bureaucratic legitimacy? Discuss.

6. Do you agree that there is a distinction between "customers" and "citizens" or is this differentiation merely a semantics game? If there is a difference, why is it significant? Explain.

7. Do you believe that recent trends to decentralize government authority and privatize some traditional functions of government are positive or negative developments? Discuss. What are the implications for public administration ethics?

Notes

[1]   Thomas Hobbes, *Leviathan* (Indianapolis: Bobbs-Merrill, 1958), 107.

[2]   Herbert J. Storing, "American Statesmanship: Old and New," in *Bureaucrats, Policy Analysts, Statesmen: Who Leads?*, Robert A. Goldwin, ed. (Washington, D.C.: American Enterprise Institute, 1980), 96-97.

[3]   William D. Richardson, *Democracy, Bureaucracy, and Character: Founding Thought* (Lawrence: University Press of Kansas, 1997), 43-47.

4   Michael E. Milakovich and George J. Gordon, *Public Administration in America* (Belmont, Calif.: Wadsworth/Thomson, 2004), 23-26; Terrence R. Mitchell and William G. Scott, "The Barnard-Simon Contribution: A Vanished Legacy," *Public Administration Quarterly* 12 (Fall 1988): 354-56.

5   Graham T. Allison, Jr., "Public and Private Management: Are They Fundamentally Alike in All Unimportant Respects?" in *Setting Public Management Research Agendas* (Washington, D.C.: Office of Personnel Management, February 1980), 27-38; Milakovich and Gordon, *Public Administration in America*, 24-26; Alex W. Thrower and J. Michael Martinez, "Hazardous Materials Transportation in an Age of Devolution," *American Review of Public Administration* 29 (June 1999): 183; Sidney Tarrow, *Power in Movement: Social Movements, Collective Action and Politics* (New York: Cambridge University Press, 1994).

6   Garret Hardin, "The Tragedy of the Commons," *Science* 162 (December 1968): 1243-48.

7   Richard J. Stillman II, "American or European Public Administration: Does Public Administration Make the Modern State, or Does the State Make Public Administration?" *Public Administration Review* 57 (July/August 1997): 332-38.

8   Vernon Greene, Sally Coleman Selden, and Gene Brewer, "Measuring Power and Presence: Bureaucratic Representation in the American States," *Journal of Public Administration Research and Theory* 11 (July 2001): 379-402; John J. Hindera, "Representative Bureaucracy: Further Evidence of Active Representation in the EEOC District Offices," *Journal of Public Administration Research and Theory* 3 (October 1993): 415-29; Gregory B. Lewis, "Progress Toward Racial and Sexual Equality in the Federal Civil Service?" *Public Administration Review* 48 (May-June 1988): 700-707; Kenneth J. Meier and Lloyd G. Nigro, "Representative Bureaucracy and Policy References: A Study in the Attitudes of Federal Executives," *Public Administration Review* 36 (July-August 1976): 458-69.

9   John Locke, *Two Treatises of Government*, Thomas I. Cook, ed. (New York: Hafner Press, 1947), Second Treatise, V. See also Paschal Larkin, *Property in the Eighteenth Century: With Special Reference to England and Locke* (London: Cork University Press, 1930); Richardson, *Democracy, Bureaucracy, and Character: Founding Thought*, 84-86; Paul P. Van Riper, "Some Anomalies in the Deep History of U.S. Public Administration," *Public Administration Review* 57 (May/June 1997): 218-23.

10   Locke, *Two Treatises of Government*, V, 133-34.

11   Ibid., 134.

12   Richardson, *Democracy, Bureaucracy, and Character: Founding Thought*, 84-86.

13   Martin Diamond, "Ethics and Politics: The American Way," in *The Quest for Justice: Readings in Political Ethics*, 3d. ed., Leslie G. Rubin and Charles T. Rubin, eds. (Needham Heights, Mass.: Ginn Press, 1992), 295.

14   The Motherland experiences of the settlers certainly affected the ways in which the various regions of the new nation evolved. Indeed, Tocqueville claimed that the striking differences between the South, Northeast, and West were directly attributable to the character, mores, beliefs and habits the original settlers brought to their new homes. Cf. Alexis de Tocqueville, *Democracy in America*, ed. Harvey C. Mansfield and Delba Winthrop (Chicago: University of Chicago Press, 2002), 27-45.

[15]   Frank Donovan, *Mr. Madison's Constitution: The Story Behind the Constitutional Conven-tion* (New York: Dodd Mead & Company, 1965), vi-vii; John P. Roche, "The Founding Fathers: A Reform Caucus in Action," in *American Government: Readings and Cases*, 3d. ed., Peter Woll, ed. (Boston: Little, Brown & Company, 1969), 55-78.

[16]   Alexander Hamilton, James Madison, and John Jay, *The Federalist Papers*, Clinton Ros-siter, ed. (New York: New American Library, 1961), 435.

[17]   Jeremy Rabkin, "Bureaucratic Idealism and Executive Power: A Perspective on *The Fed-eralist*'s View of Public Administration," in *Saving the Revolution: The Federalist Papers and the American Founding*, Charles Kesler, ed. (New York: Free Press, 1987), 196-98.

[18]   Morton Grodzins, "The Federal System," in *Classic Readings in American Politics*, 2d. ed., Pietro S. Nivola and David H. Rosenbloom, eds. (New York: St. Martin's Press, 1990), 61-77; Richardson, *Democracy, Bureaucracy, and Character: Founding Thought*, 85-86.

[19]   Milakovich and Gordon, *Public Administration in America*, 3-9; Richard Stillman II, *American Bureaucracy: The Core of Modern Government*, 3d. ed. (Belmont, Calif.: Wads-worth/Thomson, 2004), 7-9.

[20]   Stephen Page, "What's New About the New Public Management? Administrative Change in the Human Services," *Public Administration Review* 65 (November 2005): 713-14.

[21]   Milakovich and Gordon, Public Administration in America, 38-41; Stillman, *American Bureaucracy: The Core of Modern Government*, 112.

[22]   Donald F. Kettl, *The Global Public Management Revolution*, 2d. ed. (Washington, D.C.: Brookings Institution Press, 2005), 36-37; James R. Thompson, "Reinvention as Re-form: Assessing the National Performance Review," *Public Administration Review* 60 (November/December 2000): 517-18.

[23]   Michael Spicer, "Public Administration, the History of Ideas, and the Reinventing Gov-ernment Movement," *Public Administration Review* 64 (May/June 2004): 357-59; Larry D. Terry, "From Greek Mythology to the Real World of the New Public Management and Democratic Governance (Terry Responds)," *Public Administration Review* 59 (May/June 1999): 274-76.

[24]   Milakovich and Gordon, *Public Administration in America*, 39-40.

[25]   Milakovich and Gordon, *Public Administration in America*, 39; Stillman, *American Bu-reaucracy: The Core of Modern Government*, 211.

[26]   Wendell L. French, Cecil H. Bell, Jr., and Bobert A. Zawaci, eds., *Organization Devel-opment and Transformation: Managing Effective Change* (Boston: McGraw-Hill, 2000); Robert T. Golembiewski, *Ironies in Organizational Development*, 2d. ed. (New York: Marcel Dekker, 2003); Robert T. Golembiewski, *Managing Diversity in Organizations* (Tuscaloosa: The University of Alabama Press, 1995).

[27]   Kettl, *The Global Public Management Revolution*, 33-35; Jon Meacham, "What Al Gore Might Learn the Hard Way," *Washington Monthly* 25 (September 1993): 16-21; Ronald C. Moe, "The 'Reinventing Government' Exercise: Misinterpreting the Problem, Mis-judging the Consequences," *Public Administration Review* 54 (March/April 1994): 111-22; Thompson, "Reinvention as Reform: Assessing the National Performance Review," 516-19.

28   Carolyn J. Hill, and Laurence E. Lynn, Jr., "Is Hierarchical Governance in Decline? Evidence from Empirical Research," *Journal of Public Administration Research and Theory* 15 (April 2005): 187.

29   Milakovich and Gordon, *Public Administration in America*, 154-56; Max Weber, "Bureaucracy," in *Classics of Organization Theory*, 2d. ed., Jay M. Shafritz and J. Steven Ott, eds. (Pacific Grove, Calif.: Brooks/Cole Publishing Company, 1987), 81-86.

30   Andrew Heywood, Political Ideas and Concepts: An Introduction (New York: St. Martin's Press, 1994), 89-93; Weber, "Bureaucracy," 81-86.

31   David Osborne and Ted Gaebler, *Reinventing Government: How the Entrepreneurial Spirit is Transforming the Public Sector* (Boston: Addison-Wesley, 1992), 327.

32   Linda deLeon and Robert B. Denhardt, "The Political Theory of Reinvention," *Public Administration Review* 60, 2 (March/April 2000): 89-92.

33   Ibid., 92.

34   Terry, "From Greek Mythology to the Real World of the New Public Management and Democratic Governance (Terry Responds)," 275. See also Spicer, "Public Administration, the History of Ideas, and the Reinventing Government Movement," 353-62.

35   Michael Barzelay and Babak J. Armajani, *Breaking Through Bureaucracy: A New Vision for Managing in Government* (Berkeley, Calif.: University of California Press, 1992), 8-9; Milakovich and Gordon, *Public Administration in America*, 429-32; Stillman, *American Bureaucracy: The Core of Modern Government*, 210

36   Richardson, *Democracy, Bureaucracy, and Character: Founding Thought*, 20-21; Roche, "The Founding Fathers: A Reform Caucus in Action," 55-78.

37   Hamilton, Madison, and Jay, *The Federalist Papers*, 322.

38   Diamond, "Ethics and Politics," 47-48; Richardson, *Democracy, Bureaucracy, and Character: Founding Thought*, 18-26, 85.

39   Spicer, "Public Administration, the History of Ideas, and the Reinventing Government Movement," 360-61; Terry, "From Greek Mythology to the Real World of the New Public Management and Democratic Governance (Terry Responds)," 275-76.

40   Terry, "From Greek Mythology to the Real World of the New Public Management and Democratic Governance (Terry Responds)," 276.

PART TWO:
BUREAUCRATIC POWER *and* DECISION-MAKING:
RULE *by* GIANT PYGMIES?

Chapter Three
Bureaucratic Power

The concept of "power"—its sources, uses, and potential abuses—raises a variety of ethical issues for the concerned public servant. In a regime founded on democratic principles, political power exercised by elected officials who receive their authority through free elections is legitimate because it is based on the consent of the governed. Presumably, if the governed are dissatisfied with their elected representatives, they can, and will, make changes in the next election. Thus, elected officials are accountable to the voters for their decisions, including decisions about how power should be wielded. Although it is true that many an unscrupulous politician has misused power behind the scenes, far away from the prying eyes and ears of the uninformed electorate, it is also true that the threat of exposure and a subsequent fall from grace generally serve as a strong deterrent against the most egregious misbehavior, especially in an era of "Gotcha" journalism where multitudes of crusading reformers use the electronic media and the Internet as weapons in the information wars. For every corrupt congressman and senator who accepts bribes, engages in sleazy sexual escapades, or even doles out plentiful piles of pork to constituents—which is not in and of itself a legal or ethical violation—many other elected officials are wary of misusing power in overt ways that will haunt, or possibly end, their public careers.

As discussed in many places throughout this text, the direct constitutional correctives that ensure the continued good faith of elected officials are not present in the bureaucracy. Because public administrators are never required to face voters (with some minor exceptions below the federal level), they need not fear the loss of their jobs or their public persona. Legislators oversee the bureaucracy and statutes and regulations place undeniable limits on the use of unfettered administrative discretion, but in the end public administrators nonetheless possess wide latitude for making decisions. This enormous discretion with little direct accountability naturally causes observers to question the factors that motivate bureaucrats.

Public administrators do not have a profit motive except in extreme cases where a rogue administrator embezzles public funds for private gain. Although some administrators act from a sense of public spiritedness, for many bureaucrats the ability to exercise power is a strong motivator. Bureaucratic power is a function of how much responsibility an agency has, how many clients the agency serves, the importance of its mission to the well-being of the nation, and the size of the agency's budget. Public administrators often engage in political infighting and intrigue, just at their elected counterparts do, to increase their power. Increased power is the reward that falls to an agency that creates a strong domain, which is essentially a claim that an organization stakes out in terms of programs covered, populations served, or services rendered.

Researcher James D. Thompson (1967) contends that all complex, purposive organizations, regardless of whether they exist in the public or the private sector, strive to establish a domain. Without a clearly defined domain, an organization cannot justify its existence to members, client groups, or third parties. Moreover, establishing a domain cannot be "an arbitrary, unilateral action" but "the organization's claims to a domain must be recognized by those who can provide needed support by the task environment." If an organization fails to make a case that it offers some desirable knowledge or expertise that cannot be offered elsewhere, the organization ultimately will not survive. Thus, establishing and maintaining a domain is a paramount objective for any organization if it is to withstand repeated competition and assaults from its foes.[1]

In a heightened political atmosphere where many organizations seek to establish and maintain a domain, individual administrators must recognize that competition exists among public agencies. Scarce budgets, limited personnel, incomplete knowledge, and looming deadlines make it imperative that bureaucrats practice politics in an effort to enhance their power. In light of the scarcity of resources and the possibility of intergovernmental competition, political concerns are never far from the forefront when public bureaucracies compete in the policy-making arena to establish and maintain a policy domain.

The ethical administrator recognizes that he or she must engage in political infighting, to some extent, if the agency is to retain and perhaps expand its domain, thereby increasing its power. At the same time, the ethical administrator recognizes that power must not be an end in itself but a means toward accomplishing the mission and objectives of the organization. To say the ends justify the means it to mistake the ultimate "public interest" of providing goods and services to citizens in a fair and equitable manner consistent with the concept of a democratic regime.

Bureaucratic power has long been a topic of concern. The study of public administration has come full circle since Publius wrote in "Federalist 72" that, "[t]he administration of government, in its largest sense, comprehends all the operations of the body politic, whether legislative, executive, or judiciary...."[2] The Founders envisioned a regime where democratic and bureaucratic power were one and inseparable, the latter a necessary derivative of the former. Moreover, because the power of the bureaucracy depended on the power of elected officials, accountability was implicit in the exercise of administrative functions. In fact, to Publius it would have been nonsensical to evaluate public administration without using political standards of accountability.[3]

In some ways, it is no exaggeration to conclude that the Founders understood public administration far better than the generations that immediately succeeded them. During the nineteenth century, observers came to regard politics and administration as dichotomous. It would take scholars and political scientists of the mid-twentieth century to return to an understanding of public administration as part of a continuum rather than as a discrete realm of government.[4]

In appreciating the Founders' perspicacity, however, we should not credit them with more than their due. For the simpler world of the eighteenth century, bureaucratic dominance in affairs of state would have seemed strange and unthinkable. Public administrators were little more than technicians, clerks who faithfully carried out the orders of elected officials without unduly affecting policy. It was no small conceptual leap to view public administration as an auxiliary function of the political realm when administrators were deemed little more than scribes.[5] If this view seems quaint today, it is because we have seen the mushrooming of the administrative state in the twentieth century and with it the development of a concept unknown to the Founders: administrative discretion. Far more important than the public concern with "crude wrongdoing" (to use Paul Appleby's phrase), administrative discretion involves public administrators implementing public policy by using their own interpretations of legislative requirements.[6] Sometimes this interpretation is unsupported by articulated standards, but a lack of legislative oversight is not the core issue. The debate over administrative discretion is a concern about elected officials delegating authority to unelected officials who are left to their own devices—not because they are usurpers of power (although sometimes that may be the case), but because someone must decide and no one else can or has chosen to do so. In short, public administrators fill in the gaps in public policy intentionally or unintentionally left by elected officials.[7]

This "gap-filling" function holds enormous repercussions for bureaucratic power, to say nothing of ethical considerations. When a legislature delegates authority to an executive branch agency, invariably this leaves the agency with broad discretion in developing the details of a policy. If agencies were staffed by clerks who did not need to exercise discretion, the ethical administrator would need only to discern what the guidelines required and act accordingly. The assumption that discretion was not part of the administrator's role characterized much of the early literature on public administration, but the thesis has been rejected (or at least substantially modified) in the years since the growth of the administrative state demonstrated the inevitability of bureaucratic discretion.[8]

When public administrators are viewed as more than mere clerks fulfilling the expressed will of elected representatives, this means that their decisions have real or potential political repercussions. When a group of unelected officials exercises political power in a regime purportedly founded on democratic principles, the question naturally arises as to why this group legitimately should make political judgments.[9] Heredity and direct public accountability through election—the two major sources of legitimacy for western governments—were never serious sources of bureaucratic authority.[10] This leaves expertise and political neutrality as the twin pillars of bureaucratic legitimacy.[11]

Expertise is the idea that public administrators rule because they have knowledge that is not available to the general population. As government—especially the federal government—exercises ever more control in the American regime, the need for expertise increases. Regulating airline safety, transportation infrastructure, environmental controls, food and drug safety, homeland security, and so forth requires an educated work force. Thus, public administrators answer Herbert Storing's "Who says?" question about the legitimacy of exercising power by presenting their credentials and making a case for administrative expertise. Why does Congress delegate authority to the U.S. Environmental Protection Agency (EPA) to promulgate rules and regulations governing clean air and water? Congress is comprised of generalists who do not necessarily understand the scientific and technical issues associated with environmental issues. EPA, however, employs many career specialists with training in the scientific processes necessary to extend policy from the conceptual realm to a place "where the rubber meets the road," in the words of the old adage.[12]

Political neutrality is highly desirable in a political system that depends on unelected experts to make decisions that have political repercussions. As one commentator has remarked, "[a]lthough in and of itself political neutrality was an insufficiently persuasive foundation for the discretion public administration necessarily had to be allowed in our democratic republic, it proved to be an impressive support for the claim of expertise."[13] If unelected public administrators were not at least theoretically neutral in developing and implementing policy, they would become overtly political actors in an apolitical arena. This tension between democracy/bureaucracy and expertise/neutrality—that is, between politics and administration—is a classic conundrum of American public administration.[14]

The Political Context

Understanding how bureaucrats exercise power requires an understanding of the nature and extent of bureaucratic power, which became a topic in much of the literature during the twentieth century, especially in the 1940s and 1950s. In 1949, Norton Long, a well-known public administration theorist, published an influential essay titled, "Power and Administration." Not satisfied to reiterate the platitudes of the past, Long argued that, contrary to the assumptions held by an earlier generation of scholars, the "lifeblood" of public administration is power—who has it, how they got it, and how they use it. In his view, scholars who subscribe to the traditional view of politics and administration as bifurcated and forever separated are myopic; they fail to grasp the essential characteristics of a bureaucracy. Because legislators necessarily compromise and draft language in vague terms to ensure the passage of key legislation, they leave a power vacuum that must be filled by someone or something. In interpreting a statutory mandate, public administrators fill the power vacuum by exercising discretion. Depending on congressional oversight or instructions passed down through the chain of command is insufficient to control the actions of a bureaucrat because legislators seldom involve themselves in the minute technical details of a given policy.[15]

Long was not the first theorist to explore the politics-administration dichotomy, nor was he especially profound in discussing the problems inherent in the congressional delegation of power to administrative agencies. Long's contribution was his insight into the nature of bureaucratic power; he highlighted the consequences of allowing the bureaucracy to exercise enormous discretionary authority. To repeat a cliché: power abhors a vacuum. Long recognized that administrators will fill the vacuum where it exists. In doing so, they wield enormous power. Business enterprises may rise or fall depending on how an agency interprets its mandate and develops standards for formulating and implementing a policy. The lives of every American are affected by whether a certain drug is authorized for sale, which transportation mode is preferred over another, how pollution controls are designed, if one tax regulation supersedes another, and so forth.

It is logical to infer that in places where political power exists, interest groups invariably appear in the quest to influence the exercise of that power. In an influential book, the pluralist David B. Truman contended that interest group politics plays an integral role in the operation of the bureaucracy precisely because bureaucrats exercise tremendous political power. If the traditional notion of a passive bureaucracy that blithely accepts instructions from Congress were an accurate depiction of reality, the involvement of interest groups at the administrative level would be nonsensical. No self-respecting lobbyist would attempt to influence the formulation of policy at the administrative level if the process was clear, unequivocal, and not subject to interpretation. A lobbyist would focus on Congress or the appropriate state or local legislative authority, concentrating his resources in one place before a bill could be enacted and thereafter handed off to automatons for implementation and enforcement. Yet the halls of administrative agencies are filled with interest group representatives who seek to influence the formulation of policies in virtually every area regulated by governments.[16]

The notion of "bureaucratic politics," which the pluralists propound, moves away from a focus on formal, legalistic analyses toward a more informal process of developing public policy. Public administrators are almost as involved in politics as legislators, albeit they focus on a different point in the policy process. Where legislators debate a policy at its broadest point—for example, where the United States should set standards for ground-level ozone emissions—public administrators debate the specific standards themselves. If Congress decided that ground-level ozone should be regulated, EPA bureaucrats must develop the numerical standards, searching the literature or commissioning research to determine if x parts per million is more appropriate than y parts per million.

The pluralist movement raises a variety of issues concerning the representative nature of a bureaucracy. The core tenet of pluralism is the belief that groups will compete with each other and out of that competition efficacious public policy will emerge, phoenix-like, from the ashes. Accordingly, if bureaucrats exercise broad discretion and craft policies, they must in some sense reflect the values of the democratic system in which they work. They must understand the interests of the various parties affected by a given policy and they must take into account those interests, to the extent possible. At the same time, they must take care not to become "captured" by the private interests with which they deal. The "public interest," however it is defined, must be protected.

To accomplish their goals, according to this view, individual bureaucrats should understand what John Rohr calls "regime values," that is, those core principles upon which the nation was founded and still stands. This is a tall order. As discussed in Chapter 2, bureaucrats must be cognizant not only of the fundamental concepts inherent in the American political system, but also of the changing political climate and mores reflected in various pronouncements of positivist legal authorities, especially the U.S. Supreme Court.[17]

In short, the representativeness so favored by pluralists is the idea that the values and interests of affected parties and the public are properly factored into bureaucratic decision-making. If an agricultural bill has been passed by Congress and must be implemented by the U.S. Department of Agriculture (USDA), presumably the department will want to receive input from affected parties. Farmers, truckers, grocers, and other interested groups may wish to point out practical difficulties in implementation or pitfalls to avoid in drafting workable regulations. Not only can affected parties educate bureaucrats on the issues involved in implementation, but it is far easier to ensure that affected parties buy into rules and regulations when they have input into the process than when it is forced on them through a heavy-handed command-and-control process.

The difficulty in the pluralist conception of bureaucratic politics is that it highlights the tension between democracy and bureaucracy without offering a solution to the conundrum. Ideally, unelected bureaucrats will diligently work to identify regime values and act in a manner consistent with those values. Problems arise owing to differences between elected and unelected officials. Elected officials have a direct connection with "regime values." If their constituents do not approve of the choices that elected officials make, they can vote for another candidate in the next election. The faith expressed by pluralists that unelected bureaucrats will be self-policing and voluntarily seek out regime values begs the question of what happens if bureaucrats are unwilling or unable to identify values consistent with the will of the majority. If unelected officials exercise discretion and act in ways that are patently unconstitutional or beyond the scope of their legislative mandate, who is to say that they have ignored regime values? Moreover, who has the proper authority to determine the nature and scope of regime values?[18]

An even more fundamental issue is the difficulty in determining regime values in the first place. As a matter of general policy in a democratic political system, the interests of affected parties should be considered in the policy-making process at all levels—in agencies as well as in legislatures. But what happens when multiple parties express conflicting interests and it falls to the agencies to navigate these stormy seas? Administrative agencies have constituencies just as elected representatives have constituencies. If the pluralists are correct that interest groups play a role in the exercise of bureaucratic power, ensuring that bureaucrats do not pander to their constituencies is a genuine concern. Unfortunately, finding one easily understood universal principle to guide bureaucrats in choosing which groups to listen to and which groups to ignore is an almost impossible task. The problem of group formulation and access always has been a sore spot for pluralists. Not all groups are equally well situated. Some groups, especially large, well-endowed corporations, invariably can marshal more resources than smaller, public-interest-oriented groups can hope to command. Elitism inevitably intrudes into the pluralist landscape. Who, then, protects the public interest? How is it that broad, desirable public policy that provides the greatest good for the greatest number emerges from a political process that is based on the advancement of narrow self-interest?[19]

This insight highlights the central issue in any discussion of bureaucratic power: bureaucrats exercise no small degree of political power owing to their expertise and the reality of legislative delegation. Determining how they should use their discretion in exercising power is the crucial issue, as we have discussed, but it is by no means free of controversy. If the "iron law of oligarchy" holds true and all power tends to become centralized, hence autocratic, over time, the problem is in legitimizing bureaucratic power when the expertise of unelected bureaucrats ostensibly undermines the democratic process. Bureaucrats can invite public participation, to some extent, in their activities, but this generally leads to a proliferation of interest groups competing to catch the ear of their regulators. The proponent of democratic systems will cry, "then bureaucrats should discern the public will and act accordingly," but this is far easier said than done. What exactly is the "public will" and how does someone recognize it, assuming it even exists?[20]

If bureaucrats are to act as agents of the legislative branch and guardians of the public trust in exercising power, it is incumbent upon them to follow proper courses of action—based on "regime values," in Rohr's parlance—even in situations that seem pedestrian and devoid of political repercussions. In broad terms, this translates into a search for safeguards to ensure that bureaucrats behave in a manner consistent with the regime. At this point, legal safeguards are an important factor in bureaucratic power because they serve as a key external control on the discretion exercised by unelected officials.[21]

The Legal Context

Whenever government provides goods and services, invariably one group will benefit while other groups must shoulder the burden. If goods and services were available without regard to cost or scarcity, such questions would not arise, but they always do in an imperfect, finite world. Providing welfare benefits to impoverished peoples, for example, means that taxes must be imposed on one group to pay for the transfer of wealth to another group. All kinds of arguments exist for and against this transfer, but undeniably each group is affected. Deciding how to fashion rules and regulations in light of this imbalance among and between competing groups can be accomplished through several means, including the development and maintenance of legal standards and procedures, especially the concepts of equal protection of the law and due process of law.[22]

Broadly speaking, the concept of equal protection of law refers to the idea that no individual or group will be deliberately harmed or benefited solely on the basis of the individual's status or the group's identity. That is not to say that an individual or group will avoid bearing a burden or always gain a benefit, but only that the burden or benefit will not be apportioned based solely on inequitable considerations such as race, ethnicity, gender, age, or wealth. A regulation may provide Social Security payments for senior citizens at the expense of younger persons, but this distinction does not constitute an impermissible violation of the equal protection of the law. The statute that was passed by Congress and implemented by the agency included a mandate, as a matter of policy, to benefit senior citizens. If enough Americans disapprove of the policy and the reasons behind it, they may complain and vote for Members of Congress to change the policy. In this instance, senior citizens received a benefit not because they were afforded preferential treatment *solely* based on their age. They were a population specifically targeted by Congress based on a perceived need to correct a problem or improve an existing condition that affected the group. This goal is a far cry from imposing harm or bestowing a benefit on a group without due consideration for individual circumstances.[23]

Classification of individuals is constitutionally permissible in the American political system if a legitimate, compelling reason exists for the classification. Because older people have clearly defined characteristics that differentiate them from the rest of the population, targeting such a group of people for legislation or administrative regulations is constitutionally permissible if the targeting does not discriminate against them unreasonably. Firing a worker merely because he is a certain age generally is not allowable, but providing for retirement at a certain age or allowing senior citizens to withdraw funds from an Individual Retirement Account at a certain age is a reasonable use of the classification.

Some classifications—especially those based on race and, to a lesser extent, gender—are considered by the courts to be "suspect" classifications. On its face, classifying people based on race is considered to be impermissible and, in cases where racial discrimination is alleged, courts have approached the matter using "strict scrutiny." In effect, this means that the state or the party that has imposed the racial classification has an extremely difficult burden of proof to show how and why the classification was related to a legitimate governmental objective. In the vast majority of cases, the racial classification cannot be defended, and it fails to pass constitutional muster. Gender classifications, by contrast, receive "intermediate scrutiny" from the courts, which means that the party making such a classification has a high burden of proof to meet, but it can be met. For example, women may be denied certain types of hazardous employment if the employer can show studies or other convincing data that women as a group are subjected to unusually high risks. As a result, it is extremely difficult to justify racial and gender classifications, although the instances where gender classifications are held to be constitutionally permissible exceed instances where racial classifications are upheld.[24]

The core issue is whether a law upholds a discriminatory purpose. In some cases, it is clear that legislators drafted a law expressly to harm or benefit a certain classification of people. Such statutes clearly violate the constitutionally mandated equal protection of the law found in the Fifth Amendment and the Fourteenth Amendment. In other cases, it may be that legislators did not intend to discriminate, but the result is the same as if they did. In essence, the law has a discriminatory effect. Depending on how the law was drafted and/or how it was implemented, it is possible that the courts will consider it a law that upholds a discriminatory purpose. In such a case, the law cannot stand unless and until the discriminatory purpose is ameliorated or abolished.[25]

Due process is closely related to the notion of equal protection of the law. At its core, due process is the idea that every individual possesses a set of rights that cannot be abrogated by government without going through a series of steps to ensure that individuals are protected. Thus, according to the concept of procedural due process, every person charged with a crime is entitled to his or her "day in court." A speedy trial must be held and the defendant has the right to present evidence and witnesses in his or her behalf as well as confront accusers and examine evidence and witnesses on the opposing side. In John Rawls's words, due process can be understood as "a process reasonably designed to ascertain the truth, in ways consistent with the other ends of the legal system, as to whether a violation has taken place and under what circumstances."[26]

In the context of public administration, procedural due process refers to whether, and in what manner, administrative agencies can take actions that might harm citizens' constitutionally protected rights. Every person who falls into a category that is the subject of an agency's actions has the right to be notified of the action, respond orally or in writing, and have an appeal if he or she loses. For example, when an agency changes the eligibility requirements for receiving welfare benefits, all welfare recipients who will be affected must be notified of the impending change. If the recipient wishes to do so, he or she then must be afforded an opportunity to comment on the change. Such comments may be in writing or at a public hearing or, in a few instances, in an individual adjudicatory hearing. Even if the recipient loses at this stage, he or she can request an appeal. The concept of due process does not promise a particular outcome—the welfare recipient may lose benefits even if many hearings are held—but at least the recipient has his or her day in court.[27]

In light of the discussion above, it should be clear that the legal context of bureaucratic power contains many constraints on the exercise of that power. Constitutional and other legal constraints on the unbridled use of power at all levels of government are hallmarks of the American political system. The purpose of the Bill of Rights was to impose limits on what the federal government (and, later, the states) could do to the liberty and property of its citizens. Laws and regulations have been adopted since the ratification of the Constitution specifically to ensure that democratic government does not degenerate into a tyrannical political system.

For the ethical administrator, following explicit legal requirements is not the core issue. Obviously, an administrator must follow the letter of the law if that law is clear and unambiguous. The difficulty lies in following a law that is not context-specific. In cases where the law is anything but clear, the ethical administrator must use his or her discretion to find the "spirit" of the law. Determining the spirit of the law is akin to ascertaining regime values, but it is the task of every unelected public official who wishes to act ethically in government service.

The Management Context

Accountability always has presented a problem for bureaucratic politics. For elected officials, this connection between the electorate and its representatives is fairly straightforward. If the masses do not approve of their representatives' performance in office, theoretically they can vote for other candidates. They may have practical reasons for reelecting incumbents—a reluctance to forfeit the gains that accrue through seniority, an uninformed electorate that does not bother to obtain information on challengers, or alienation from the political process—but they have a choice in the matter.[28]

By contrast, the overwhelming majority of public administrators are career civil servants. Their decisions may hold enormous repercussions for citizens, but they are not directly accountable to the electorate. How, then, are bureaucrats held accountable? This question often is phrased as "who guards the guardians"? If public administrators are charged, at least in part, with protecting the public interest, safeguards must exist for those occasions when administrators, for whatever reasons, fail to do so.[29]

Public administrators sometimes are mistaken in their conception of the public interest. They might be well meaning and earnest in their attempts to discern regime values, but for a variety of reasons they fail to grasp the "higher good." This kind of myopia can occur especially in highly specialized or technical agencies where an administrator becomes so close to a project and so emotionally and intellectually invested in the agency's work that he or she cannot see beyond that work. It is only natural that someone working in an agency finds the job rewarding because he or she believes in the agency's mission. While such zeal generally is praiseworthy, it can have a deleterious effect when the administrator loses sight of the place of the agency in the context of the regime. Thus, an administrator at the U.S. Environmental Protection Agency may be wholeheartedly in favor of protecting the natural environment, but in some instances this concern must be set aside in favor of other interests. Emergency response personnel removing debris from the site of the World Trade Center terrorist attacks in 2001 would not have been amenable to arguments that burying construction debris in the Fresh Kills landfill creates enormous environmental problems. No question about it, dumping tons of debris in the landfill harms the natural environment, but in this case other considerations outweighed environmental considerations. Administrators must be sensitive to such contextual concerns, especially when more prosaic issues arise.[30]

Public administrators may have less laudable reasons for their failure to discern the public interest. In some instances, they may have their own personal agendas that they elevate over and above the public interest. They may decide that a particular policy should be implemented in accordance with a vision far different from that expressed by Congress or higher-level administrators. Moreover, they may decide that they will perform their duties based on political exchanges or owing to base corruption. Although corruption often is sensationalized far beyond the realities that exist in the bureaucracy, as long as the endlessly inventive human mind is capable of crafting new schemes, corruption invariably will exist to a greater or lesser extent.[31]

Clearly, then, public administrators must be held strictly accountable. The difficulty, of course, is in designing a program that ensures that public administrators have the necessary authority to exercise discretion and carry out their duties while still being responsible for their decisions. Administrators' expertise and access to tightly controlled, and generally obscure, information ensures that attempts by generalists in Congress to curb the bureaucracy often will be frustrated. Similarly, members of the public almost always find themselves at a disadvantage when they confront administrators. Only lobbyists and other representatives of interest groups can hope to match public administrators' resources and access to information, and even in such instances the ensuing "battle of the experts" does little to ensure that the "public interest," however it is defined, is protected.[32]

Accountability also is undermined when legislators commit what one political scientist has called "legiscide." In an effort to appeal to voters, elected officials sometimes prefer to delegate authority for making difficult political decisions to administrative agencies. This effort certainly is understandable; cutting government programs and services seldom enhances political careers. It is human nature to avoid blame and seek praise, and elected officials are especially attuned to the need for continued popularity. Consequently, they want to tell their constituents that they have accomplished goals that the public will appreciate—building new military bases, bringing federal dollars into the state or district, and providing government largesse to meet a variety of constituent objectives.[33]

This preference for making popular decisions means that legislators sometimes push unpopular decision-making authority into agencies. Afterward, when agency officials indicate that new pollution standards must be instituted or budget cuts must be implemented or a previously promised government service or program must be curtailed, legislators can avoid the resultant hue and cry. In fact, savvy legislators can heap blame on the agencies and promise their constituents that the legislature will investigate bureaucratic abuses.

This delegation of political power invests enormous authority in agencies, despite the subsequent criticism. In extreme cases, it transforms the legislative body into little more than a rubber-stamping organization. Yes, the legislature retains oversight authority to set standards for agencies and require a measure of accountability, but for all practical purposes a legislature that is unwilling or unable to make difficult decisions is an ineffectual body. A decrease in legislative power almost always leads to an increase in bureaucratic power.[34]

The ethical public administrator must strive never to stray too far from the public will. Even if the administrator does not personally agree with a particular policy, he or she must remember to make decisions, to the extent possible, in accordance with regime values. As long as administrators act as though they were directly accountable to an informed electorate, even though they may not be, they can be confident that they are acting on sound principles of accountability.

Conclusion: Bureaucratic Power and Ethical Controls

Bureaucratic power as well as the propensity of bureaucrats to engage in political maneuvering is a widely accepted feature of American public administration. With the growth in size and complexity of government operations after the middle of the twentieth century, the question of how bureaucratic power can be exercised is an important inquiry. Some theorists have argued that the only appropriate control on bureaucratic power is to educate public administrators so they develop an individual sense of moral responsibility as an internal control on their behavior. The literature on this point recommends that courses on ethics and identifying regime values be taught in schools of public administration and seminars on ethics be offered in public agencies. If teachers can only provide good, credible information to well-meaning individuals, bureaucratic power can be used in a responsible manner that comports with the public interest.

The alternate view suggests that external controls are a more appropriate method of controlling bureaucratic power. Formal codes of ethics, legal rules, and frequent checks on the power of bureaucrats are the only assurances that unelected officials will not abuse their positions and hide behind a veneer of civil service protection. "Moral responsibility is likely to operate in direct proportion to the strictness and efficiency of political responsibility, and to fall away in all sorts of perversions when the latter is weakly enforced," Herman Finer once observed.[35]

In recent years, public administration theorists have begun to argue in favor of fusing both internal and external controls. Writers such as John Rohr and Terry L. Cooper contend that public administrators must search for guidance on appropriate regime principles—and the quest is a kind of internal control on behavior—but they take their cues from the formal organizations in which they serve. If organizations do not function properly, the administrator owes a higher duty to the public to act ethically above and beyond what is required by a particular organization.[36]

Ethical controls can be developed to allow bureaucratic power to be used, as necessary, and to curb it when appropriate. Internal and external controls, combined, seem to offer the best approach. Kathryn G. Denhardt suggests that the two controls can be fused to provide "a better-developed theoretical framework...more grounded in philosophy, and...ultimately more practical in that it considers and accommodates the exigencies of the environment in which public administrators must practice."[37] In Cooper's view, all such controls must promote core American values: "The beneficial aspects of pluralism of interests, the creative possibilities in conflict, the sovereignty of the public, the rights of the minority, the importance of citizen participation in government, [and] the societal values of freedom of expression." When these values are embraced and bureaucrats adhere to them, bureaucratic power can be exercised in the name of the public interest.[38]

Exercises and Discussion Questions

1. Is bureaucratic expertise desirable in the United States? Why or why not? If bureaucratic expertise is desirable, discuss the pros and cons of allowing unelected "experts" to make political decisions. If it is not desirable, discuss the pros and cons of having elected officials make decisions on highly complex or technical matters in lieu of leaving those questions for experts.
2. Discuss the concept of bureaucratic politics. Do you believe that unelected public administrators should make political decisions? Why or why not? What are the pros and cons of bureaucratic politics?
3. Discuss the issue of accountability. How are accountability and legitimacy related? In your opinion, what are the best ways to ensure bureaucratic accountability? For example, should public administrators be rotated from one position to another? Discuss.
4. What is meant by the term "due process of law"? Does classifying persons based on their physical attributes violate due process? Explain. How are due process and administrative ethics related, if at all? What obligations, if any, does an ethical administrator have with respect to due process of law?
5. You are working as an inspector general for the U.S. Department of the Interior (DOI), which makes you, in effect, a roving overseer. In that position, you must ensure that each office within DOI performs its work in accordance with its congressional mandate and departmental policy. Late one afternoon, you learn that the president's new nominee to head up the department is a conservative Republican who has vowed to "remake DOI so it does not interfere in the administration's desire to use western lands

for new, moneymaking, profitable purposes." The department is in charge of western lands—supposedly acting as a "steward of the people." Consequently, the new nominee's stated desire to use public land for profit is worrisome. By a strange coincidence, you have mutual friends who knew the nominee years ago, when he was in college, and they have supplied you with photographs showing the youthful nominee from 30 years ago engaging in what can only be described as "indecent" (although not criminal) behavior. What should you do in this situation?

a. Ignore the photographs because they are not relevant to the current situation and, besides, it is not your job to politicize the department.
b. Send the photographs, or at least information about the photographs, to the U.S. Senate committee in charge of holding hearings to determine whether the nominee should be confirmed as the Secretary of the Interior. If the nominee was engaged in "indecent" behavior, no matter how long ago, the Senate—and, ultimately, the American people—have a right to know about it when deciding whether the nominee is fit to serve at a high level in government service.
c. Anonymously send the photographs, or at least information about the photographs, to the press.
d. Ignore the photographs because, although they are relevant to the current situation, you are supposed to be politically neutral. It is not your job to politicize the department.
e. You should perform more than one of the actions listed above (be specific.)

Notes

1   James D. Thompson, *Organizations in Action: Social Science Bases of Administrative Theory* (New York: McGraw-Hill, 1967), 28.
2   Alexander Hamilton, James Madison, and John Jay, *The Federalist Papers*, Clinton Rossiter, ed. (New York: New American Library, 1961), 435.
3   Jeremy Rabkin, "Bureaucratic Idealism and Executive Power: A Perspective on *The Federalist*'s View of Public Administration," in *Saving the Revolution: The Federalist Papers and the American Founding*, Charles Kesler, ed. (New York: The Free Press, 1987), 196-98.
4   See, e.g., Reinhard Bendix, "Bureaucracy and the Problem of Power," *Public Administration Review* 5 (1945): 194-209; Gerald E. Caiden, "In Search of an Apolitical Science of Public Administration," in *Politics and Administration: Woodrow Wilson and American*

Public Administration, Jack S. Rabin and James S. Bowman, eds. (New York: Marcel Dekker, 1984), 51-76; Wallace S. Sayre, "Premises of Public Administration: Past and Emerging," *Public Administration Review* 18 (1958): 102-5.

[5] William D. Richardson, *Democracy, Bureaucracy & Character: Founding Thought* (Lawrence: University Press of Kansas, 1997), 41-43; Sayre, "The Premises of Public Administration," 102-3.

[6] Paul H. Appleby, *Morality and Administration in Democratic Government* (Baton Rouge: Louisiana State University Press, 1952), 56; John P. Burke, *Bureaucratic Responsibility* (Baltimore: Johns Hopkins University Press, 1986), 11-15; Wayne A. R. Leys, "Ethics and Administrative Discretion," *Public Administration Review* 3 (Winter 1943): 10-23.

[7] David H. Rosenbloom, *Public Administration: Understanding Management, Politics, and Law in the Public Sector*, 3d. ed. (New York: Random House, 1993), 54,56,382.

[8] See, e.g., Luther Gulick, "Science, Values, and Public Administration," in *Papers on the Science of Administration*, Luther Gulick and Lyndall Urwick, eds. (New York: Augustus M. Kelley, 1937), esp. 191-95; Woodrow Wilson, "The Study of Administration," *Political Science Quarterly* 56 (December 1941): 494 (originally published in *Political Science Quarterly* 2 [June 1887]: 209-17). See also J. Michael Martinez, "Law Versus Ethics: Reconciling Two Concepts of Public Service Ethics," *Administration & Society* 29 (January 1998): 705-6.

[9] Herbert Storing once characterized the quest for legitimacy as "Who says?" In other words, the query is why I should obey your authority as opposed to some other entity's claim to authority. The discussion of bureaucratic power at its core is a question of how a bureaucracy exercises discretion and thereby exercises power legitimately. Herbert J. Storing, "American Statesmanship: Old and New," in *Bureaucrats, Policy Analysts, Statesmen: Who Leads?* Robert A. Goldwin, ed. (Washington, D.C.: The American Enterprise Institute, 1980), 88-113.

[10] See, e.g., Richardson, *Democracy, Bureaucracy, & Character*, 45-47.

[11] Richardson, *Democracy, Bureaucracy, & Character*, 45-46;Rosenbloom, *Public Administration*, 482-4.

[12] See, e.g., Steven Ferrey, *Environmental Law: Examples and Explanations* (New York: Aspen Law & Business, 1997), 2-4; Olga L. Moya and Andrew L. Fono, *Federal Environmental Law: The User's Guide* (St. Paul, Minn.: West Publishing, 1997),3-7; Leonard Ortolano, *Environmental Regulation and Impact Assessment* (New York: John Wiley & Sons, Inc., 1997), 45-48.

[13] Richardson, *Democracy, Bureaucracy, & Character*, 46.

[14] The classic discussion of this point is found in Dwight Waldo, *The Administrative State* (New York: Holmes & Meier, 1984), 15-16. See also Arthur S. Fleming, "The Civil Servant in a Period of Transition," *Public Administration Review* 13 (1953): 73-79; David Levitan, "The Neutrality of the Public Service," *Public Administration Review* 2 (1942): 317-23; Dwight Waldo, "The Perdurability of the Politics-Administration Dichotomy: Woodrow Wilson and the Identity Crisis in Public Administration," in *Politics and Administration: Woodrow Wilson and American Public Administration*, Jack S. Rabin and James S. Bowman, eds. (New York: Marcel Dekker, 1984), 219-33.

[15] Norton Long, "Power and Administration," *Public Administration Review* 9 (Autumn 1949): 257-64.

[16] David B. Truman, *The Governmental Process: Political Interests and Public Opinion* (New York: Alfred A. Knopf, 1951).

[17] John A. Rohr, *Ethics for Bureaucrats: An Essay on Law and Values*, 2d. ed. (New York: Marcel Dekker, 1989), 285-91.

[18] See, e.g., Henry Kariel, *The Decline of American Pluralism* (Palo Alto, Calif.: Stanford University Press, 1961), 51.

[19] Burke, *Bureaucratic Responsibility*, 20-22.

[20] Andrew Heywood, *Political Ideas and Concepts: An Introduction* (New York: St. Martin's Press, 1994), 40-43. See also Robert Michels, *Political Parties* (New York: The Free Press, 1962).

[21] Rohr, *Ethics for Bureaucrats*, 285.

[22] Marshall Dimock, *Law and Dynamic Administration* (New York: Praeger, 1980), 31.

[23] Henry Campbell Black, *Black's Law Dictionary*, 5th ed. (St. Paul: West Publishing Company, 1979), 481-82; Rosenbloom, *Public Administration*, 493-96.

[24] William Cohen and David J. Danelski, *Constitutional Law: Civil Liberty and Individual Rights*, 4th ed. (Westbury, N.Y.: The Foundation Press, Inc., 1997),1021-23.

[25] Rosenbloom, *Public Administration*, 496-98. So much has been written about discrimination, especially regarding race, that it is difficult to narrow the sources in this area. Two especially good books on this point are Brian K. Landsberg, *Enforcing Civil Rights: Race, Discrimination and the Department of Justice* (Lawrence: The University Press of Kansas, 1997), and Paul M. Sniderman and Thomas Piazza, *The Scar of Race* (Cambridge, Mass.: The Belknap Press of the Harvard University Press, 1993).

[26] John Rawls, *A Theory of Justice* (Cambridge, Mass.: The Belknap Press of Harvard University Press, 1971), 239.

[27] Cohen and Danelski, *Constitutional Law*, 1152-54.

[28] Burke, *Bureaucratic Responsibility*, 38-54.

[29] The problem is stated most famously by Publius in "Federalist 51," but for more modern sources, see, e.g., Terry L. Cooper, *The Responsible Administrator: An Approach to Ethics for the Administrative Role*, 3d. ed. (San Francisco: Jossey-Bass, 1990), 123-54; Harold F. Gortner, *Ethics for Public Managers* (Westport, Conn.: Praeger, 1991), 21-22; Frederick Mosher, *Democracy and the Public Service* (New York: Oxford University Press, 1968), 5; and John Rehfuss, *The Job of the Public Manager* (Chicago: The Dorsey Press, 1989), 270-75.

[30] For more on mistaken impressions of the public interest, see Samuel Krislov and David H. Rosenbloom, *Representative Bureaucracy and the American Political System* (New York: Praeger, 1981), Chapter 2.

[31] Michael Johnston, *Political Corruption and Public Policy in America* (Monterey, Calif.: Brooks/Cole, 1982), 3; Rosenbloom, *Public Administration*, 512-17.

[32] Rosenbloom, *Public Administration*, 507-11.

[33] The point on "legiscide" is most famously made in Theodore J. Lowi, *The End of Liberalism* (New York: W.W. Norton, 1969), esp. 71.

[34] Rosenbloom, *Public Administration*, 54-58.

[35]   Herman Finer, "Administrative Responsibility in Democratic Government," in *Combating Corruption/Encouraging Ethics: A Sourcebook for Public Service Ethics*, William L. Richter, Frances Burke, and Jameson W. Doig, eds. (Washington, D.C.: American Society for Public Administration, 1990), 44.

[36]   Rohr, *Ethics for Bureaucrats*, 68; Cooper, *The Responsible Administrator*, 166-67.

[37]   Kathryn G. Denhardt, *The Ethics of Public Service: Resolving Moral Dilemmas in Public Organizations* (Westport, Conn.: Greenwood Press, 1988), ix.

[38]   Cooper, *The Responsible Administrator*, 167.

Chapter Four
Decision-making and the Ethical Administrator

Bureaucrats by definition make decisions that affect the day-to-day operation of administrative agencies. If they did not have the authority to sift through data, weigh alternatives, formulate a plan for implementing legislative will, and pursue an appropriate course of action, a bureaucracy would be, at best, a superfluous form of organization, and, at worst, a colossal waste of resources. Bureaucracies are created and maintained because they allow bureaucrats to make informed decisions on a variety of technical and complex issues that might otherwise never be addressed.[1]

"Bureaucracy" is a much-maligned concept at the beginning of the twenty-first century, but the idea did not always meet with opprobrium. In the early days of public administration theory, the concept was hailed as an innovative approach to structuring government operations, free from the taint of nepotism and corruption that ran rampant through the federal government during much of the nineteenth century. With its emphasis on impersonal decision-making, hierarchical control, specialization, expertise, and merit, the bureaucratic model seemed to be the most efficacious design for governmental decision-making imaginable.[2]

Features of a Bureaucracy

One feature often cited as a damning characteristic of bureaucracy originally was touted as its saving grace. For early theorists, the impersonal nature of a bureaucracy was a welcome change from the cronyism that infected so much of executive branch government service during the first 100 years of the American experiment. Rather than emphasizing whom a candidate knew, a bureaucratic model focused on *what* the candidate knew. According to the bureaucratic model, it was far more important to recruit competent, skilled, well-educated bureaucrats than well-connected friends and relatives of office-holders. Civil service examinations and merit-based competition became the paramount considerations in determining who would become a civil servant.[3]

According to early theorists, the best method for ensuring that impersonal decision-making would thrive was to create a formal hierarchical organization. At the top would be a single individual—a chief executive officer, a president, a chairman, an administrator, or whatever terminology was appropriate—who would be the final arbiter of disputes and the highest authority in that hierarchy. Below him would be assistants and departmental managers who would report up the chain of command. Although the highest-ranking officer in the hierarchy retained ultimate responsibility for decision-making, each person in the hierarchy exercised authority for the persons and issues within his or her span of control. By working within a clearly defined role with clear rules and regulations and with a superior officer who was responsible for passing information up and down the vertical chain, the organization could ensure that decisions were made in the most efficacious manner possible.[4]

The hierarchical structure of bureaucratic organizations was especially well suited for encouraging specialization. When specialists were assigned particular tasks, they would be afforded precise tools and specific instructions for carrying out their work. This kind of precision and clarity would ensure that bureaucrats could implement the fuzzy and often nebulous policies delegated to a federal administrative agency by the legislative branch.[5]

Much like an assembly line in a manufacturing plant, bureaucratic specialization allows its practitioners to develop expertise. If an administrator works in a single field within a single agency for most of his or her career, the administrator develops a level of competence and mastery of the subject matter that probably would not be possible in a less structured setting. Who better to understand the intricacies of food and drug testing but a physician who has tested foods and drugs for two decades?

Merit is the most prized attribute of the bureaucratic model because it suggests that persons knowledgeable about the technical issues appropriate to a particular agency must administer government programs, just as lawyers, physicians, and other professionals are expected to be well versed in the subject matter of their respective fields. If a would-be bureaucrat does not possess the knowledge and skills necessary to perform well within an agency, he or she is not deemed qualified. Unlike a democracy, where all citizens of a certain age are considered qualified to vote for candidates and take part in political life, a bureaucracy seeks out those persons who stand above the crowd owing to their specialized expertise.[6]

Rational-Comprehensive Decision-making

At first blush, the characteristics of a bureaucracy seem to lend themselves well to rational-comprehensive decision-making. This kind of decision-making requires a bureaucrat to develop the details of a particular policy. Ideally, the goals will be stated by Congress at the time the policy is adopted, but this kind of explicit statement is not always included in the statutory language. In its absence, bureaucrats must discern the proper purpose of the policy by using discretion to discover the goal and develop a detailed implementation plan.[7]

The task of implementing a policy can be more daunting than it sounds. Depending on the nature and scope of the policy, innumerable means may be sufficient for achieving the objective. At this stage, seasoned bureaucrats must review all possible means, assess opportunities and potential obstacles, and determine whether one approach is preferable to another.[8]

Finally, the bureaucrat must select the approach that achieves the goal most efficiently and effectively. In many cases, this calculation will involve a straight cost-benefit analysis. Accordingly, the preferred alternative is an approach that bestows the greatest benefit with the least burden. In other cases, such as instances involving environmental quality or affirmative action, the calculation may involve broader goals that extend beyond a strict cost-benefit analysis. It may cost more money and tax businesses in the short-run to install pollution control devices on smokestacks, but the goal of improving the health of the natural environment and human beings in the long run may necessitate the implementation of such a policy. Similarly, while it remains a contested concept, ensuring that members of historically disadvantaged groups are afforded opportunities in jobs, housing, and education may cost money in the short run, but some policy-makers believe that the benefits of ensuring diversity in American life are worth the short-term costs.[9]

In any event, once a bureaucrat goes through the process of identifying a goal, considering the range of options for implementation, and finally choosing the preferred option, the policy can be implemented. This decision-making style is orderly, rational, and takes into account virtually every relevant factor necessary for arriving at a reasonable decision. In theory, the rational-comprehensive model of decision-making is ideally suited for the bureaucratic model of government in place in the United States in the twenty-first century.[10]

Unfortunately, the model does not seem to reflect the reality of bureaucratic decision-making. Any model is only as accurate and useful as its assumptions, and the rational-comprehensive model assumes that the decision-making process is far more orderly than it is in reality. Consider the identification of a policy goal. In some cases, the goal of a policy is self-evident either because it is stated explicitly in a statute or because the nature of the statute makes the goal obvious to anyone working in the field. The Clean Air Act Amendments of 1990 (CAA) clearly is a statute designed to clean up the poor air quality in and around most of America's major cities. Even if Congress had not specified these goals in the act it would have been obvious in light of the provisions contained in the law. Despite the clear objective of cleaning up air in general, the more precise goal of cleaning up specific types of atmospheric pollution is not as evident. If the perpetually under-funded Environmental Protection Agency is forced to choose between regulating two chemicals—for example, particulate matter or lead—which substance should the agency choose to regulate? EPA scientists can weigh in on one side or the other based on their interpretation of the relevant scientific data, but that decision is not based on a clearly defined goal. It is the responsibility of the agency to specify a goal based on a reading of the appropriate scientific data and literature, but this conclusion can be a matter of much debate and contention.[11]

The rational-comprehensive model also assumes that decision-makers possess ample resources with which to consider alternatives and draw conclusions. In an ideal situation, bureaucrats would have the time, expertise, and funding necessary to implement the best possible program to achieve the desired goal. Unfortunately, the ideal situation rarely exists. In some cases, multiple programs must be implemented simultaneously. Owing to the complexity of the issues involved, even bureaucrats who have labored in a particular specialization for decades may be hard-pressed to acquire the necessary expertise for making an informed decision. With new advances in technology, the plethora of scientific and technical studies published each year, and the pressure to master many issues, bureaucrats may be overwhelmed by the data and information at their disposal. Even when they do have the proper information and can discover the key issues, bureaucrats may not have the requisite funds with which to implement the program. In an age of scarcity, Congress often slashes budgets or diverts funding to other programs, leaving bureaucrats with options that are far from ideal.[12]

Aside from these practical problems, the rational-comprehensive model suffers from a fundamental design flaw. Although specialization generally is cited as a benefit in designing a bureaucracy, it can be a liability when bureaucrats make decisions. The inclination is for specialists to see the world from the perspective of their specialties. Because they focus on the narrow confines of their agencies or professional fields, bureaucrats, in the words of the old cliché, may miss the forest for the trees. Operating in their environment with their own unique set of pressures, challenges, and difficulties, they naturally view the world through a prism formed by their specialties.[13]

The fragmented nature of bureaucracies can lead to many problems. Duplicated efforts, contradictions in policy formulation and implementation, and internecine rivalries often undermine the effectiveness of agencies. Moreover, because a single agency may not take the lead in designing or implementing a policy, multiple agencies occasionally pursue multiple goals at the expense of an overall vision. The example often cited is the 1971 war between India and Pakistan where the U.S. State Department supported one side and the U.S. Department of Defense supported the other. Diplomats may choose to back both sides in a conflict as an effective global geopolitical strategy, but bureaucracies seldom evince such deliberate strategies. They work at cross-purposes because they fail to coordinate their efforts and one agency does not know what the other agency is doing.[14]

Ultimately, the rational-comprehensive model fails because it assumes that decision-makers work in a rational, trouble-free environment. As an abstract proposition, the model works well because it identifies and quantifies the necessary ingredients in effective decision-making. Abstractions seldom work in an agency setting, however, owing to the limitations previously discussed. Accordingly, bureaucrats must act in the face of vague or ambiguous goals, incomplete or conflicting data, scarce resources, and incomplete knowledge. In Herbert Simon's words, they must "satisfice." An ideal solution rarely can be found, but satisficing means that they make the best decision they can in light of the conditions under which they labor.[15]

Incrementalism

If rational-comprehensive decision-making is not an adequate explanation for how bureaucratic decision-making works, some other theory must be preferable. For most public administration theorists, incrementalism—the "science of muddling through"—remains a far more realistic model for understanding bureaucratic decision-making. In its most basic form, incrementalism is the idea that government policies are developed and implemented in small, piecemeal steps. Instead of identifying a goal in broad terms, as the rational-comprehensive model suggests, the incremental model recognizes the reality of bureaucratic politics. Bureaucrats identify goals in the context of the agency's resources, funding, and political capital. Although preferable alternatives might exist, a particular course of action generally is pursued because the likelihood of success is considerably higher than it is with the theoretically ideal, but practically unworkable solution.[16]

Thus, a bureaucrat in the Department of Transportation might recommend that the department approve funding for a new road in a highly congested city as long as that road is coupled with a highway beautification program to plant more trees and bushes along the median. Technical studies might conclude that a light rail system would be ideal to solve the problems associated with constructing more roads—traffic congestion, atmospheric pollution, more highway fatalities, urban blight, and so forth—but the smart administrator knows that the analysis does not stop with an assessment of technical requirements. In some cities, the public simply has shown no inclination to use mass transit systems in place of automobiles even when such systems are readily accessible and affordable. Moreover, lawmakers sometimes talk about the need for light rail systems and similar mass transit concepts, but they respond to constituents who want to keep their automobiles. As a result, no matter how desirable a light rail system might be from a theoretical standpoint, the practical bureaucrat would have to recommend using more highway construction funds to build roadways. By arguing for highway beautification funds to accompany the funding for new roads, at least the bureaucrat has done something for the natural environment. This recommendation may not be an ideal solution, at least insofar as urban planners are concerned, but it represents the kind of real-world considerations that bureaucrats face every day.

The incremental model leaves room for compromise and deal making in a way that the rational-comprehensive model does not. In the example cited above, a bureaucrat championing the highway beautification program has decided that half a loaf is better than no loaf; consequently, he or she has in all likelihood lobbied for consensus on this issue. Not everyone will agree with the final outcome, but as long as enough people within the hierarchy support the position, it stands a reasonable chance of being implemented.[17]

The insight here is that incrementalism leads to a satisfactory, but not a perfect solution. Compromising, deal making, pushing for a partial solution and bargaining with other bureaucrats may seem to be bizarre ways of addressing essentially technical or scientific problems, but they serve as an efficacious means for resolving problems that boast of no clear-cut solutions. For every "expert" who supports building a light rail system, another expert can think of reasons why the money could be used better in some other program. Despite the expertise that many bureaucrats possess in a given policy area, this does not mean that they have a corner on truth or wisdom. Incrementalism is an effective policy when a policy-maker is not too sure that he or she is right. If it turns out later that a given policy was misguided, it is far easier to backtrack on a partially implemented policy than to start from scratch, as a policy implemented under a rational-comprehensive model would require—assuming the policy were implemented in the first place.[18]

Incrementalism is especially well suited to bureaucracies. With a hierarchical structure and a generally secretive organizational culture, bureaucracies perform well when they handle small pieces of a problem. By focusing on one issue, investigating its permutations and combinations, and implementing a program in accordance with the agency's expertise, a bureaucracy can deliver satisfactory results as long as it does not have to stray beyond its strengths. The rational-comprehensive model would push a bureaucracy to visualize all aspects of a problem and enlarge the context of decision-making beyond the agency's parameters. The incremental model makes no such demands.[19]

For all of its strengths, the incremental model is not without problems and weaknesses. It is a conservative approach to change, which, depending on the context, may be beneficial or detrimental to policy-making. Incremental changes ensure a measure of order and stability in government programs, which provides continuity. A business owner who is forecasting whether a new warehouse or manufacturing plant ought to be built generally can depend on a stable, orderly business climate. The economy may travel through boom and bust cycles, but the business owner can rest assured that laws and policies in place today probably will not change radically in the next decade or two. This may assist the business owner, but persons harmed by current policies may see the incremental process as unconscionably slow. When Dr. Martin Luther King, Jr. and other civil rights leaders of the 1960s were pushing for changes in discriminatory laws, the glacial speed with which change occurred was maddening. It was little wonder that Dr. King titled one of his books *Why We Can't Wait.*[20]

Whenever a new policy has to be implemented in small steps over time, the snail's pace may frustrate policy. In 2001, President George W. Bush called for the consolidation of intelligence agency functions into a new cabinet-level agency, the Department of Homeland Security. Despite Americans' concerns about future terrorist attacks, the pace of change was slow and clumsy. Each agency involved in the consolidation had its own jurisdictional and bureaucratic turf, and navigating through all of the interests and the organizational milieu was no simple task.[21]

Incrementalism may have unintended consequences owing to the cumulative effect of taking small steps in policy implementation. When a policy is created out of whole cloth as suggested by the rational-comprehensive model, policy-makers have relatively tight control over how the policy is implemented. The shorter the time between policy formulation and implementation, the less likely it is that an intervening factor or a series of factors will wreak havoc on the policy. Unfortunately, the incremental model suggests that many months or years often pass between the time a policy is created by Congress and when it is implemented by the appropriate agency. This span of time means that new data, subsequent events, and the tendency of policies to shift and evolve may result in ineffective policies being put into place.[22]

Two examples may illustrate the point. When Congress enacted the Clean Air Act Amendments in 1990, they envisioned cleaning up the nation's polluted atmosphere through several measures. One means of accomplishing this goal was to regulate some or all of 189 hazardous air pollutants (HAPs) identified in the legislation. In the years since the act was passed, the U.S. Environmental Protection Agency has struggled to implement congressional policy by collecting data and information on the HAPs referenced in the statute. As the world changes, however, so do chemicals. By the time EPA concludes its scientific investigations, the nature and relative percentage of HAPs in the atmosphere may have changed markedly. The risk arises that the agency may find a good solution to a problem that no longer exists or was solved many years earlier.[23]

A second example of the perils of incrementalism concerns the terrible events of September 11, 2001, when terrorists attacked targets in New York and Washington, D.C. The administration of President George W. Bush had come into office with a goal of reducing the power of a big, fat, bloated federal government. Throughout the 2000 presidential campaign, Bush repeatedly criticized his Democratic opponent, Vice President Al Gore, for Gore's emphasis on "big," bloated, inefficient government and for the Democrats' willingness to use the American military for extended "peacekeeping" missions across the globe. After he took office in January 2001, Bush was poised to follow up his words with action as he instructed political appointees in the federal agencies to implement policies designed to cut back on federal government involvement in the day-today lives of citizens.

Bush's policy initiatives were disrupted by the terrorist attacks that occurred eight months after he moved into the White House. In the years that followed, circumstances required him to detour widely from his stated objectives at the outset of his presidency. Ironically, Bush began to consolidate power in a manner he had decried as a candidate. The Department of Homeland Security became one of the largest and most ambitious cabinet agencies created in American history. In undertaking military operations in Afghanistan, Iraq, Liberia, and other areas of the world, Bush engaged troops in far more dangerous versions of the very missions that he had criticized previously.

These actions do not necessarily imply that President Bush was a hypocrite. Rather, they indicate that events sometimes intervene in the policy process. Bush's early efforts to remake American life would have taken many months to realize. The period between the development of his administration's goals and the implementation of policy obviated, at least in part, some of the objectives. The problem with incrementalism, therefore, is that slow change in policy formulation and implementation can retard the decision-making process.[24]

A Postbureaucratic Model: The Flow of Work

Some public administration scholars have called for the development of a new model to supplant both the rational-comprehensive and incremental models. The new model travels under different names and often is cast in slightly different ways, but one of the more promising approaches is dubbed the "flow-of-work" model. The idea in this post-bureaucratic concept is to design an organization that can adapt to changing needs without relying on the traditional, hierarchical structure of a bureaucracy. Instead of having work flow down from line managers who must then funnel information up to their bosses and pass resources back down to their subordinates, the flow-of-work model envisions a less rigidly hierarchical organization where workers form teams. Each team reports to a leader and the leader in turn reports to the chief executive or a similar officer at the top of the organization. The flow-of-work model ensures that a "cookie cutter, one size fits all" approach will be avoided. Teams dictate how goals will be identified, work will be performed, and results measured. The actions of one team will not necessarily affect the actions of another team.[25]

According to proponents of this new approach, the bureaucratic model promotes degenerative interactions. In other words, the bureaucratic model flows from the top down and is standardized regardless of the circumstances that prevail in a given agency. Decisions are made in more or less the same manner regardless of the size of the agency or the subject matter under consideration. As a result, the quality of decision-making suffers because each cog in the large machine is discouraged from stepping outside the bureaucratic norms to seek innovative, creative solutions. In fact, any efforts to solve problems that stray beyond the confines of the hierarchy threaten to disrupt operations. It is similar to the idea of "rate busting" on a manufacturing assembly line. A rate buster is an assembly-line worker who seeks to produce at a rate beyond the established norm, thereby disrupting the entire line and garnering resentment from others who do not wish to perform at a faster rate. In a bureaucratic organization, the incentive for all workers is to perform at a minimal level and eschew ambition for anything better, faster, cheaper, or more innovative.[26]

By contrast, the flow-of-work model envisions small groups of workers organized into teams. The workings of one team do not necessarily enhance or impede the workings of another team, although teams sometimes are pitted against each other in the spirit of good-natured competition. If a particular worker proves to be a rate buster, he or she can be moved into a team for high achievers. That team can be suitably rewarded as well. Information and resources can be channeled to different teams, as needed, depending on a team's performance and the importance of the team's work to the goals of the entire organization.[27]

The flow-of-work model allows for a flexibility in decision-making that is not possible in the bureaucratic model. Job-sharing arrangements, flexible work hours and time off, compensation tied to performance, and other relatively new and innovative management techniques and tools can be applied in a postbureaucratic model. When changes occur in the outside world, teams can change their approach relatively quickly so that the policy solutions implemented by the organization are not designed for an issue that has already been resolved or obviated by intervening events. An organization that performs in this manner can encourage regenerative interactions—that is, interactions and decisions that encourage bureaucrats to act more responsibly with an eye toward consequences.[28]

The flow-of-work model holds many repercussions for ethics. In the rigid bureaucratic, incremental model, bureaucrats often avoid blame and escape responsibility for their actions with the excuse, "I did not know what I was working on, so how can I be held responsible?" Alternatively, they may argue that "I had very little discretion in performing my job, and even when I did have discretion I had to follow the dictates of the organization's mission, structure, culture, and leadership directives." Incremental decision-making in a bureaucratic organization can lead to decisions that rest on the status quo and stifle new ideas at a time when such ideas would enhance policy goals and ultimately benefit everyone affected by the work of the organization.[29]

Perhaps in the years to come, when later authors pen a book on public administration ethics, a chapter on decision-making in administrative agencies will chronicle the death of incrementalism and highlight the ways in which the flow-of-work or an alternative post-bureaucratic model trounced its predecessors. That day has not yet arrived. For all of the potential benefits of instituting widespread change in public bureaucracies in the United States, as of this writing incrementalism remains the order of the day. In fact, the idea of promulgating bureaucratic rules and regulations in a society that grew increasingly litigious and rule-oriented in the twentieth century seems stronger than ever. For that reason, bureaucrats must know at least rudimentary concepts about bureaucratic decision-making in accordance with external legal controls.[30]

External Legal Controls on Decision-making

Perhaps even more troubling than how bureaucrats make policy decisions is whether they should make such decisions in the first place. Moreover, if they must make decisions, how should they govern themselves as they make decisions? One way to approach this issue is to rely on external legal controls and requirements.

In the past three or four decades, legal controls on bureaucratic behavior have grown tremendously. As more rules have been put into place, the legal requirements and mandates that must be followed have increased to provide guidance on appropriate procedures. The process of adjudication, discussed in more detail in Chapter 6, often is cited as an effective legal control over bureaucratic decision-making. If an affected party believes that a bureaucratic regulation does not apply in a particular case, the complainant can request a trial-type hearing before an administrative law judge (ALJ). This process serves as a check on bureaucratic behavior because it provides an external control. If a bureaucratic organization has applied a regulation in an arbitrary or discriminatory manner, the ALJ has the authority to modify or vitiate its application in a particular case.[31]

Because adjudication is the administrative version of a trial, it has the same strengths and weaknesses as a judicial proceeding. Allowing parties to contest the application of a regulation by presenting witnesses, testimony, and documents provides a process which ensures that bureaucratic decisions will not go unchallenged, especially as they affect individual rights. Moreover, the outcome of the adjudication can serve as a precedent for later decisions, giving the ALJ authority to modify the application of a regulation that was vaguely or ambiguously written and inappropriately applied.[32]

Unfortunately, adjudication is a difficult way to affect public policy owing to its incremental nature. Adjudications can take years to consider and decide, leaving the interpretation of a regulation unresolved. In addition, the decisions announced in adjudications are not always clear and consistent. Because the facts in a given case can determine the outcome, in some instances the resolution of a new case may be ambiguous or confusing because the situation differs from the situations considered in previous adjudications.[33]

Another possibility for imposing external controls on bureaucrats as they make decisions is for a particular agency to consider instituting an ombudsman program. An ombudsman is a roving investigator with the authority to ensure that administrators within an agency are carrying out legislative mandates in an appropriate manner. Ombudsmen search for waste, inefficiency, and even fraud and report back to Congress with recommendations for improving on the maladministration they have uncovered. Although ombudsmen can assist in ensuring that administrators work in accordance with legislative dictates, sometimes they can cause friction within an agency if they are seen as policemen embarking on a quest to criticize or embarrass the agency. The resulting resentment can harm the morale of agency officials and actually hinder their work. Moreover, the existence of an ombudsman program may encourage bureaucrats to avoid personal responsibility for their own behavior or other behavior they witness. "That's not my problem," they might say. "That's for the ombudsman to discover and correct."

As part of the increased emphasis on external legal controls to influence bureaucratic decision-making while also allowing for a measure of personal responsibility, some commentators have called for the development of a codified system of ethics, with enforceable sanctions and penalties for non-compliance. Two difficulties arise in this endeavor. First, the field of public administration is so diverse and amorphous that it is difficult to design a system of ethics that would apply to all or almost all public administrators working in the various agencies, departments, and organizations at all levels of government. Some codes have been developed, most notably the American Society of Public Administration Code of Ethics and Guidelines, the International City Management Code of Ethics with Guidelines, the National Contract Management Association Code of Ethics, and the U.S. Code of Ethics of 1980. Although these systems are preferable to having no code at all, they apply in relatively narrow situations where administrators meet certain guidelines or work in particular agencies at relatively high levels of responsibility. To date, no single code of ethics applies to all public administrators.

An even more fundamental difficulty concerns whether a code of ethics is desirable in the first place. Obviously, the existence of a codified system of ethics provides guidance on expected behavior and clarifies confusing or ambiguous situations to some extent. But no code, regardless of how expertly crafted it may be, can guide a bureaucrat's behavior in every instance. Invariably, situations arise that were not anticipated in the code and, once again, a bureaucrat is called upon to exercise good judgment in identifying an appropriate course of conduct and taking action.

A code of ethics also must not be used to avoid personal responsibility. "I was just following the rules found in the code" should not be allowed to serve as a mantra for an administrator seeking to avoid blame. The code provides general guidelines; an administrator is responsible for adapting those guidelines to real-world situations. In some cases, the ethical administrator must set aside the code and in other cases he or she must follow it zealously.

"The fact is that there is no way of avoiding the introduction of personal and private interests into the calculus of public decisions," one commentator has wisely observed.[34] Another commentator, while praising the development of ethical codes, nonetheless highlights the personal nature of ethical decision-making. "I contend that a sense of responsibility and sound practical judgment depend not only on the quality of one's professional training," Gerald Postema writes, "but also on one's ability to draw on the resources of a broader moral experience."[35]

The Central Role of Ethics in Bureaucratic Decision-Making

Ultimately, the question of personal responsibility is at the heart of bureaucratic decision-making. If a bureaucrat exercises little or no personal autonomy or administrative discretion, he or she might argue against the assumption of personal responsibility for decisions he or she made while working within an organization. In one sense, this is a logical argument, especially for persons who work in the lower echelon of an organization. The lowly claims adjustor, janitor, or computer data entry specialist cannot decide to accept a dubious claim from a marginal applicant or reverse an adverse decision by the organization. The organization is much larger and more powerful than the individual. If the individual makes a decision because the choices were limited or non-existent owing to organizational rules or norms, why should negative consequences be assigned to the individual? Even if the bureaucrat took a principled stand and vehemently argued against the result in a particular case, it is unlikely that the organization would change the outcome, especially if the outcome already had been decided through formal channels. The bureaucrat might lose his or her position, and the final result would not be altered.

In another sense, however, if an individual can avoid responsibility because "I was just following orders," managers at the top of the organization can set an example of "appropriate behavior," however unethical it may appear to the outside world, and individuals lower in the hierarchy must obey with little or no argument. Even in a modern organization where a rigid hierarchy does not exist, allowing the individual to escape responsibility on the grounds that an exterior source has determined what constitutes right conduct beforehand can lead to a moral blindness that harms both the individual and the organization. Consider two egregious examples of individual moral blindness attributed to the failures of a larger organization.

William L. Calley, Jr., by all accounts, led an undistinguished life. Before he enlisted in the U.S. Army, he had dropped out of junior college with poor grades and little direction. Afterward, he drifted from one dead-end job to another. By 1966, he enlisted in the service just as Vietnam was becoming the most pressing issue of the era. Within two years, the unpopular, untalented junior grade lieutenant was commanding a platoon in Charlie Company, 1ˢᵗ Battalion, 20ᵗʰ Infantry Regiment, 11ᵗʰ Brigade, Americal Division, stationed in the Quang Ngai Province of South Vietnam.

The opening months of 1968 were difficult for the U.S. military. In January, the North Vietnamese launched the Tet Offensive, an effort coordinated by the Viet Cong and the People's Army of Vietnam to strike at civilian and military sites in the Republic of Vietnam and topple the ailing South Vietnamese government. As U.S. troops chased fleeing Viet Cong into the countryside following one especially fierce round of fighting, intelligence reports indicated that the enemy had taken refuge in the Village of Song My, comprised of a number of smaller hamlets, including My Lai 1, 2, 3, and 4. While military leaders planned to assault the hamlets, Captain Ernest Medina claimed that his superior officers ordered him and his men to pursue the enemy "aggressively," even if that meant killing innocent women and children.

On 16 March 1968, around eight o'clock in the morning, Charlie Company entered the village of My Lai with orders to root out the enemy. Although subsequent accounts varied in their details, in a little over three hours the company executed between 350 and 500 civilians, including children, women, and the elderly. Perhaps some of the victims were Viet Cong guerilla fighters or sympathizers, but the platoon did not stop to distinguish between the guilty and the innocent as they unloaded their guns into their prisoners' bodies.

The massacre was covered up until a year later when a soldier, Ronald L. Ridenhouer, sent a letter to the president and several high-ranking military leaders detailing second-hand reports he had heard about the incident. The matter already had been investigated internally by the army, but an additional round of inquiries found that many soldiers in Charlie Company had herded civilians into a throng and summarily executed them at My Lai. Far from disciplining his men or imposing a sense of restraint, Lieutenant Calley actively engaged in the slaughter, apparently firing on a group of at least 80 defenseless civilians and ordering his men to line up other civilians so they could be shot and their bodies deposited in ditches.

In September 1969, Calley was charged with premeditated murder. Although other officers were included as co-defendants, Calley faced the most serious charges. In his defense, the young lieutenant argued that he was following orders from his superiors and should not be made a scapegoat for actions that occurred not only at My Lai, but throughout many areas of

Vietnam. The defense failed to secure an acquittal and, in March 1971, Calley was found guilty, dishonorably discharged from the army, and sentenced to hard labor for life. The sentence was later reduced, and Calley won his parole in 1974 after serving approximately three and a half years in prison.[36]

An even more infamous case involves Adolf Eichmann, a high-ranking officer in the German Army during World War II. Recognized for his organizational skills after he joined the Nazi Party in 1932, Eichmann became the chief overseer of the mass deportation and extermination of millions of Jews when Reinhard Heydrich, the ruthless Nazi officer in charge of preparing a "final solution" for the "Jewish problem," tapped him for a leadership role. Eichmann was not a disaffected loser seething with anger and resentment or an ardent anti-Semite eager to transform Jews into a subhuman scapegoat for the ills of German society. Instead, he was a mild-mannered administrator who carefully studied the problem with a degree of thoughtfulness and attention to the detail that stunned, and continues to stun, students of Nazi history. Eichmann approached his duties as if they were a challenging engineering and logistics exercise; he seemed oblivious to the scale of human suffering he caused.

At the end of the Second World War, the "desk murderer," as he came to be known, was among a handful of high-ranking Nazi officials who fled from Germany to avoid capture by the victorious allies. He escaped detection in various European countries by traveling on falsified passports until he landed in Argentina, where he lived throughout the 1950s. In 1960, the Mossad, the Israeli intelligence agency, kidnapped the former Nazi and brought him back to Israel where he was tried for his role in engineering the Holocaust. He was found guilty and executed in 1962.

During his trial, Eichmann contended that he should not be punished because he was obeying the orders of a totalitarian state. To disobey would have cost him his job and probably his life. If he had died, someone else would have taken his place. Therefore, because he essentially exercised no free will in discharging his duties on behalf of the Nazi regime, he should not be convicted of a war crime. "When the state leadership is good, the subordinate is lucky," Eichmann said in his defense. "I was unlucky because the head of state at that time issued the order to exterminate the Jews."[37]

The Calley and Eichmann cases, and many less dramatic examples, illustrate the difficulties that occur when individuals make decisions as part of a larger organization. These are extreme cases, to be sure, but both Calley and Eichmann contended, with some justification, that they were not outside the mores of their respective institutions. They were exemplars. To indict William Calley, his defense team asserted, was to indict the entire U.S. war effort in Vietnam because, after all, Calley only did what many other soldiers in his position did. He aggressively cleared out villages where the enemy was thought to be hiding.

Eichmann's argument is even stronger than Calley's. Eichmann was part of a political system that had dehumanized and exterminated Jews. Calley's detractors could argue that he overzealously interpreted the orders of his superior officers and crossed a line between fighting the enemy and upholding the respect for human life that theoretically serves as an integral feature of the American tradition. Eichmann, in the meantime, did not cross a line; far from it. He efficiently carried out his orders much as a machine stamps out metal parts in a factory with no regard for the consequences or collateral damage caused by those actions. The Nazi regime was dedicated to Jewish extirpation, and Eichmann merely saw himself as an instrument of his masters, a cog in a larger machine. Calley repulses us because he was so enthusiastic in carrying out his orders. Eichmann repulses us because he was so nonchalant in carrying out his duties. It was little wonder that the political theorist Hannah Arendt famously proclaimed this little man who seemed so ordinary and unassuming the embodiment of the "Banality of Evil."[38]

Calley and Eichmann dramatically illustrate the problems inherent in bureaucratic decision-making. At what point must an individual assume personal responsibility for his or her actions and at what point can he or she contend that the organization is in control? The premise of this book is that individuals working within the context of a public organization do not abandon their individual ethical precepts. They must first learn the organizational structure, culture, and formal rules and, afterward, try to operate within the appropriate administrative context. The difficulty arises when they are forced by the organization to act in ways the individual deems unethical.

Individuals assume a particular role within an organization and in no small measure that role affects the person's ethical duty. Generally, the more decision-making responsibility a person assumes within his or her organizational role, the more responsibility the individual retains. A small cog working in a large machine may seem powerless to act against the organization, but such powerlessness does not allow the ethical administrator to turn a blind eye to ethical quandaries. The incremental nature of decision-making in most public sector organizations might induce a bureaucrat to say, "I was only following orders and, besides, it's not my place to interfere in the policy process" as a way of avoiding personal responsibility. Unfortunately, if everyone in the chain of command were to reach this same conclusion, no one would step forward to challenge a policy that contained ethical pitfalls.[39]

At the same time, a bureaucrat must recall that disagreeing with a particular policy may or may not raise ethical issues. If he objects to a policy because it violates the law, compromises the public's right to know, deceives the public, or hides some important fact that might cause direct harm to others, clearly he is justified in assuming a moral posture and opposing the policy openly. In situations where the objection is based on strongly felt opinions that do not raise issues of honesty of integrity, the bureaucrat nonetheless must support the policy or leave the organization. Distinguishing between legitimate disputes over public policy and ethical lapses is not always an easy task, but it is a necessary one.[40]

The difficulty in discussing ethics in public administration is that ethical precepts do not have the same precision and cohesion as law. Even a code of ethics does not possess the same clearly delineated, relatively well-articulated standards that positivist law exhibits. Ethical administrators are expected to "walk their talk." While ethics standards may or may not be written down and publicized, they are still lived and practiced. Ethical administrators constantly strive to "do the right thing," even if it is not always clear what that is in a particular situation.[41]

What is a conscientious administrator to do when confronted with an ethical dilemma during the decision-making process? Two general answers spring to mind: external and internal controls. In the case of the former, if a code of ethics exists and the answers can be found in a code provision, the administrator would be wise to follow the code to the extent possible. Reading applicable statutes, case law, and regulations also would inform the administrator of the requirements that must be met and thereby provide him or her with a yardstick by which to judge whether decisions are being made in accordance with applicable external sources.[42]

Internal sources may be even more important. Instilling values into administrators is an ongoing, never-ending process. Parents, friends, social and civic organizations, schools, peers, and governmental organizations all play an important role in inculcating the values of a democratic society into a person who may one day serve the public interest at any level of American life. When a bureaucrat who has been schooled in the ways of the regime confronts an ethical dilemma in decision-making, for example, he or she must look to external sources for guidance, if possible, but the first line of defense is a well-developed internal sense of right and wrong.[43]

Conclusion

Decision-making is an integral component of a bureaucracy; accordingly, it is important to understand the decision-making process. For many reasons, the rational-comprehensive model fails to explain the nuances and reality of bureaucratic decision-making. By assuming that decision-making is a rational orderly process that can be understood through abstractions divorced from the context of bureaucratic politics, proponents of the rational comprehensive model fail to grasp the difficulties associated with decision-making in public agencies and the piecemeal approach used in developing and implementing most policies.

Incrementalism is a far more comprehensible model for understanding bureaucratic decision-making. With its emphasis on policy-making in small steps—a piecemeal approach to handling complex issues—the incremental model captures the policy-making process better than the rational-comprehensive model because it more accurately reflects the characteristics of decision-making within a public agency. It is not a perfect model—in some cases, decisions should be made with a broader perspective in mind—but it does reflect the way bureaucracies generally operate.

If it displaced incrementalism, the flow-of-work concept might be an improved model for improving the effectiveness of decision-making in public organizations. With its focus on regenerative interactions and an innovative approach to making decisions, this post-bureaucratic model holds many advantages. Until such a transformation occurs on a large scale, however, the incremental model remains the most accurate reflection of bureaucratic decision-making in existence. Moreover, with the emphasis on external controls on bureaucratic behavior—including quasi-judicial proceedings such as adjudications as well as the quest to implement a code of ethics—decision-makers in public agencies are well-advised to reply on a combination of internal and external controls on behavior.

It is not enough to say, as Calley and Eichmann said, that an autonomous individual is merely following orders when he or she makes decisions.

The ethical administrator does not follow orders that clearly violate legal or moral precepts. A choice always exists. An individual can contact a higher-level officer within the organization and point out an ethical dilemma. In some organizations, an ombudsman or older mentor may provide counsel. In extreme cases, a person can resign his or her position. Even Adolf Eichmann, faced with a choice that might have meant his death, could have resisted serving the Nazis by refusing to participate or by participating with such gross incompetence that he would be dismissed from his position. That he chose to participate and hide behind the organization that fed him his orders does not absolve him of his sins; it reveals the essence of his character.

Exercises and Discussion Questions

1. Why does bureaucratic decision-making raise fundamental questions about personal responsibility? Discuss the merits of the argument that "I was just following orders." Why might this defense be justified in some cases and not in others? Does it matter where a person works inside an organization—at the top or at the bottom? Why or why not?
2. How does rational-comprehensive decision-making differ from incrementalism? What are the strengths and weaknesses of each approach? Which approach do you prefer? Why?
3. The flow-of-work model has been touted as a more creative approach to bureaucratic decision-making. Do you agree? Why or why not? What are the pros and cons of this model?
4. How are formal codes of ethics similar to and different from external legal controls on bureaucratic decision-making? In your opinion, are codes of ethics positive or negative developments in a bureaucracy? Explain.
5. Discuss the debate between internal and external controls in bureaucratic decision-making. In your opinion, which type of control is preferable? Explain.
6. You are a mid-level manager within a regional office of the Social Security Administration (SSA) and you have decided to develop a new policy for administering Social Security funding to the states in your region. Although the congressional statute recently passed—the Social Security Reauthorization Act (SSRA)—did not specifically mention a new policy for distributing funding to the states, neither did it prohibit a new approach. Accordingly, you have two innovative plans to improve the way

the SSA operates. One potentially controversial change is to alter the number of checks that are distributed. Instead of paying recipients every two weeks, you want to distribute checks on the 15th and on the last day of the month. Under the proposal, the amount of money that each recipient receives will not change, but the plan will reduce the number of times that checks are distributed in a calendar year, thereby reducing administrative costs. This plan sounds innovative, although it might hurt people living from paycheck to paycheck or desperately waiting for their Social Security benefit checks to arrive.

Building on the flow of work model for your second innovative idea, you designate five different teams to handle a variety of issues. One team will focus on improving eligibility criteria for Supplemental Security Income while another focuses on improving eligibility criteria for retirement income. Each of the remaining groups will brainstorm on related disbursement issues. The teams will exercise independent authority for improving management operations and report back to you periodically.

As you set up the new teams, one of your long-time employees comes to you and says, "Aren't we going far beyond our congressional mandate? These kinds of changes require a lot more decision-making at the legislative level. These ideas sound good in theory, but it's a lot different when you have to implement them." Is your employee correct? How should you respond?

a. You should explain to the employee that the SSRA provides you with broad discretion to manage the SSA regional office as you see fit, and your innovations are "in the spirit of the new statute." If your SSA superiors don't like it, they will countermand your proposals.
b. You should draft a memorandum outlining your ideas and send it to your SSA superiors in Washington, D.C. before you develop the new teams.
c. You should contact key members of Congress and explain how you intend to interpret the SSRA and reveal your new implementation plans.
d. You should initiate the process of formal rulemaking so that affected parties will have an adequate opportunity to provide comments on your proposed changes.

e. You should abandon your plans to change anything about the management of the agency. If Congress wanted such changes made, the authors of the statute would have specified it in the language of the SSRA.

f. You should perform more than one of the actions listed above (be specific.)

Notes

1   Donald F. Kettl, "The Perils—and Prospects—of Public Administration," *Public Administration Review* 50 (July/August 1990), 413; Charles Lindblom, "The Science of 'Muddling Through,'" *Public Administration Review* 19 (Spring 1959): 79-88.

2   R. Kenneth Godwin and John C. Wahlke, *Introduction to Political Science: Reason, Reflection, and Analysis* (Fort Worth, Tex.: Harcourt, Brace & Company, 1997), 252-53; Thomas E. Patterson, *We The People: A Concise Introduction to American Politics*, 6th. ed. (Boston: McGraw-Hill, 2006), 447-48; David H. Rosenbloom, *Public Administration: Understanding Management, Politics, and Law in the Public Sector*, 3d. ed. (New York: Random House, 1993), 320-25; James Q. Wilson, *Bureaucracy* (New York: Basic Books, 1989), 368.

3   William D. Richardson, *Democracy, Bureaucracy, & Character: Founding Thought* (Lawrence: University Press of Kansas, 1997), 41-43.

4   Rosenbloom, *Public Administration*, 322-323; Wilson, *Bureaucracy*, pp. 31-49; Douglas T. Yates, Jr., "Hard Choices: Justifying Bureaucratic Decisions," in *Public Duties: The Moral Obligations of Government Officials*, Joel L. Fleishmann, Lance Liebman, and Mark H. Moore, eds. (Cambridge, Mass.: Harvard University Press, 1981): 32-51.

5   Peter M. Blau and W. Richard Scott, "The Concept of Formal Organization" in *Classics of Organization Theory*, 2d. ed., Jay M. Shafritz and J. Steven Ott, eds. (Pacific Grove, Calif.: Brooks/Cole Publishing Company, 1987), 187-92; John P. Burke, *Bureaucratic Responsibility* (Baltimore: Johns Hopkins University Press, 1986), 79-83; Harold F. Gortner, *Ethics for Public Managers* (Westport, Conn.: Praeger, 1991), 108-113; Rosenbloom, *Public Administration*, 322-23; John Rehfuss, *The Job of the Public Manager* (Chicago: The Dorsey Press, 1989), 121-23; Dwight Waldo, *The Administrative State* (New York: Holmes & Meier, 1984), 12-13.

6   Gortner, *Ethics for Public Managers*, 91-93; Wilson, *Bureaucracy*, 139-42.

7   Rosenbloom, *Public Administration*, 325-31.

8   Burke, *Bureaucratic Responsibility*, 79-99; Benny Hjern and David O. Porter, "Implementation Structures: A New Unit of Analysis," *Organizational Studies* 2 (1981): 211-27; Rehfuss, *The Job of the Public Manager*, 36-37.

9   Vicki Norberg-Bohm and Mark Rossi, "The Power of Incrementalism: Environmental Regulation and Technological Change in Pulp and Paper Bleaching in the US," *Technology Analysis & Strategic Management* 10 (June 1998): 225-26; Rosenbloom, *Public Administration*, 325-29.

10 Burke, *Bureaucratic Responsibility*, 2-4; Rosenbloom, *Public Administration*, 325-31.

11 Steven Ferrey, *Environmental Law: Examples and Explanations* (New York: Aspen Law & Business, 1997), 162-89; Olga L. Moya and Andrew L. Fono, *Federal Environmental Law: A User's Guide* (St. Paul, Minn.: West Publishing Company, 1997), 233-87; Rehfuss, *The Job of the Public Manager*, 34-37; Denise Scheberle, *Federalism and Environmental Policy: Trust and the Politics of Implementation* (Washington, D.C.: Georgetown University Press, 1997), 24-26.

12 Stephen H. Linder and B. Guy Peters, "A Design Perspective on Policy Implementation: The Fallacies of Misplaced Perception," *Policy Studies Review* 6 (February 1987): 459-67; Rosenbloom, *Public Administration*, 329-31.

13 Larry E. Greiner and Virginia E. Schein, "Defining a Political Model of Organizations" in *Organization Development and Transformation: Managing Effective Change*, 5th ed., Wendell L. French, Cecil H. Bell, Jr., and Robert A. Zawacki, eds. (Boston: Irwin, McGraw-Hill, 2000), 342-46; Linder and Peters, "A Design Perspective on Policy Implementation," 467-74; Robert S. Montjoy and Laurence J. O'Toole, Jr., "Toward a Theory of Policy Implementation: An Organizational Perspective," *Public Administration Review* 39 (September/October 1979): 465-67.

14 Thad E. Hall and Laurence J. O'Toole, Jr., "Structures for Policy Implementation: An Analysis of National Legislation, 1965-1966 and 1993-1994," *Administration & Society* 31 (January 2000): 667-86; Jeffrey L. Pressman and Aaron Wildavsky, *Implementation* (Berkeley: University of California Press, 1973), 110-24; Rosenbloom, *Public Administration*, 330-31.

15 Burke, *Bureaucratic Responsibility*, 10-15; Amitai Etzioni, "Mixed Scanning: A 'Third' Approach to Decision-Making," *Public Administration Review* 27 (December 1967): 385-92; Hal G. Rainey, *Understanding and Managing Public Organizations*, 3d. ed. (San Francisco: Jossey-Bass, 2003), 34-36; Rehfuss, *The Job of the Public Manager*, 45-49; Richard Stillman II, *The American Bureaucracy: The Core of Modern Government*, 3d. ed. (Belmont, Calif.: Wadsworth, 2004), 330-32. For a full discussion of this point, see especially Herbert A. Simon, *Administrative Behavior: A Study of Decision-Making Processes in Administrative Organizations*, 3d. ed. (New York: The Free Press, 1976).

16 Burke, *Bureaucratic Responsibility*, pp. 16-22; Lindblom, "The Science of 'Muddling Through,'" 79-88; Daniel A. Mazmanian and Paul A. Sabatier, *Implementation and Public Policy* (Lanham, Md.: University Press of America, 1989), 7-9; Rosenbloom, *Public Administration*, 331-37.

17 Burke, *Bureaucratic Responsibility*, 56-69; Rosenbloom, *Public Administration*, 331-337; Stillman, 331.

18 Anne Larason Schneider and Helen Ingram, *Policy Design for Democracy* (Lawrence: University Press of Kansas, 1997), 21-28.

19 Rehfuss, *The Job of the Public Manager*, 45-49; Rosenbloom, *Public Administration*, 331-33.

20 Burke, *Bureaucratic Responsibility*, 20-23; Rosenbloom, *Public Administration*, 331-333. Dr. King's book is: *Why We Can't Wait* (New York: New American Library, 1964).

21 Rainey, *Understanding and Managing Public Organizations*, 3-4.

22 Rehfuss, *The Job of the Public Manager*, 46-47; Rosenbloom, *Public Administration*, 334-37.

[23]   Ferrey, *Environmental Law*, 162-89; William H. Rodgers, Jr., *Environmental Law*, 2d. ed. (St. Paul, Minn.: West Publishing Company, 1994), 140-56.

[24]   Kenneth Janda, Jeffrey M. Berry, and Jerry Goldman, *The Challenge of Democracy*, 7th ed. (Boston: Houghton-Mifflin, 2002), 95, 252, 371-72; Rainey, *Understanding and Managing Public Organizations*, 3-4.

[25]   Robert T. Golembiewski, *Ironies in Organizational Development*, 2d. ed. (New York: Marcel Dekker, 2003), 146-50; Robert T. Golembiewski, *Managing Diversity in Organizations* (Tuscaloosa: The University of Alabama Press, 1995), 120-29; Robert A. Zawacki and Carol A. Norman, "Successful Self-Directed Teams and Planned Change: A Lot in Common," in *Organization Development and Transformation: Managing Effective Change*, 5th ed., Wendell L. French, Cecil H. Bell, Jr., and Robert A. Zawacki, eds. (Boston: Irwin, McGraw-Hill, 2000), 228-34.

[26]   Golembiewski, *Ironies in Organizational Development*, 105-13.

[27]   Golembiewski, *Managing Diversity in Organizations*, 93-110; Jerry I. Porras and Robert C. Silvers, "Organization Development and Transformation," in *Organization Development and Transformation: Managing Effective Change*, 5th ed., Wendell L. French, Cecil H. Bell, Jr., and Robert A. Zawacki, eds. (Boston: Irwin, McGraw-Hill, 2000), 80-99.

[28]   Golembiewski, *Managing Diversity in Organizations*, 89-132.

[29]   Warren R. Nielsen, Nick Nykodym, and Don J. Brown, "Ethics and Organizational Change," in *Organization Development and Transformation: Managing Effective Change*, 5th ed., Wendell L. French, Cecil H. Bell, Jr., and Robert A. Zawacki, eds. (Boston: Irwin, McGraw-Hill, 2000), 460-70.

[30]   Burke, *Bureaucratic Responsibility*, 10-16; Rosenbloom, *Public Administration*, 337-41.

[31]   Walter Gellhorn, Clark Byse, Peter L. Strauss, Todd Rakoff, and Roy A. Schotland, *Administrative Law: Cases and Comments* (Mineola, N.Y.: The Foundation Press, Inc., 1987), 291-95.

[32]   Alfred C. Aman, Jr. and William T. Mayton, *Administrative Law* (St. Paul, Minn.: West Publishing Company, 1993), 199-255.

[33]   Rosenbloom, *Public Administration*, 339-41.

[34]   Stephen K. Bailey, "Ethics and the Public Service," *Public Administration Review* 24 (December 1964): 236.

[35]   Gerald Postema, "Moral Responsibility in Professional Ethics," *New York University Law Review* 55 (1980): 64.

[36]   Much has been written on the Calley case. For one of the earliest sources, see Lt. Gen. W. R. Peers, USA (Ret.), *The My Lai Inquiry* (New York: The Notable Trails Library, 1993).

[37]   Quoted in David Cesarani, *Becoming Eichmann: Rethinking the Life, Crimes, and Trial of a "Desk Murderer"* (New York: Da Capo Books, 2004), 281

[38]   Ibid., 349-50.

[39]   Debra Stewart, "Ethics and the Profession of Public Administration: The Moral Responsibility of Individuals in Public Sector Organizations," *Public Administration Quarterly* 8 (Winter 1985): 487-95; Susan Wakefield, "Ethics and the Public Service: A Case for Individual Responsibility," *Public Administration Review* 36 (November-December 1976): 661-66.

40 J. Michael Martinez, "Law Versus Ethics: Reconciling Two Concepts of Public Service Ethics," *Administration & Society* 29 (January 1998): 698-99; R.G. Tugwell, "Implementing the General Interest," *Public Administration Review* 1 (1940): 32-49.

41 Terry L. Cooper, "Hierarchy, Virtue, and the Practice of Public Administration: A Perspective for Normative Ethics," *Public Administration Review* 47 (July/August 1987): 320-28; Gregory D. Foster, "Law, Morality, and the Public Sector," *Public Administration Review* 41 (January/February 1981): 29-34; Phillip Monypenny, "A Code of Ethics as a Means of Controlling Administrative Conduct," *Public Administration Review* 13 (Summer 1953): 184-87.

42 Martinez, "Law Versus Ethics," 712-18; John A. Rohr, *Ethics for Bureaucrats: An Essay on Law and Values*, 2d. ed. (New York: Marcel Dekker, 1989), 285-91; Wakefield, "Ethics and the Public Service," 665-66.

43 Bailey, "Ethics and the Public Service," 234-43; Saul M. Katz, "A Model for Educating Development Administrators," *Public Administration Review* 28 (November/December 1968): 530-38; Martinez, "Law Versus Ethics," 712-18; Bob L. Wynia, "Federal Bureaucrats' Attitudes Toward a Democratic Ideology," *Public Administration* 34 (March/April 1974): 156-62.

PART THREE:
THE ORGANIZATIONAL *and* LEGAL ENVIRONMENT
of the ADMINISTRATIVE STATE

Chapter Five
Organizational Theory and Behavior: Implications for Ethics

Students of public administration may ask whether the study of organizational theory and behavior has an ethical dimension. One well-established view suggests that ethical questions are misplaced in this field because organizations are large, impersonal structures impervious to the kinds of moral dilemmas that human beings face every day. Consequently, organizational theory should be taught in schools of business and public administration by focusing on the macro-system and ignoring the personal characteristics of individuals who staff the organization. If an organization is structured properly, it will be efficient, effective, and morally neutral. Questions of ethics and human relations should unquestionably be addressed, but in the context of disciplines that emphasize the individual, such as psychology or personnel administration, rather than in the realm of organizational theory, which seeks to understand large, complex systems through empirical research. This "macro" view has received widespread support since the early days of public administration theory in the United States, but increasingly the perspective has been dismissed as antiquated and myopic at the dawn of a new, progressive century.[1]

A rejoinder to this view of morally neutral organizational structure envisioned by early administrative theorists begins with an analysis of the concept, stated above, that "if an organization is structured properly" it will function well. The idea of properly structuring an organization suggests that value judgments are inherent in any enterprise involving organizations. Public organizations reflect social values regardless of whether those values are stated explicitly. In establishing a public agency, for example, Congress can choose to create mechanisms for effective legislative oversight, public participation in rulemaking activities, and transparent policy-making procedures. Such values determine in no small measure how individuals who staff the organization will perform their roles. Moreover, strict organizational controls help to ensure that an organization performs in accordance with the values underlying the creation of the organization in the first place.[2]

As the traditional understanding of organizational theory and behavior has been assailed and this broadened perspective on the link between organizations and administrative ethics has been explicated, ethical questions have been raised with greater frequency, although the nature and extent of the questions depend in no small measure on the presuppositions that underlie a given school of thought. Accordingly, the purpose of this chapter is to review the early history of organizational theory and behavior to understand how the so-called Orthodox School adopted the traditional approach of moral neutrality and how later theorists attacked it. In rejecting the idea that organizations can be structured or operated independently of ethical considerations, the new theorists have acknowledged—sometimes explicitly, sometimes not—that ethics are an integral component of organizational theory.

Organizational Theory: The Early Years

"Organization" is a loaded term pregnant with many meanings; accordingly, it should be defined with some precision. An organization can be thought of simply as a group of people working together to achieve a common goal. Of course, such a simple definition fails to convey the variety and complexity of organizations at work in the modern world. For the purposes of this chapter, however, an organization can be defined as a public association that works as part of a government agency to deliver goods and/or services.[3] Notice that this limited definition means that private organizations are not included in the discussion; it is the public nature of organizations, as best expressed through the study of public administration, that takes center stage here. Moreover, if this textbook explanation sounds incomplete, it is little wonder. Since the early years of the administrative state, public administration theorists have struggled to define and understand public organizations, how they are structured and operate, and their strengths and weaknesses.

In a famous 1887 essay, political scientist and future president of the United States Woodrow Wilson contended that public administration, like business administration practiced in the private sector, should be studied and practiced using a scientific methodology. Writing at the end of a century of enormous scientific progress and change, Wilson was influenced by the scientific movement that pervaded virtually every human endeavor from philosophy and medicine to the humanities and the fine arts. In the wake of the Darwinian revolution, the influence of the German universities, the advances achieved during the Industrial Revolution, and the rise of powerful corporations, especially railroads, Wilson wanted to place the business of operating public agencies on an equal footing with other empirically grounded disciplines.[4] If he could identify the scientific principles of public administration, he could subject the discipline to the precise, exacting standards and empirical research required of "hard" sciences such as chemistry, physics and biology.[5]

Wilson was not nearly as dogmatic in his quest to ground a "science" of administration as later writers concluded. Nonetheless, he was the progenitor of a movement away from the politics/administration marriage so elegantly discussed by earlier theorists, most notably Publius in *The Federalist Papers*.[6] Subsequent commentators picked up on threads in the Wilsonian argument and developed them to their illogical conclusion. Max Weber, the German sociologist writing at the beginning of the twentieth century, arguably was the most renowned of these later thinkers. Weber was not satisfied merely to call for scientific standards as a general proposition. He sought to develop "ideal types" that would provide clear examples of scientific principles. In defining the concept of "bureaucracy," he focused on developing a strict hierarchical structure that outlined the duties of workers without reference to personal factors such as charisma. In that era, when "bureaucracy" was not viewed negatively, Weber argued that a bureaucratic organizational system was preferred over the partisan, internecine struggles that characterized nineteenth century political life.

As Weber explained it, an "ideal type" of bureaucracy required each worker to undertake a clearly defined role. The primary advantage of this arrangement was that a clear chain of command existed and the personality quirks of individuals were minimized or eliminated altogether. Each worker could be hired, supervised, trained, evaluated, or fired in accordance with rules that were known or knowable to every worker beforehand. Under the Weberian scheme, workers were ensured equitable treatment and neutral enforcement of the rules. This structure improved an organization's operations because it removed "non-scientific" factors from consideration.

While Weber focused almost exclusively on the work of large bureaucratic organizations, management theorist Frederick Taylor, writing not long after the beginning of the twentieth century, examined the activities of individual workers to determine the most efficient method of working. A leading proponent of what came to be called the "Scientific Management" school, Taylor contended that each task could be assigned to the appropriate worker based on that worker's skills. Moreover, the worker could be sufficiently trained in the most efficient method of accomplishing the specified goal. Thus, if a worker were assigned the task of shoveling rice coal, a manager's job was to instruct the worker on the most efficient method of shoveling. Assuming that a person of sufficient strength was employed and offered the proper incentives for hard work, he would excel after he learned the appropriate procedure. In short, using the shoveling metaphor, Taylor argued in favor of scientific management as necessary to produce "the power which comes to the man who knows the science of shoveling."[9]

Taylor sought to establish principles of scientific management that could be applied across all organizations, whether public or private, thereby leading to higher yields and improving the standard of living for everyone. Higher yields would lead to fewer incidents of favoritism and political patronage because everyone eventually would understand that all persons would benefit from neutral rules equitably applied. He would have been appalled at the suggestion that political and administrative decisions are similar in content. In Taylor's view, the proper method of shoveling coal does not depend on political considerations, nor does it result in political consequences. It depends on the science of human labor.[10]

The so-called Orthodox School of public administration and organizational theory grew from the early work of theorists such as Wilson, Weber and Taylor. Frank Goodnow, an early innovator in the development of administrative law, built on this distinction between politics and administration as a central theme in his influential books *Politics and Administration* and *The Principles of the Administrative Law of the United States*. In his view, the business of government can—and should—be separated into two distinct functions: first, the expression of a political will by the people and, second, the implementation of policies that fulfill the expression of that will by public administrators. In broader terms, the citizenry articulates its goals for a regime and, afterward, managers within a public organization work out the necessary details and design appropriate programs to accomplish those goals.[11]

During the 1920s, Leonard D. White was one of the most important contributors to the Orthodox School. His influential textbook, *Introduction to the Study of Public Administration*, contained the principles and insights of a newly developed field that were taught to a generation of scholars.[12] In White's view, public administration could be understood as a single, ongoing process that, once mastered, would apply to all organizations in all situations.[13] Thus, the "correct" structure for a public agency in the United States would be correct for a public agency at any level of government or in any country. This "process" theory of administration was a logical corollary to the scientific management school. Despite later criticisms by a generation of theorists who came of age after World War II, White was celebrated as a strong champion of the Orthodox School. Herbert Storing once observed that, "Leonard D. White did not plant the seeds from which the field of public administration grew; but for four decades he tended that garden with unexcelled devotion."[14]

Perhaps the best known articulation of the tenets of the orthodox school came in a 1937 volume titled *Papers on the Science of Administration* edited by Luther Gulick and Lyndall Urwick.[15] Gulick famously employed a mnemonic device—POSDCORB—to explain how a chief executive can divide work within a department to ensure maximal efficiency. POSDCORB—planning, organizing, staffing, directing, coordinating, reporting, and budgeting—was the tool for ensuring that "scientific" principles of management were implemented within a public organization. "POSDCORB is, of course, a made-up word designed to call attention to the various functional elements of the work of a chief executive because 'administration' and 'management' have lost all specific content. If these seven elements may be accepted as the major duties of the chief executive," Gulick explained, "it follows that they *may* be separately organized as subdivisions of the executive."[16]

Gulick accepted Weber's insights into the necessity of a hierarchical structure, but he refined them further by developing additional intellectual distinctions. In Gulick's view, an organization must be structured according to a core principle such as its purpose, process, clientele, or geographical place. This conceptualization has been influential in public administration since it was first articulated in the 1930s and represented the apex of the Orthodox School. By carefully explicating "scientific" principles of bureaucracy, Gulick sought to reduce the ambiguity and partisan nature of government operations and place the discipline of public administration on a firm foundation.[17]

Members of the Orthodox School saw radical differences between politics and administration because the decision-making process itself was radically different. Scientific decisions concerning efficiency and political neutrality are by their nature separate and apart from decisions rendered at the ballot box. This conclusion, of course, presupposes that science, however it is defined, is value-neutral. A "right" or "wrong" way (i.e., demonstrably efficient or inefficient) of administering government programs exists, and the task of the public administrator is to differentiate between the two without relying on patronage or other political tools to resolve the issue.[18]

Orthodoxy Comes Under Attack

The Orthodox School came under attack beginning in the 1940s owing to its over-reliance on "value-neutral" scientific principles. Ironically, the impetus for the initial assault on orthodoxy originated much earlier with the so-called "Hawthorne experiments" conducted in the 1920s. As is often the case with experiments, the Hawthorne study produced serendipitous results. A group of researchers in a Westinghouse Electric Corporation plant designed a test to determine the effect, if any, of certain physical conditions, especially lighting, on the productivity of factory workers. Their hypothesis was that workers would be more productive if physical conditions were improved because they would be able to respond positively to changes in external stimuli. The researchers discovered, much to their surprise, that lighting and productivity were related, but not in the manner in which they had hypothesized. The factory workers' productivity increased owing to the attention and feedback they received from the researchers. This startling conclusion was a small crack in the foundation of the Orthodox School, but it would widen into a fistula in subsequent decades.[19]

In the years following World War II, many theorists in the social sciences followed up on the Hawthorne experiments with their own research on human motivations in organizational design and operation. Abraham Maslow developed a hierarchy of needs ranging from physiological needs such as food, shelter, and clothing to higher-order needs such as self-esteem and self-actualization.[20] Frederick Herzberg identified factors such as an adequate base salary and well-functioning office equipment as necessary conditions for workers to be productive. Yet, as important as these factors are, they are not in themselves sufficient. Workers need intangible motivators such as promotions, praise, and a sense of accomplishment if they are to be productive.[21] In *The Functions of the Executive*, Chester Barnard argued that workers will perform tasks that fall within a "zone of indifference," but if they are directed to work beyond this scope or if they must make untenable sacrifices, they will rebel openly or in subtle, passive-aggressive ways. Management must therefore determine where this zone of indifference lies and direct workers accordingly.[22] In the meantime, Douglas McGregor developed his Theory X (the indolent worker) and Theory Y (the industrious worker) to explain why some workers advance the goals of an organization and others do not. In his view, managers within an organization must establish the conditions by which industrious workers proliferate and indolent workers are excluded.[23] The cumulative effect of this new, so-called "human relations school" was to undercut the rigid formalism of the Orthodox School. By ignoring human psychology, orthodoxy failed to account for important variables in understanding how organizations function.[24]

Herbert Simon and Dwight Waldo set forth perhaps the most cogent analyses of orthodoxy's failings in their landmark works, *Administrative Behavior* and *The Administrative State*, respectively.[25] Simon argued that the Orthodox School had unwittingly accepted certain assumptions as true without investigating them to determine whether they were value neutral, as orthodox theorists claimed. Unfortunately, this meant that standard principles asserted by public administration scholars—such as the notion that administrative efficiency can be increased through a specialization of labor—contained hidden and unexamined presuppositions. Simon labeled these presuppositions "proverbs" and cautioned against accepting theories without first explicating their underlying bases. "Most of the propositions that make up the body of administrative theory today share, unfortunately, this defect of proverbs," Simon observed. Thus, mutually contradictory pairs of assertions (such as "look before you leap" and "he who hesitates is lost") could be accepted as true and yet provide no guidance on organizational structure or operation. "Although the two principles of the pair will lead to exactly opposite organizational recommendations, there is nothing in the theory to indicate which is the proper one to apply."[26]

Simon's critique applied a ruthless *reductio ad absurdum* technique to undermine the logical consistency of the Orthodox School. Dwight Waldo also attacked orthodoxy, but in many ways his analysis was even more devastating than Simon's because Waldo used orthodox concepts against the school itself. The Orthodox School claimed to be value neutral, but this claim contained an implicit value, namely, that public administration could be value neutral in the first place. Moreover, the values of neutrality and impersonality are at odds with democratic political theory, which prizes individual rights and representativeness above neutrality and administrative values such as efficiency. Even if supposedly value neutral concepts such as "efficiency" and "economy" are accepted as desirable goals, the terms themselves are not operational. In other words, the terms do not provide sufficient direction to public administrators who were required to use discretion in implementing policies.[27]

Waldo was disturbed by the long-held notion that politics and administration could be separated. Even if such a separation occurred, he questioned the wisdom of bifurcating democratic and bureaucratic values. "Until lately," Waldo wrote, "administrative students have been generally concerned with excluding 'democracy' from administration by making the latter unified and hierarchical, and with confining democracy to what is deemed to be its proper sphere, decision on policy." As practitioners and scholars alike began to attack the tenets of orthodoxy, however, a strict division between politics and administration no longer seemed possible or, for that matter, desirable. "It is only in more recent years that some writers have challenged the notion that politics and administration can be or should be separated and have urged that democracy is a way of life which must permeate the citizen's working as well as his leisure hours."[28]

Organizational Theory After Orthodoxy

In the wake of the attacks on Orthodoxy, public administration theorists turned their attention away from efficiency and rationality as well as formal processes such as law and legal authority as sufficient explanations of organizational behavior. Instead, they began to explore psychology and social relations as productive fields for understanding how organizations work. In the words of theorists Harold Gortner, Julianne Mahler, and Jeanne Bell Nicholson, "after a certain point in the development of productivity programs and increasing rationality in structures, the individuals operating in organizations began to resist further change. To comprehend the attitudes and reactions of employees, it became important to focus on both the individuals and groups in the organizations and how they interacted outside the formal structures and procedures."[29]

Modern psychology was a natural field of inquiry for the opponents of Orthodoxy. If organizations are more than machines, then by implication the individuals who staff them must be understood as more than cogs in a vast organizational structure. The study of psychology seems ideal for undertaking this new exploration because it suggests that understanding individual motivations and behavior is instrumental in understanding how organizations operate. In public administration, for example, this has meant that personnel managers must focus on tests that measure aptitude, skills, and personalities of workers in public agencies. Despite successes in these and other areas, psychology remains a difficult, hard-to-pinpoint field; moreover, establishing satisfactory personnel policies, for example, remains an elusive goal. Even the tests themselves have been challenged in recent years. Nonetheless, work in the area of organizational psychology continues, especially as researchers seek to understand how some individuals act as effective leaders within organizations and others do not.[30]

Similar to psychology, the sociological approach to administration suggests that organizations can be understood by exploring how the parts come together to create a larger whole. Sociologists insist that the unit of analysis is the group, not the individual. Thus, the sociological approach is founded on a key insight, namely, that understanding group behavior and dynamics can yield insights into the behavior of complex organizations. This perspective requires researchers to examine the form and function of formal and informal groups within an organization. Formal groups are those subunits of an organization identified on an organizational chart as important components of the whole. In many cases, they are divided into departments and staffed by officers of the organization.

By contrast, informal groups are those often *de facto* groups that arise within an organization but fall outside the formal, identifiable structure of formal groups. They may include department heads and other executives, but not necessarily so. Individuals who do not hold formal positions of leadership within the organization sometimes lead informal groups; they provide leadership in fulfilling some tasks by virtue of their expertise, longevity or personality instead of their formal positions of authority. Informal groups are much more difficult to identify than formal groups, yet they may be extremely important to the successful operation of an organization. These groups exhibit recognizable patterns of behavior and the literature indicates that theorists can learn much about how an organization behaves by examining group dynamics, that is, how groups are formed, structured, and operated.[31]

As the sociological approach came to be accepted by public administration theorists, the focus shifted to a field labeled "organization development," or "OD." Proponents of OD seek to discover the factors that create an organizational culture, that is, an accepted method of acting within the organization. According to this perspective, if researchers understand the culture of a bureaucracy, they can examine the factors that influence its behavior. An organization's culture affects virtually all of its aspects, including how groups within the organization interact. Moreover, combining the individual and the group can provide insight into how organizations operate. In the words of one influential organization theorist, Talcott Parsons, "like any social system, an organization is conceived as having a describable structure. This can be described and analyzed from two points of view, both of which are essential to completeness." In short, OD theory requires researchers to examine the larger organization as well as its subunits. "The first is the 'cultural-institutional' point of view which uses the values of the system and their institutionalization in different functional contexts as its point of departure," Parsons writes. "[T]he second is the 'group' or 'role' point of view which takes suborganizations and the roles of individuals participating in the functioning of the organization as its point of departure."[32]

One final perspective on organizational behavior might be described as "political culture," or power and politics. Public administration has come a long way from the days of the Orthodox School's emphasis on the relatively neat and clean division between politics and administration. Modern theorists recognize that all administrative decisions, even those made by low- or street-level bureaucrats, potentially hold political ramifications. Thus, it is nonsensical to speak of political decisions and administrative decisions as though the two were separate spheres. Researchers have spent a great deal of time and devoted much attention to studying how politics and political culture influence organizations and their behavior.[33] We will have much more to say on this subject elsewhere in this book.

With the surge of research into political culture, it is little wonder that the topic of communications has received no small degree of emphasis. In fact, the subject has been the focus of so much research that it merits detailed analysis in many articles and books. Suffice it to say that, insofar as communications relate to the present discussion, the formal and informal nature of communications within organizations is the paramount consideration. Formal communications are networks of clearly delineated channels so that, for example, subordinates ideally convey information up the hierarchy to decision-makers who then make informed decisions based on the information and provide feedback to subordinates. Researchers who study formal communications networks tend to review organization charts, policies and procedure manuals, official correspondence files, bylaws and articles of incorporation and other indicia of the "official" messages conveyed by and to an organization.

Would that all relevant information about communications networks was so easily discerned. Alas, researchers in this field have identified a second type of communications within an organization. Unlike formal communications, informal communications tend to be task-oriented or dependent on social or interpersonal relationships. Thus, it is not uncommon to find a self-styled "expert" on a particular topic lurking, unidentified and unheralded, within an organization. Nowhere on the organizational chart is the person's position identified as that of an expert in this area, but it is widely acknowledged by his or her co-workers. Similarly, someone working within an organization may emerge as a natural leader or extraordinary communicator through sheer force of personality. Such informal networks and relationships often are difficult to discover, but seldom are they absent from even small organizations.[34]

Although it is difficult to point to any one seminal development that gave rise to these "new" views on public administration and OD theory, when pressed many researchers point to the 1968 Minnowbrook Conference at Syracuse University as a logical starting point.[35] According to Frank Marini, editor of *Toward a New Public Administration: The Minnowbrook Perspective*, a compilation of essays that emerged from the conference, the New Public Administration could be characterized by five integral themes. First, public administration should be taught in conjunction with organizational humanism and other emerging social science disciplines so that the field will be relevant to new developments in thinking and research. Second, the new thinking in public administration must extend beyond the stodgy, rule-bound limitations inherent in positivism. The theoretical premises inherent in previous views of organizations, for example—that they are value-neutral and should be autocratic—are inherently flawed and ultimately damaging to both the individuals and the organizations they serve. Third, the New Public Administration must consider systems theory as a method of integrating various disciplines, a move that requires managers to adopt a longer range perspective on the work of their organizations. Fourth, the New Public Administrators recognize that the standard hierarchical model championed by Weber and his adherents need not be employed in every case. Different types of organizations require different organizational forms. Finally, organizations must be "client-focused." Building on Maslow's insight, this theme suggests that equity and social justice require organizations to consider the social ramifications of their actions as well as what those actions will achieve for the organization in the short run.[36]

Shortly after the Minnowbrook conference concluded, H. George Frederickson and David K. Hart emerged as the most visible leaders of the new school of thought. They contended that the field of public administration had come a long way since the late nineteenth century when Woodrow Wilson argued that politics and administration could and should be separated. Public administrators and OD theorists no longer needed to adhere to that obsolete perspective. Because public managers exercise a large measure of discretion, which in turn makes them part of the political process in a democratic society, the role of public administrators and ODers is transformed by this new responsibility. Ethical behavior in this altered landscape requires managers at all levels of organizations, public as well as private, at least to consider questions of social justice and equity in their decision-making processes.[37]

OD Culture in the Twenty-First Century

Building on the work of theorists who stormed the gates of Orthodoxy, ODers at the dawn of the twenty-first century often focus on organizational dynamics and change. Thus, the context of ethics shifts from mechanistic questions about how an organization is structured to a question of how organizations can use human resources as effectively as possible. For orthodox theorists, an ethical manager was required to discern the "public will" (perhaps as it was expressed through a legislative mandate) and implement programs that allowed that will to be fulfilled. For new public administrators, the ethical manager must do more than merely act as an automaton. A manager must exercise a large measure of discretion and consider political issues that result from the behavior of the organization.[38]

In light of this change in thinking about public administration and organizational theory and behavior, leadership studies have emerged from the field as an integral component of OD. Textbooks devote chapters to the methods by which effective leaders promote an ethical climate and oppose unethical practices. Common prescriptions for effective leadership include suggestions for managers to set an example of ethical behavior, facilitate the development of codes of ethics, intervene into conflicts in an effort to encourage ethical outcomes, and recognize and reward ethical behavior in subordinates. According to this view, an ethical leader sets the tone for the organization by refusing to tolerate unethical behavior, speaking out publicly against unethical behavior, and, in egregious situations, providing the appropriate authorities with assistance and information to oppose unethical decisions or practices. In the wake of corporate scandals that plagued the American landscape early in the twenty-first century, the concern with promoting the proper values within an organization has received more attention than ever before. Whether that attention will prove to be a permanent focus or merely a passing phase remains to be seen. In any event, as of this writing, ethical issues at least need to become part of an organization's agenda if its leaders want to avoid the kinds of unethical and sometimes illegal practices that have damaged many modern organizations.[39]

Ethical issues also emerge in the context of organizational change. As the nature and context of organizations continue to evolve, the classic conception of a large hierarchy—Weber's "ideal type" bureaucracy—has become outmoded. If a conglomerate is going to survive in a world where the pace of change continues to accelerate, organizations must adapt to their new environment with a rapidity and flexibility unfathomable to an earlier age.

As a result of this emphasis on remaking organizations, new approaches have garnered much attention in the literature. ODers speak of "systems theory" as a way of identifying patterns of activity and how they are related to everything that occurs within an organization. In the words of one OD theorist, the traditional "machine model" of an organization is predicated on the idea that an organization can best be understood and improved by disassembling it, that is, by taking it apart piece by piece and understanding how the pieces fit together. Systems theory suggests an alternative approach. Instead of taking things apart, systems theorists concentrate on putting things together. They speak of a "synthesis" or "synergy," by which they mean that three conditions exist in an effective organization: (1) the behavior of each component affects every other component within the system; (2) the behavior of the components is interdependent; and (3) in whatever manner the components are arranged within an organization, each component has an effect on the system and no one component has an independent effect. Systems theory requires ODers to see the forest, not the trees, to consider the effect of each tree on the entire system. The accounting department should not act on its own behalf if those actions harm the marketing department and vice versa. Each department must work with the others to ensure the survival and prosperity of the whole.[40]

Another strategy for revitalizing an organization is to reject the traditional Weberian model of a "tall" hierarchy where a chief executive officer sits at the head and passes down orders while various bureaus report up to him. The modern notion of a "flat" hierarchy is used to refine the bureaucratic model so that power and communications flow horizontally instead of vertically. Teams and other semi-autonomous units work to resolve problems within the larger organizational structure. Instead of competing, teams assist each other and build coalitions as necessary. The argument in favor of these new approaches is that the old bureaucratic model is unworkable. It assumes that top management possesses skills and insight into the organization and its operations that are lacking among lower echelon employees. This kind of "factory mentality" may have been a useful approach to organizational structure and operation when the Industrial Revolution transformed the nature of the workplace in the nineteenth and twentieth centuries, but new times require new approaches.[41]

New approaches also require new vocabularies, some of which have become so familiar in recent years that they border on being clichés. The notion of "empowering" employees is bandied around frequently and its meaning often is difficult to discern. At its core, empowerment is the idea that employees can contribute far more to the success of an organization when they are afforded the responsibility and the tools to undertake projects without constant and repetitive approval from officers higher up in the organization. This objective is easier to discuss than it is to implement, but ultimately it requires a commitment from managers to delegate responsibility and authority in return for a commitment from workers to perform their tasks using creative methods with little or no direct supervision.

In the traditional bureaucratic model of an organization, top management develops the organization's mission and vision as well as the tasks required to accomplish the organization's goals. Managers must then communicate the appropriate actions to be undertaken by their subordinates and ensure that the employees perform those tasks in an acceptable manner. This process generally is referred to as external commitment because it occurs outside of the employees. Internal commitment, by contrast, requires managers to explain the objectives to their employees and leave it to teams of employees to define the tasks, set an appropriate level of work and behavior, and, to some extent, manage themselves. The role of top management changes from a patriarch that controls virtually every aspect of the employees' working life to a wise mentor that sets the stage for success by providing the proper equipment, motivating employees, and allowing them the room and space to act on their own impetus.[42]

The new OD attempts to transform the nature of organizations from autocratic institutions to democratic institutions. This terminology may sound strange, but it belies an important point. Just as the human relations school sought to alter management concepts from a focus on treating organizations as though they were staffed by automatons devoid of human strengths and frailties to an emphasis on psychological factors, so, too, modern theorists have sought to change the nature of OD. Organizations must allow individuals to grow and assert themselves in order to reach their potential, to the extent possible, consistent with the goals of the organization. In Robert Golembiewski's words, the healthy, workable organization is one that operates in a way that "enlarges the area of discretion open to us in organizing" and, moreover, "increase[s] individual freedom."[43]

According to proponents of the new school of OD, in a democratic society organizations function properly when they allow workers to participate in decision-making in an open process subject to political accountability. If this perspective holds true, many issues that plague democratic theorists also confound OD theorists who subscribe to this new understanding. First, workers who decline to participate or who remain uninformed even after they have been afforded ample opportunity to participate in the process raise issues of whether a democratic organization can actually exist and function or whether democratic governance is a myth. Moreover, the difficult feature of a democratic organization is that it is deliberately inefficient and at times chaotic. Allowing opposing viewpoints to clash invariably complicates matters and ensures that an organization will encounter criticism and occasional redirection as coalitions form and power changes hands. The traditional view of organizations avoided these problems by establishing a monarchical structure where one supreme executive ensured that efficiency was achieved and dissent was all but stifled.[44]

This new championing of democracy within organizations is a tall order, but not an impossible one. It requires managers to open themselves and their organizations up to new possibilities, many of which hold enormous repercussions for ethics. The enlightened manager, according to the new perspective, develops and nurtures certain core beliefs, values, and ethical precepts. The beliefs focus on how managers view workers—not as fungible cogs in some large, mechanistic machine that can be replaced by other, interchange-able pieces, but in accord with the Kantian perspective that human beings are never the means to an end, but ends in themselves. Thus, human beings that work within an organization are to be treated with dignity and respect and allowed to take charge of their lives and grow within the context of the or-ganization. In addition, organizations are seen as human systems; that is, they are part of a chain of communities, countries, and transnational systems that are interdependent socially, culturally, politically, economically, and spiritually. According to modern ODers, organizational change that does not consider these factors is deficient.[45]

The fundamental values that underlie this view of OD are that freedom, responsibility, and self-control are desirable ends for all individuals laboring within an organization. Managers who wish to succeed in the future must be cognizant of these values and strive to inculcate them into everyone within the organization. This task requires a measure of flexibility and proactive willingness to change and experiment to ensure the continued growth and prosperity of the organization. The ethical precepts necessary to encourage these kinds of organizational changes include a commitment to moral rules and ideals inherent in the Judeo-Christian tradition, such as prescriptions to do no harm, honor promises, obey the law, and attend to duties and obliga-tions. For some organizations, it makes sense to develop a codified system of ethical rules that can be published and disseminated, while other organiza-tions can exist with an unwritten series of moral guidelines that are implicit in the behavior of ethical managers who lead by example. Whatever the ap-proach, all organizations must place ethical issues at the forefront if they hope to thrive in the new century.[46]

Indeed, the dynamic sense of change in modern organizations at the dawn of the twenty-first century has enormous repercussions for administra-tive ethics. Accountability questions contain crucial ethical considerations in a democratic regime, but changing the form of an organization also changes the underlying values of an organization. When public organizations are re-structured to ensure a more entrepreneurial focus and greater decentraliza-tion of authority, the resultant organization is less accountable to a legislative body or an authority placed higher in an administrative hierarchy. A hierar-chical structure helps to ensure stability and control while a more fluid, de-centralized organization helps to ensure flexibility and change, which are markedly different values. Thus, whatever else reorganization does, it rearranges the values of the new organization.[47]

In a traditional, stable bureaucracy where lines of authority are clear and change seldom occurs, high-level managers make decisions and are held accountable to their superiors within the hierarchy or in the legislative branch, as appropriate. Administrative discretion is used only at relatively high levels inside the organization. Lower level employees are expected to perform their duties in accordance with directions from their superiors, in effect shifting accountability to the organization's upper echelon. These organizations are staid and often resistant to change, but they are fairly predictable and can be evaluated in accordance with a series of rules set forth ahead of time. Effective leaders know the rules, follow them, and occasionally adapt them to changing needs and circumstances.

By contrast, a more decentralized organization that subscribes to the new OD theory is more fluid and far less hierarchical than a traditional bureaucracy. Accordingly, the behavior of these organizations is dictated by events that occur in the marketplace or by external actions that affect the organization's context. Effective leaders are risk takers who value intuitive knowledge, flexibility, and adaptive skills. Teams and creative problem-solving are important; administrative discretion is exercised by virtually every employee at every level. Accountability is a question of function, not a person's title or placement within the hierarchy.[48]

The accountability expectations and values embraced by the two types of organizations are markedly different. Obviously, both a traditional organization and a modern, fluid organization seek an organizational structure that avoids egregious cases of maladministration resulting from fraud and corruption. More commonly, both types of organizations also can be subject to what Van Wart and Denhardt refer to as "maladministration…due to organizational dysfunction." Organizational dysfunction occurs when an organization is structured in a manner that makes it difficult, if not impossible, to achieve its goals. Sometimes this happens when rigid conformity to the rules displaces the underlying goals of the organization so that an agency slavishly upholds the letter of the law or policy without adequately considering its spirit or intent. In other instances, an agency adheres to a "command and control" mentality that emphasizes the power of the organization and its officers with little or no regard for an appropriate course of action to achieve the desired ends.[49]

The new type of fluid "flat" hierarchy holds great promise for expanding the accountability of public employees and ensuring that an individual public administrator cannot hide behind the excuse of "I was just following orders. Don't blame me." When every employee at every level of an organization is expected to "take ownership" of his or her job, he or she must be willing and able to answer for decision-making. A difficulty arises when employees are empowered to assume greater responsibility but fail to do so owing to inability, negligence, or outright hostility toward shouldering a heavy burden. In such situations, managers will be called upon to ensure that change occurs in an orderly way and that training programs clarify the new expectations placed on employees.

Another difficulty is that leaner, "flat" organizations may be more in line with external market forces, but an emphasis on efficiency and quality may ignore issues surrounding representation and democracy. If the new public manager in a modern organization places efficiency ahead of equity and the right of constituents to be heard and protected through due process mechanisms—which often increase the time and money spent on public safeguards, thereby decreasing efficiency—the change may be detrimental to larger societal values. Ironically, this bifurcation between the efficiency of the marketplace and the needs and desires of the citizenry to participate in government decisions seems tantamount to a return to the old politics and administration dichotomy prevalent in the early years of American public administration.[50]

Whatever else may be said, it should be clear that the structure of an organization is based on and determines the underlying values of the organization. Thus, restructuring traditional bureaucracies must be undertaken with the realization that what constitutes an ethical public administrator will change, at least in part, as a result of the restructuring. As long as this fundamental concept is recognized and accounted for, an organizational change can be a positive occurrence.

Exercises and Discussion Questions

1. What did Woodrow Wilson, Max Weber, and Frederick Taylor contribute to organizational theory? What were the strengths and weaknesses of their theories? How does the Orthodox School of organizational theory affect the study of administrative ethics?

2. What is POSDCORB and how did this idea influence the development of public administration as a field of study? Overall, do you find the concept useful? Why or why not?

3. How did Herbert Simon and Dwight Waldo attack the Orthodox School of organizational theory? If Simon and Waldo are correct that public administration is not value-neutral, what are the implications for administrative ethics?

4. How have principles of modern psychology affected the development of public administration? Do you see pitfalls in relying on psychological theories in the study of public organizations? Discuss.

5. What was the result of the 1968 Minnowbrook Conference at Syracuse University? In your opinion, was this a positive or negative development in the evolution of public administration as a field of study? What are the strengths and weaknesses of New Public Administration? Explain.

6. The chapter mentions that "ODers speak of 'systems theory' as a way of identifying patterns of activity and how they are related to everything that occurs within an organization." Do you agree with this statement? Explain the concept of Organizational Development and how it attacks the "machine model" of an organization. What is systems theory? In your opinion, is this concept an improvement over the traditional "machine model"? Why or why not?

7. Do you find terminology and concepts such as "flat versus tall hierarchies" and "empowerment" useful in the study of public administration? Why or why not?

8. Oliver Martin has worked with the Xerxes Corporation, a large manufacturer of plastic casings for the defense industry, since he graduated from college 38 years ago. It has been his one and only job apart from stints as a part-time worker in the food service industry during his high school and college days. He graduated from the gargantuan State University with a b[51]achelor's degree in business administration in the halcyon days before student protests rocked college campuses and fundamental changes in American labor dictated that loyalty to one company was the exception rather than the rule. Six weeks after he finished college, he married his childhood sweetheart, Olivia, who stayed at home to care for the house and bore him six children, five sons and a daughter, the youngest of whom is a sophomore at the State University this year.

During his tenure with Xerxes, Oliver has prided himself on his loyalty to the company. Although not exactly shy, he has never been comfortable in the limelight, preferring to perform his tasks competently but without the flare for the dramatic that seems to have characterized many of his peers. As a result, he has labored in the shadows for most of his professional career, watching as many less talented coworkers have risen through the ranks while he stayed in a mid-level management position far past the customary 8-10-year period that most employees take to move into upper management.

Fortunately, now, in the twilight of his career, Oliver has been promoted to the position of Manager of the Traffic Department. His job is to ensure that orders routed from Sales & Marketing are loaded onto the appropriate trucks in the warehouse for distribution. If more orders arrive than trucks, he must contact common carriers to transport the finished product to distribution warehouses throughout the country. When trucks break down or employees fail to show up for work, Oliver must find suitable replacements. The company's motto is "Always Right, Always on Time"; consequently, he is under a great deal of pressure to ensure that all orders leave the warehouse as soon as possible, or in any case within 24 hours of the arrival of the order.

Oliver is somewhat nervous about his new position because he is stepping into mighty big shoes. His predecessor, Richard Goodson, was a star on the rise. Only 34 years old, Goodson had earned degrees in business from Princeton and the Wharton School of Finance and joined Xerxes after working in a variety of managerial positions in the communications technology industry. Everyone believed that Goodson would be the CEO of Xerxes or another firm before he turned 50. He had been overseeing Traffic for slightly over two years when he was killed in a senseless traffic accident on his way home from work a month earlier.

Goodson's management style had been what some workers called "loosey-goosey." As one of the new breed of OD thinkers, he believed that the Traffic Department functioned well when he established small teams of employees within the department and left them alone to ship the orders. He was a "hands off" manager, often "interfacing" with other department managers and serving on Xerxes's many management committees to improve the company's public relations efforts, especially with the all-important contract officers at the U.S. Department of Defense.

When he was on site, he preferred to leave the details to team leaders, asking them for a quick monthly briefing unless problems arose in the meantime.

A born practical joker, Goodson enjoyed wearing funny masks or bringing toys like whoopee cushions to work to keep "my people" laughing. He also believed in recognizing the accomplishments of his employees. He was the first to send cards and flowers to employees on special occasions—the death of a loved one, an employee's child's high school graduation, or birthdays, for example—and he was known to surprise long-time workers with certificates of appreciation, plaques, and other tokens of his esteem.

Even when a particular team fell short of its monthly or quarterly shipping goals, Goodson exhibited an almost superhuman patience in working with his subordinates to get back on track. Although the department was not grossly deficient in shipping orders, it had fallen far below its historically high 94 percent on-time delivery rate achieved in the years before Goodson took the helm. Nonetheless, Goodson was almost uniformly beloved by the 46 employees in the department. They were still mourning his loss when the company announced that Oliver would become the new department manager.

Many employees had never heard of Oliver Martin, but those who had were not optimistic about his management style. A self-professed proponent of the "old school," Oliver believed that hard work was its own reward, that the company had the right to expect loyalty from its employees, and that Goodson's "showboating" had no place in the Traffic Department. Work was serious and people should leave their problems and biases out in the parking lot. For Oliver, the "hot shot M.B.A. types" were merely riding the wave of silly trends that would come and go, but a manager's real job was to ensure, day in and day out, that the orders got shipped on time. Anything that interfered with that objective had to be eliminated.

As many people expected, Oliver left a terrible first impression on the employees in the Traffic Department. Less than a week into his new position, he called a meeting of the department and outlined his plans. First, the teams were to be disbanded. In addition, he would develop production schedules for the department and require that the schedules be met unless something occurred outside their control, such as problems in another department. Failure to meet the schedules would result in written warnings issued to the offending parties. Egregious or continuing failures could result in termination.

One afternoon about a week after the meeting, as he was walking to his car in the parking lot, Oliver overheard two Traffic Department employees discussing plans for the Autoworkers Union, Local #182, to unionize the plant. They indicated that they intended to arrive a few minutes before their shift started the next morning and leave leaflets explaining the benefits of union membership in the employee break room. Incensed at such obvious disloyalty, Oliver decided that he would not sit by idly and allow the union to interfere with Xerxes' operations. He arrived an hour early the next day and waited until he spotted the two men he had seen discussing the union. After the two employees had entered the break room, deposited a stack of papers, and left the area, Oliver entered through another door, grabbed the leaflets, and threw them in the trashcan behind the plant.

a. Comment on the different management styles employed by Oliver Martin and Richard Goodson. What are the strengths and weaknesses of each style?

b. If you could ask Oliver Martin how an ethical manager should behave, what do you think he would say? Defend his point of view.

c. If you could ask Richard Goodson how an ethical manager should behave, what do you think he would say? Defend his point of view.

d. Given the fact that he was taking over the department from an enormously popular manager, what should Oliver Martin have done to ensure a smooth transition?

e. What, if anything, should Oliver Martin have done when he learned of the attempt to unionize the plant? Could he have behaved differently and still accomplished his goal in an ethical (and legal) manner? Why or why not?

f. Apart from the issues discussed above, what ethical considerations are relevant to the work of the traffic department or, for that matter, the Xerxes Corporation? Is efficiency an ethical issue? Does it matter that Xerxes performs work for the U.S. Defense Department?

Notes

[1]   See, e.g., Richard M. Cyert and James G. March, *A Behavioral Theory of the Firm* (Englewood Cliffs, N.J.: Prentice-Hall, 1963); Richard M. Cyert and James G. March, "A Behavioral Theory of Organizational Objectives," in *Classics of Organization Theory*, 2d. ed., Jay M. Shafritz and J. Steven Ott, eds. (Pacific Grove, Calif.: Brooks/Cole Publishing Company, 1987), 155-65; James G. March, ed., *Handbook of Organizations* (Chicago: Rand McNally, 1965); Robert K. Merton, *On Theoretical Sociology* (New York: The Free Press, 1967), esp. 39.

[2]   Montgomery Van Wart and Kathryn G. Denhardt, "Organizational Structure: A Reflection of Society's Values and a Context for Individual Ethics," in *Handbook of Administrative Ethics*, 2d. ed., Terry L. Cooper, ed. (New York: Marcel Dekker, 2001), 227-41.

[3]   Harold F. Gortner, Julianne Mahler, and Jeanne Bell Nicholson, *Organization Theory: A Public Perspective* (Pacific Grove, Calif.: Brooks/Cole Publishing Company, 1989), 2-3.

[4]   See, e.g., Albert Somit and Joseph Tannenhause, *The Development of American Political Science: From Burgess to Behavioralism* (New York: Irvington Publishers, 1982).

[5]   See, e.g., Kathryn G. Denhardt, *The Ethics of Public Service: Resolving Moral Dilemmas in Public Organizations* (Westport, Conn.: Greenwood Press, 1988), 2-3.

[6]   Philip J. Cooper, "The Wilsonian Dichotomy in Administrative Law," in *Politics and Administration: Woodrow Wilson and American Public Administration*, Jack S. Rabin and James S. Bowman, eds. (New York: Marcel Dekker, 1984), 79-94; William D. Richardson, *Democracy, Bureaucracy, & Character: Founding Thought* (Lawrence: University Press of Kansas, 1997), 38-39.

[7]   Andrew Heywood, *Political Ideas and Concepts: An Introduction* (New York: St. Martin's Press, 1994), 89-93.

[8]   Max Weber, "Bureaucracy," in *Classics of Organization Theory*, 2d. ed., Jay M. Shafritz and J. Steven Ott, eds. (Pacific Grove, Calif.: Brooks/Cole Publishing Company, 1987), 81-87. See also Gortner, Mahler, and Nicholson, *Organization Theory*, 58-64.

[9]   Frederick Winslow Taylor, "The Principles of Scientific Management," in *Classics of Organization Theory*, 2d. ed., Jay M. Shafritz and J. Steven Ott, eds. (Pacific Grove, Calif.: Brooks/Cole Publishing Company, 1987), 74. See also Frederick Taylor, *The Principles of Scientific Management* (New York: Harper & Brothers, 1917).

[10]   David H. Rosenbloom, *Public Administration: Understanding Management, Politics, and Law in the Public Sector*, 3rd. ed. (New York: Random House, 1993), 145-47.

[11]   Frank Goodnow, *Politics and Administration* (New York: MacMillan, 1900), and Frank Goodnow, *The Principles of the Administrative Law of the United States* (New York: G. P. Putnam's Sons, 1905). See also John P. Burke, *Bureaucratic Responsibility* (Baltimore and London: Johns Hopkins University Press, 1986), 10; Rosenbloom, *Public Administration*, 183; Carl Joachim Friedrich, "Public Policy and the Nature of Administrative Responsibility," in *Combating Corruption/Encouraging Ethics: A Sourcebook for Public Service Ethics*, William L. Richter, Frances Burke, and Jameson W. Doig, eds. (Washington, D.C.: American Society for Public Administration, 1990), 43-44.

[12]   Leonard D. White, *Introduction to the Study of Public Administration* (New York: MacMillan, 1926).

[13] In his words, the book "assumes that administration is a single process, substantially uniform in its essential characteristics wherever observed...." White, *Introduction to the Study of Public Administration*, I, vii.

[14] Herbert J. Storing, "Leonard D. White and the Study of Public Administration," *Public Administration Review* 25 (1965): 38.

[15] *Papers on the Science of Administration*, Luther Gulick and Lyndall Urwick, eds. (New York: Augustus M. Kelley, 1937).

[16] Luther Gulick, "Notes on the Theory of Organization," in *Classics of Organization Theory*, 2d. ed., Jay M. Shafritz and J. Steven Ott, eds. (Pacific Grove, Calif.: Brooks/Cole Publishing Company, 1987), 96.

[17] Rosenbloom, *Public Administration*,167-69.

[18] A large body of literature, especially books and articles in the fields of cognitive science, refutes the idea that science is value-neutral. The landmark work in this field is Thomas Kuhn, *The Structure of Scientific Revolutions* (Chicago: University of Chicago Press, 1970). See also, e.g., Ronald N. Giere, *Explaining Science: A Cognitive Approach* (Chicago: University of Chicago Press, 1988); Larry Laudan, *Progress and Its Problems: Towards a Theory of Scientific Growth* (Berkeley and Los Angeles: University of California Press, 1977); Helen E. Longino, *Science as Social Knowledge: Values and Objectivity in Scientific Inquiry* (Princeton, N.J.: Princeton University Press, 1990); and Theodore M. Porter, *Trust in Numbers: The Pursuit of Objectivity in Science and Public Life* (Princeton, N.J.: Princeton University Press, 1995).

[19] Rosenbloom, *Public Administration*, 147-48, 156.

[20] Gortner, Mahler, and Nicholson, *Organization Theory*, 348-49.

[21] See, e.g., Frederick Herzberg, *Work and the Nature of Man* (Cleveland, Ohio: World Publishing, 1966).

[22] Rosenbloom, *Public Administration*, 148-49, 153.

[23] See McGregor's two most important works, *The Human Side of Enterprise* (New York: McGraw-Hill, 1960), and Douglas McGregor, *The Professional Manager* (New York: McGraw-Hill, 1967).

[24] See, e.g., Burke, *Bureaucratic Responsibility*, 12-15; D.W. Martin, "The Fading Legacy of Woodrow Wilson," *Public Administration Review* 48 (March/April 1988): 631-36; Rosenbloom, *Public Administration*, 147, 157-58; and Dwight Waldo, "Development of the Theory of Democratic Administration," *American Political Science Review* 46 (March 1952): 81-103.

[25] Herbert Simon, *Administrative Behavior*, 2d. ed. (New York: The Free Press, 1957), and Dwight Waldo, 2d. ed., *The Administrative State* (New York: Holmes & Meier, 1984).

[26] Herbert Simon, "The Proverbs of Administration," in *Classics of Organization Theory*, 2d. ed., Jay M. Shafritz and J. Steven Ott, eds. (Pacific Grove, Calif.: Brooks/Cole Publishing Company, 1987), 103.

[27] Rosenbloom, *Public Administration*, 171.

[28] Waldo, *The Administrative State*, 2d. ed., 16.

[29] Gortner, Mahler, and Nicholson, *Organization Theory*, 69.

[30] See, e.g., Paul Hersey and Kenneth H. Blanchard, *Management of Organizational Behavior: Utilizing Human Resources*, 4th ed. (Englewood Cliffs, N.J.: Prentice-Hall, 1982) and

Floyd Hunter, *Community Power Structure: A Study of Decision Makers*. Chapel Hill: University of North Carolina Press, 1953. The literature on leaders is quite lengthy but see, e.g., James W. Doig and Erwin C. Hargrove, eds., *Leadership and Innovation: Entrepreneurs in Government* (Baltimore, Md.: Johns Hopkins University Press, 1990); T.O. Jacobs, *Leadership and Exchange in Formal Organizations* (Alexandria, Va.: Human Resources Research Organization, 1971); Norma M. Riccucci, *Unsung Heroes: Federal Execucrats Making a Difference* (Washington, D.C.: Georgetown University Press, 1995); Gary Yukl, *Leadership in Organizations*, 5th ed. (Upper Saddle River, N.J.: Prentice Hall, 2002).

[31]   The literature on this point is extensive. See, e.g., Peter M. Blau, *The Dynamics of Bureaucracy* (Chicago: University of Chicago Press, 1955); Dorwin Cartwright and Alvin F. Zander, *Group Dynamics: Research and Theory* (New York: Harper & Row, 1968); Daniel Katz and Robert L. Kahn, *The Social Psychology of Organizations*, 3d. ed. (New York: John Wiley & Sons, 1982).

[32]   Talcott Parsons, "Suggestions for a Sociological Approach to the Theory of Organizations," in *Classics of Organization Theory*, 2d. ed., Jay M. Shafritz and J. Steven Ott, eds. (Pacific Grove, Calif.: Brooks/Cole Publishing Company, 1987), 134.

[33]   See, e.g., Robert Dahl, *Who Governs? Democracy and Power in an American City* (New Haven, Conn.: Yale University Press, 1961).

[34]   A good discussion of this point is found in Gortner, Mahler, and Nicholson, *Organization Theory*, 154-60. For an extended discussion of communications networks, see, for example, Anthony Downs, *Inside Bureaucracy* (Boston: Little, Brown & Company, 1967); Gerald Goldhaber, *Organizational Communication* (Dubuque, Ia.: William C. Brown, 1974); Everett M. Rogers and Rekha Agarwala-Rogers, *Communication in Organizations* (New York: The Free Press, 1976); and Lee Thayer, *Communication and Communication Systems: In Organization, Management, and Interpersonal Relationships* (Homewood, Ill.: Richard D. Irwin, 1968).

[35]   Terry L. Cooper, *The Responsible Administrator: An Approach to Ethics for the Administrative Role*, 3d. ed. (San Francisco: Jossey-Bass, 1990), 148.

[36]   Frank Marini, "The Minnowbrook Perspective and the Future of Public Administration," in Frank Marini, ed., *Toward a New Public Administration: The Minnowbrook Perspective* (New York, NY.: Chandler, 1971), 346-67.

[37]   See, e.g., H. George Frederickson, *New Public Administration* (Tuscaloosa, Al.: University of Alabama Press, 1980) and David K. Hart, "Social Equity, Justice, and the Equitable Administrator," *Public Administration Review* 34 (January 1974): 3-11

[38]   J. Michael Martinez, "Law Versus Ethics: Reconciling Two Concepts of Public Service Ethics," *Administration & Society* 29 (January 1998): 706-12.

[39]   Yukl, *Leadership in Organizations*, 401-22.

[40]   Gary E. Jusela, "Meeting the Global Competitive Challenge: Building Systems That Learn on a Large Scale," in *Organization Development and Transformation: Managing Effective Change*, 5th ed., Wendell L. French, Cecil H. Bell, Jr., and Robert A. Zawacki, eds. (Boston: Irwin, McGraw-Hill, 2000), 252-55.

[41]   Gortner, Mahler, and Nicholson, *Organization Theory*, 168-69.

42 A good summary of the empowerment process can be found in Chris Argyris, "Empowerment: The Emperor's New Clothes," in *Organization Development and Transformation: Managing Effective Change*, 5th ed., Wendell L. French, Cecil H. Bell, Jr., and Robert A. Zawacki, eds. (Boston: Irwin, McGraw-Hill, 2000), 452-59.

43 Robert T. Golembiewski, *Men, Management, and Morality* (New York: McGraw-Hill, 1965),65.

44 Michael M. Harmon and Richard T. Mayer, *Organization Theory for Public Administration* (Glenview, Ill.: Scott, Foresman and Company, 1986), 232-36.

45 William S. Gellerman, Mark S. Frankel, and Robert F. Ladenson, "A Statement of Values and Ethics by Professionals in Organization and Human Systems Development," in *Cases in Organization Development: Four Perspectives on Value-Guided Consultation* (Itasca, Ill.: F.E. Peacock Publishers, 2000), 233-35.

46 Gellerman, Frankel, and Ladenson, "A Statement of Values and Ethics," 235-37; Robert T. Golembiewski, *Ironies in Organizational Development*, 2d. ed. (New York: Marcel Dekker, 2003), 197-204; Martinez, "Law Versus Ethics," 708-18.

47 See, for example, Richard H. Hall and Robert E. Quinn, *Organization Theory and Public Policy* (Beverly Hills: Sage Publications, 1983).

48 Van Wart and Denhardt, "Organizational Structure: A Reflection of Society's Values and a Context for Individual Ethics," 235-36.

49 Ibid., 236-39.

50 Linda deLeon and Robert B. Denhardt, "The Political Theory of Reinvention," *Public Administration Review* 60, 2 (March/April 2000): 90-92; Michael Spicer, "Public Administration, the History of Ideas, and the Reinventing Government Movement," *Public Administration Review* 64, 3 (May/June 2004): 353-62; Larry D. Terry, "From Greek Mythology to the Real World of the New Public Management and Democratic Governance (Terry Responds)," *Public Administration Review* 59, 3 (May/June 1999): 272-77.

Chapter Six
Administrative Law

Much of the structure of American government is devoted to requiring the branches of government to engage in reasoned decision-making. Rather than develop laws and rules of behavior behind closed doors or through an opaque process inexplicable to citizens, the U.S. Constitution and subsequent laws and regulations create a transparent procedure where the rules of behavior developed in the regime are known and knowable beforehand. For example, Congress engages in a complex but visible legislative process involving 535 members and numerous committee and subcommittee hearings. Similarly, the president issues executive orders and presidential directives, among other powers, and influences the legislative process through congressional lobbying and by using the bully pulpit to persuade the citizenry to adopt his recommendations. The U.S. Supreme Court, in turn, following principles of *stare decisis*, decides court cases and interprets the law. For their part, administrative agencies develop rules through two related decision-making processes: rulemaking and adjudication.

The rulemaking process resembles the legislative process (while adjudication is reminiscent of the judicial process). Article I, Section 1, of the U.S. Constitution provides, among other things, that "All legislative Powers herein granted shall be vested in a Congress of the United States." This section vests certain supreme legislative powers in the Congress of the United States. During more than 200 years of Supreme Court cases interpreting various constitutional provisions—especially the Necessary and Proper Clause, the Commerce Clause, and the Supremacy Clause—the scope of congressional authority has grown substantially, with occasional exceptions designed to preserve state authority under principles of federalism.[1]

At the dawn of the twenty-first century, Congress legislates on so many issues that affect American life that it cannot possibly expect to develop expertise in every substantive area. If federal policies and programs are to be implemented, the legislative branch must look to the federal administrative agencies (the executive branch) to execute the laws. Accordingly, Congress has legitimate policy reasons for delegating authority to federal agencies—if it provides sufficient guidance and retains oversight authority.[2]

Specialists in a wide array of policy areas staff administrative agencies. By contrast, generalists are elected to Congress. It is unrealistic to expect generalists to possess the necessary expertise to draft detailed regulations in all the policy areas under the purview of Congress. Environmental controls, transportation regulations, food and drug testing criteria, military weapons systems, nuclear waste studies, and general legal requirements for the federal government, among other issues, are so complicated that only persons immersed in the substantive areas can understand the nuances and complexity required to create efficacious public policy.[3]

Despite the advantages of congressional delegations of authority to administrative agencies, whenever one branch of government transfers power to another branch, no matter how much oversight occurs, the transfer carries an inherent risk that the recipient branch may act in ways antithetical to the original intent. To ensure that Congress does not inadvertently delegate too much authority without sufficient oversight, the courts have developed the Delegation Doctrine, a standard for distinguishing between permissible and impermissible transfers of authority. The doctrine is widely accepted as constitutional today, but it was a controversial concept during the New Deal era.[4]

Congressional Delegations of Authority and the Separation of Powers

Under the Delegation Doctrine, Congress identifies the broad dimensions of policy and establishes the parameters of policy-making through the legislative process. By framing the policy, setting guidelines, and overseeing the implementation process, Congress retains ultimate authority for the success or failure of the policy. Moreover, because Congress retains authority for appropriating money, it can determine the scope of an agency's efforts based on whether funds will be budgeted for implementing policies and programs. This arrangement is as it should be in a democratic nation. Unelected agency officials respond to Congress—which controls the agency's statutory authority and budget—and Congress, in turn, responds to the electorate.[5]

The difficulty arises when the congressional delegation of authority is overly broad, vague, ambiguous, or conflicts with existing well-established statutory and common law requirements. In such cases, agencies must look to Congress to cut through the morass and provide clear, unambiguous guidance. For a variety of reasons—inattention, a crowded agenda, a lack of the necessary expertise, reluctance to take action on unpopular issues in an election year, and so forth—Congress may not provide the necessary guidance, thereby leaving it to the agencies to resolve the dilemma, to the extent possible.[6]

The Delegation Doctrine has been a cause of concern for policy-makers fearful of power shifting away from elected to unelected officials. As the federal bureaucracy expanded in the latter half of the twentieth century, the concern became more pronounced; the power of Congress to oversee a plethora of agencies on extremely technical and complex issues repeatedly was challenged. Generally, most mainstream commentators have acknowledged that Congress must delegate authority for the reasons cited above; thus, the debate is not about *whether* authority should be delegated, but about *how much* authority should be delegated. In short, it is not an issue of principle, but a question of degree.[7]

Before the 1930s, courts examined the Delegation Doctrine in strict either/or terms. Either a particular act of Congress delegating authority to an agency was or was not constitutional. Moreover, the delegations that occurred before the New Deal generally involved the transfer of authority from one part of the federal government (Congress) to another part (an agency) in order to regulate an activity undertaken by the federal government. The question of whether Congress could delegate any of its authority to regulate the conduct of private parties remained unanswered, although it would have been reasonable to assume that such a delegation was too broad to withstand constitutional challenge.[8]

The doctrine changed during the 1930s as a result of two important Supreme Court decisions. In *Panama Refining Company v. Ryan*, the U.S. Supreme Court reviewed a provision in the National Industrial Recovery Act (NIRA) that granted the president authority to "prohibit the transportation" of "hot oil" among states. The crucial issue, according to the Court, was whether Congress had established a policy and concomitantly "set up a standard for the President's action." Although Congress had articulated an extensive series of "purposes" in the act, the Court held that simply enumerating congressional purposes was not tantamount to providing a standard. Something more was required. To delegate authority in accordance with constitutional dictates, Congress must promulgate clearly defined, well-developed standards for performance. Anything short of this requirement delegated too much authority to the party exercising discretion.[9]

A second challenge to the NIRA that same year resulted in the Court striking down an entire statute owing to its overly broad grant of authority to the National Recovery Administration (NRA). In *Schechter Poultry Corporation v. United States*, the U.S. Supreme Court reviewed the authority of the NRA. In theory, the agency was supposed to develop codes of "fair competition" to balance the desire of capitalists and entrepreneurs to earn a profit with the demand for government intervention into the marketplace during the Great Depression. The reality was far different from the theory. Congress had not provided the agency with standards to use in writing the codes, leaving it to NRA officials to use their judgment. Unfortunately, the NRA catered to business interests while neglecting input from labor and consumer groups. Thus, the agency became little more than a rubber stamp organization for business groups—a "captured agency," in bureaucratic parlance. Incensed at the arrangement, labor and consumer groups bitterly criticized the agency, but their complaints largely fell on deaf ears.[10]

The facts of the case were fairly prosaic. In Brooklyn, New York, the Schechter brothers sold kosher chickens at a price lower than the price established by the NRA under the "Live Poultry Code." The brothers argued that local markets would not support the higher price; consequently, if they wanted to sell their chickens, the Schechters had no alternative but to meet local demand at the lower price. The NRA disagreed, and prosecuted the two men for violating the code. In setting the price, the NRA was not required to consider local markets or other factors affecting pricing decisions. In fact, because Congress had created the NRA with few standards, the agency had only to consider those factors NRA officials deemed relevant.[11]

The Supreme Court eventually heard the case on appeal and agreed that Congress had delegated too much authority to the NRA by not providing sufficient means for determining when the codes complied with congressional intent and when they did not. In Justice Benjamin Cardozo's words, the situation at the NRA was "delegation running riot." If the NRA—or any agency—could establish its own standards without accountability to Congress, the Delegation Doctrine was essentially meaningless.[12]

The *Schechter* case seemed to settle the delegation issue. Over time, the courts would interfere with an agency's broad use of discretion under its delegated authority only if the agency specifically countermanded a requirement unambiguously articulated by Congress. Moreover, the courts generally deferred to a congressional delegation of authority provided an "intelligible principle" could be discerned. As of this writing, the courts have not validated a rule or a law based on delegation grounds since the New Deal era. In fact, for many years, the delegation issue was so well-settled that the U.S. Supreme Court seemed unlikely to grant *certiorari* to review delegation cases except in egregious circumstances. This situation changed in 2001 when the Court decided *U.S. Environmental Protection Agency* v. *American Trucking Association.*[13]

The case arose after the EPA developed national ambient air quality standards (NAAQS) for ozone and particulate matter under the Clean Air Act.[14] The U.S. Court of Appeals for the Fourth Circuit held that the standard for developing the NAAQS was so vague that it seemed to violate the Delegation Doctrine. The statute directed EPA to set each standard at the level "requisite to protect public health" with an "adequate margin of safety," but this language was hardly tantamount to establishing an intelligible principle. According to the court of appeals, there was "'no intelligible principle' to channel [the agency's] application of these factors; nor is one apparent from the statute. The nondelegation principle requires such a principle."[15]

The Fourth Circuit's decision in *American Trucking Association* stunned many court observers. EPA Administrator Carol Browner remarked that "the fact [is] that for the past 64 years, Congress has passed laws and then relied on executive agencies to set the particular rules to carry out those broader legislative goals rules that ultimately have protected the health, safety and security of all Americans."[16] On appeal, the U.S. Supreme Court agreed with Browner and the EPA won, highlighting the broad discretion afforded to administrative agencies and essentially interpreting an "intelligible principle" so that almost any guidance, no matter how broad or open to creative interpretation, would be permissible. Although it found the delegation of congressional authority to the agency was constitutionally permissible, the Supreme Court also ruled that the clear language found in part of the Clean Air Act could be subject to judicial review. Thus, the Court ensured that an agency would be allowed to exercise enormous administrative discretion, but agency actions were not beyond the reach of a judicial challenge.[17]

The Delegation Doctrine generally receives little attention in the new millennium. However, when it does, most commentators argue that it needs to be revamped. In a now classic law review article, University of Chicago law professor Kenneth Culp Davis wrote that the doctrine "can and should be altered to turn it into an effective and useful judicial tool. Its purpose should no longer be either to prevent delegation of legislative power or to require meaningful statutory standards; its purpose should be the much deeper one of protecting against unnecessary and uncontrolled discretionary power."[18] Despite Davis's call for change to protect "against unnecessary and uncontrolled discretionary power," the doctrine remains more or less intact.

At its core, the delegation issue raises concerns about the blurring of the separation of powers, a fundamental idea in the operation and study of constitutional and administrative law. Courts have held that, while the Congress can provide a great deal of authority to agencies, executive branch agencies must not overstep their authority and encroach on legislative powers owing to the sovereignty of the branches. Thus, in something of an anomaly, the Court decided in a 1943 case, *National Broadcasting Company v. United States*, that a broad, essentially "standardless" congressional grant of authority to the Federal Communications Commission (FCC) passed constitutional muster. *National Broadcasting* involved a heavily regulated industry—radio and, later, television—which the Court distinguished from other types of industries. As a result, the decision was not far-reaching owing to the relatively narrow holding, which limited the open-ended delegation of authority to questions of communications licensure. As long as Congress provided some kind of guidance to the FCC, no matter how vague or hastily drafted, an agency's authority was upheld.[19]

In *National Cable Television Association, Inc. v. United States*, the U.S. Supreme Court considered a congressional delegation of authority under the Independent Offices Appropriations Act. In that statute, Congress allowed several agencies, especially the Federal Communications Commission (FCC), to ensure that they were "self-sustaining" by charging the private sector a fee for "regulatory benefits." The FCC aggressively interpreted this grant of authority and sought millions of dollars from cable television stations. In reviewing the delegation of authority, the Court held that Congress could not cede "essential legislative functions," as it had in this case. By allowing the FCC to use its judgment in imposing fees on private industry without providing congressional guidelines, Congress had abdicated its responsibilities by vesting legislative authority in a non-legislative entity.[20]

The 1980 "benzene case" became famous for its effect on the fledging environmental movement. *Industrial Union Department v. American Petroleum Institute*, as the case was styled, involved actions undertaken by the Occupational Safety & Health Administration (OSHA). Congress had delegated authority to the agency to ensure that "no employee will suffer material impairment of health or functional capacity." OSHA proposed to adopt a rule that would prohibit more than one part benzene, a known human carcinogen, to one million parts of air.[21]

Industry representatives contended that the proposed rule was far too stringent. Not only would complying with such a strict requirement put many companies out of business owing to the costs of pollution control devices, but the results would not necessarily provide any appreciable health benefits. In essence, the burden of the new rule far outweighed the benefits.

The Court agreed with industry. In this case, Congress should not have left it to OSHA to decide whether the benefits of implementing a particular legislative mandate were greater than the burden. That determination was more properly a legislative function. Justice Rehnquist lectured Congress that "[i]t is hard choices and not the filling in of the blanks which must be made by the elected representatives of the people."[22]

Another important case during the 1970s, *Hampton v. Mow Sun Wong*, concerned a Civil Service Commission (CSC) rule barring aliens from holding federal jobs. The Commission argued that the rule was necessary to ensure enforcement of national immigration laws and to encourage illegal aliens to seek naturalization if they intended to remain in the United States indefinitely. The U.S. Supreme Court struck down the Commission's rule—not because the policy was flawed, but because it was a congressional duty to make such a policy. By leaving it to the CSC to determine the policy on federal employment of illegal aliens, Congress once again had evaded its responsibility.[23]

Each of these cases underscores the idea that policy decisions and choices involving broad questions of public import must be left to democratically chosen legislative entities. Similarly, those entities must be responsive to the public will expressed by voters. This fundamental principle does not preclude Congress from vesting a certain amount of authority with administrative agencies, but the delegation must not be overly broad. Moreover, in delegating authority, Congress, to the extent possible, must ensure that legislative standards and guidance are clearly and unambiguously provided.[24]

The difficulty, of course, is in articulating a workable standard. Deciding when a delegation is overly broad as opposed to when it is so narrow that it limits the options available to an agency in implementing a new regulation is never an easy determination. When a court is faced with an interpretation of the Delegation Doctrine, this new review adds a layer of complexity to the issue as well. Justice Scalia eloquently expressed the dilemma in a 1989 dissenting opinion in *Mistretta v. United States*. "Once it is conceded, as it must be, that no statute can be entirely precise, and that some judgments, even those involving policy considerations, must be left to the officers executing the law and the judges applying it, the debate over unconstitutional delegation becomes a debate not over a point of principle but over a question of degree."[25]

Rulemaking and Adjudication: The Rule of Law

The Delegation Doctrine occasionally rears its ugly head, but for the most part congressional grants of authority to agencies are an accepted practice in American public administration. Assuming that the delegation does not exceed the degree deemed acceptable by the U.S. Supreme Court, the next step is for an agency to develop an action plan for implementing the policy. The process of developing an action plan generally is called rulemaking.[26]

Rulemaking is a two-part process. The first, a decisional process, requires the agency to write a proposed rule that delineates the procedures by which the policy will be implemented. The development of a proposed rule often requires administrators to use discretion. Even if Congress provided sufficiently precise guidance on the appropriate policy, the steps necessary to implement the policy are left to the agency. As an example, if the Clean Air Act requires the U.S. Environmental Protection Agency (EPA) to control ground-level ozone emissions, EPA must review the relevant studies and scientific data, decide on the most appropriate method of controlling emissions, and publish a proposed rule in the *Federal Register*. Publication of the proposed rule provides interested parties with a chance to comment on the agency's decision plan. In the words of the federal Administrative Procedure Act (APA), "the agency shall give interested persons an opportunity to participate in the rulemaking through submission of written data, view, or arguments."[27]

The agency must respond to all comments it receives; however, it is under no obligation to consider the comments or change its proposed rule based on the comments. In fact, as long as the agency acts rationally and does not make its decisions in an "arbitrary and capricious" manner, its decisions generally will be upheld, even if they are challenged in court. Thus, when Congress delegates authority to an agency, it vests tremendous powers in these unelected "experts."[28]

This insight leads to the second part of rulemaking: the rule of law. The APA requires agencies to publish their final rules in codified form in the *Code of Federal Regulations (CFR)*. The CFR is the administrative equivalent of the *United States Code*, which is a compilation of all statutes enacted by Congress. In a sense, the two sources go hand in hand. The Code provides information on the general law enacted by Congress and the corresponding CFR citation provides specific details on how the law will be implemented. Together they contain the legal rules that form the basis for the rule of law at the federal level of American government.[29]

The "rule of law" is so often discussed and bandied about that today the phrase has become something of a cliché, but it should not be trivialized. In the view of the Founders, the idea of reaching decisions concerning public affairs according to a publicly available, clearly delineated set of rules that are known and knowable was of paramount importance to the new regime. The Constitution established the precedent that the nation should be based on rules, not the whims of men. The subsequent development of legislative statutes and administrative rules was designed to rest on the same firm bedrock principles that underlay the development of the U.S. Constitution.[30]

Would that rulemaking—or lawmaking, for that matter—were so clear and unambiguous. Owing to the imprecise nature of language and the multitude of situations that fail to unequivocally fall under the purview of a specific law, administrators must interpret the law passed by Congress in many instances. The interpretation is supposed to be reasonable and in line with legislative intent but, as we have seen, that intent is not always readily discernible. Moreover, one man's reasonable interpretation is another man's arbitrary and capricious decision. The field of administrative law, therefore, is concerned in no small degree with determining when an agency appropriately exercised discretion in rulemaking and when it acted in an arbitrary and capricious manner.[31]

Courts generally defer to agencies in determining what kinds of activities are deemed arbitrary and capricious. Many cases explore this issue, but probably the leading opinion is *Chevron U.S.A., Inc. v. Natural Resources Defense Council*. In that case, the central question was whether the U.S. EPA's "new source review" standards under the 1977 Clean Air Act were consistent with congressional intent or if the agency had stepped beyond its bounds in interpreting the statute. Initially, EPA had intended to count every new piece of equipment in a manufacturing plant as a "new source," which potentially could prevent an industrialized business from expanding in areas of the country where contaminated air was especially problematic. During the rulemaking process, however, the agency changed its approach to a "bubble" concept, which would allow a company to consider changes to an entire plant rather than to particular pieces of equipment. Such a permissive interpretation was a boon to companies that polluted the atmosphere heavily because it would allow them to trade out equipment and operate their plants with more latitude than would have been possible under EPA's original approach.[32]

When the issue reached the courts, the D.C. Circuit Court of Appeals concluded that the agency had strayed beyond the purposes of the Clean Air Act. Congress had not mentioned the bubble approach; therefore, EPA could not develop a standard that, in effect, relaxed the stringent requirements of the statute. The court based this analysis on its own interpretation of the statute, which differed markedly from EPA's interpretation.[33]

In reviewing the case, the U.S. Supreme Court reversed the court of appeals. According to the Court, "If Congress has not directly addressed the precise question at issue, the court does not simply impose its own construction on the statute as would be necessary in the absence of an administrative interpretation. Rather, if the statute is silent or ambiguous with respect to the specific issue, the question for the court is whether the agency's answer is based on a permissible construction of the statute."[34]

The difference between a court interpreting a statute and the court determining whether an agency has improperly interpreted a statute may initially seem to be a game of semantics, but the distinction is crucial to understanding the modern concept of administrative discretion. In the former instance, the court would be charged with interpreting the case based on the judges' reading of the statute. Therefore, it would be incumbent on an agency to determine what standards would satisfy the judges, not what standards might be reasonably inferred from the congressional delegation of authority. In the second case, the court does not determine whether the agency's actions were in line with the court's interpretation; rather, the court merely determines whether the agency's actions were reasonable in light of the original congressional delegation of authority.

Justice Stevens highlighted the issue succinctly in his opinion in *Chevron.* "Judges are not experts in the field, and are not part of either political branch of the Government," he wrote. "In contrast, an agency to which Congress has delegated policy-making responsibilities may, within the limits of that delegation, properly rely upon the incumbent administration's views of wise policy to inform its judgments. While agencies are not directly accountable to the people, the Chief Executive is, and it is entirely appropriate for the political branch of the Government to make such policy choices...."[35]

In the aftermath of *Chevron*, administrative agencies can exercise enormous discretion in implementing public policy during the rulemaking process. This increased discretionary authority, of course, does not mean that administrators are able to enact rules and regulations free of standards. They must work within the confines of the congressional delegation of authority and in accordance with the rule of law. Accordingly, most post-*Chevron* cases have attempted to refine the boundaries of administrative discretion; the outcome turns on whether Congress specifically addressed an issue or left it for the agency to decide. In *The U.S. Food & Drug Administration (FDA) v. Brown & Williamson Tobacco Corporation*, for example, a 2000 case concerning whether cigarettes met the definition of a "drug" or "device" under the Federal Food, Drug, and Cosmetic Act, the U.S. Supreme Court held that Congress had already decided that cigarettes were not included in the statute. The FDA could not regulate cigarettes. Writing the majority opinion for a five-four Court, Justice Sandra Day O'Connor succinctly summarized the *Chevron* requirements. "Under *Chevron*, a reviewing court must first ask 'whether Congress has directly spoken to the precise question at issue.' If Congress has done so, the inquiry is at an end; the court 'must give effect to the unambiguously expressed intent of Congress.' But if Congress has not specifically addressed the question, a reviewing court must respect the agency's construction of the statute so long as it is permissible." In this instance, O'Connor observed, "Considering the FDCA as a whole, it is clear that Congress intended to exclude tobacco products from the FDA's jurisdiction."[36]

In *Barnhart v. Walton*, the Court reached the opposite conclusion. In that case, the Court considered whether the Social Security Administration's interpretation of the statutory term "disability" was entitled to *Chevron* deference. In finding that the agency's interpretation was reasonable, Justice Stephen Breyer, writing for the Court majority, reasoned that "the legal question before us is whether the Agency's interpretation of the statute is lawful. This Court has previously said that, if the statute speaks clearly 'to the precise question at issue,' we 'must give effect to the unambiguously expressed intent of Congress.' *Chevron*, 467 U.S., at 842-843. If, however, the statute 'is silent or ambiguous with respect to the specific issue,' we must sustain the Agency's interpretation if it is 'based on a permissible construction' of the Act." In the majority's view, "the interstitial nature of the legal question, the related expertise of the Agency, the importance of the question to administration of the statute, the complexity of that administration, and the careful consideration the Agency has given the question over a long period of time all indicate that *Chevron* provides the appropriate legal lens through which to view the legality of the Agency interpretation here at issue."[37]

Chevron and its progeny are wrestling with three age-old problems: Ensuring that reasoned decision-making occurs; overseeing administrative agencies—which are staffed with unelected public servants, no less—to determine whether they have overstepped their congressionally delegated authority; and providing interested stakeholders with an opportunity to participate in the administrative process. The rulemaking process theoretically allows for all of these problems to be adequately addressed.

A question arises, however, whether an individual can oppose an agency's rules during the rulemaking process and after the rules have been developed. One of the hallmarks of the American legal and political system is that affected parties need not wait for rules to be dictated from higher authorities; they may lobby and attempt to persuade decision-makers to adopt their perspective. Once the rules have been developed, affected parties also may challenge the application of particular rules in specific instances. Throughout the history of the republic, lawmakers, regulators, and judges have explained the rule of law and the ability to take part in consensual government by referring to a related concept, "due process of law." Due process is observed when all affected parties are afforded a full and fair opportunity to be heard. In the case of administrative agencies, due process requires that parties subject to rules and regulations must be allowed an opportunity to comment on proposed rules as well as contest the application of a particular rule as applied to a specific party after the rule has been adopted.[38]

In resolving a dispute after adoption of a rule, an agency exercises adjudicatory power. Just as rulemaking is tantamount to a quasi-legislative power, adjudication is an agency's quasi-judicial power. Adjudication itself raises potentially thorny questions about whether an administrative body can exercise what amounts to a judicial function. Article III of the U.S. Constitution vests the federal judicial authority in the U.S. Supreme Court and the lower federal courts created by Congress. If an agency adjudicates disputes in a trial-type setting, this kind of activity apparently contravenes the seemingly exclusive nature of judicial authority in Article III. As with so much of administrative law, the courts have been willing to carve out exceptions to constitutional provisions—in this case Article III. Consequently, in cases where the question involves the interpretation of an agency regulation, an aggrieved party initially must submit to agency adjudication and exhaust all administrative remedies before moving into the judicial system envisioned under Article III.[39]

Adjudication and the Seventh Amendment

The more difficult question does not concern Article III of the U.S. Constitution, but one of the celebrated Bill of Rights, the Seventh Amendment, which provides for the right to a trial by jury in judicial proceedings. In the normal course of litigation, the purpose of a jury trial is to place a case before the common sense judgment of average people, not elites who might hold a particular litigant to an unreasonably high standard of behavior. Adjudication by an administrative agency, in contrast to a strictly judicial proceeding, is not subject to the provisions of the Seventh Amendment. If an agency is delegated congressional authority to resolve technical, highly specialized issues generally beyond the expertise of the general public, submitting a technical issue to a jury in an adjudicatory hearing would obviate the rationale for creating a bureaucratized body of experts.[40]

The leading case in this area is *National Labor Relations Board v. Jones & Laughlin Steel Corporation*. The 1937 case involved a steel company that had dismissed employees who participated in union activities. In a landmark ruling, the U.S. Supreme Court held that Congress had not violated the Constitution when it enacted the National Labor Relations Act, a major New Deal initiative, and thereby established the National Labor Relations Board (NLRB). As a result, the NLRB was duly authorized to develop regulations on employee dismissals. Toward the end of the opinion, the Court quickly disposed of the Seventh Amendment issue by distinguishing the language in the amendment from the congressional statute under consideration in the *Jones* case. Because the Seventh Amendment emphasized that the right to a jury trial "shall be preserved," the Court interpreted this provision to mean that the amendment referred specifically to jury trials in standard judicial proceedings. When an agency engages in quasi-judicial proceedings, however, it does so pursuant to a legislative enactment, which is not subject to the provisions of the Seventh Amendment. In other words, the issue is not whether an agency has impermissibly encroached on judicial authority. Because the agency is acting under a grant of authority by Congress, the question of judicial authority is not at issue.[41]

Predictably, this convoluted reasoning failed to convince critics of an ever-growing federal bureaucracy. The Supreme Court itself limited the *Jones* holding in a subsequent case, *Curtis v. Loether*. *Curtis* did not directly involve administrative agencies, but its holding touched on whether the right to a jury trial was an inviolable constitutional right. The case involved a litigant who contended that his landlord had violated the housing provisions of the Civil Rights Act of 1968 by refusing to lease an apartment owing to the race of a prospective tenant. A federal district court judge heard the case without a jury present and subsequently found for the plaintiff. The landlord appealed on the grounds that the judge had acted arbitrarily and capriciously by holding a bench trial in contravention of the Seventh Amendment guarantee of trial by jury.[42]

Backing away from the carefully crafted distinctions articulated in *Jones*, the court agreed with the landlord that the Seventh Amendment provided for a jury trial and, as such, the right could not be easily abrogated. According to the majority opinion, the crucial issue is in determining whether a "functional justification" exists for denying a jury trial. In other words, the court would allow for jury trials in cases where such trials customarily have been held, but in cases where they have not, denying the right might be appropriate, depending on the circumstances of the case.[43]

This "functional justification" was difficult to fathom, but the concept was reinforced in later decisions, most notably in a 1977 case, *Atlas Roofing Company v. The Occupational Safety & Health Review Commission*. In that case, the Supreme Court considered whether a company accused of violating health and safety rules could push for a jury trial or whether an agency imbued with congressional authority could impose civil penalties absent a jury trial. Atlas Roofing Company argued that *Curtis* required that any case where money fines were involved had to be decided by a jury. The Court disagreed, holding that the nature of the governmental entity was the key distinction. Because cases argued before courts were strictly judicial proceedings, the Seventh Amendment applied. Adjudications before an administrative agency, however, did not raise constitutional issues with respect to juries. Using this historical approach, the Court concluded that the "right to a jury trial turns not solely on the nature of the issue to be resolved but also on the forum in which it is to be resolved."[44]

The Administrative Procedure Act

Through a series of cases, as we have seen, the courts broadly interpreted congressional grants of authority to administrative agencies. Moreover, the Seventh Amendment requirement for jury trials generally does not apply in agency adjudications. As a result, the authority of agency officials, assuming that they do not act in an arbitrary and capricious manner, is well established. Any type of federal executive branch agency—executive departments, independent agencies, independent regulatory commissions, and public corporations—can exercise enormous discretion as long as it follows appropriate administrative procedures in accordance with its congressionally delegated authority.[45]

Recognizing the burgeoning power of administrative agencies, Congress enacted the Administrative Procedure Act (APA) in 1946. The APA established the framework for agency actions. At a minimum, agencies must publish information on their general methods of operation, procedural and substantive rules, and descriptions of any proposed changes to existing rules. All relevant information, including the text of final rules, must appear in the *Federal Register*. Adjudicatory hearings must afford affected parties with a right to be heard. In addition, when affected parties have exhausted their administrative remedies, they have an opportunity to seek judicial review if an agency violated constitutional or statutory provisions or abused its discretion.[46]

Although many debates have focused on when the APA requires a formal adjudication on the record in lieu of an informal resolution, the statute is designed to ensure that agencies do not exercise unfettered discretion. This emphasis on limiting agency actions through the use of legal means has led some commentators to conclude that legal rules determine now more than ever the extent to which bureaucracies perform their work. With this emphasis on black-letter legal rules, a student of public administration ethics may well ask how ethical issues arise in such a legalistic, rule-oriented environment.[47]

Implications for Administrative Ethics

A discussion of administrative law initially suggests that ethical considerations play little if any part in legal analysis. An administrator must identify the law and how it applies and act accordingly. Even in cases where substantial ambiguity exists, enough court decisions exist so that guidance is reasonably clear—or so the argument goes. It should be axiomatic that in cases where guidance can be found, the ethical administrator must act in accordance with any law that is legitimately developed and not deemed unconstitutional by an authoritative governmental entity. The more difficult ethical issues arise in cases where guidance is not forthcoming or a law seems to violate the Constitution on its face. The overriding question is how an ethical administrator should behave in such instances.[48]

The core inquiry is to ask what constitutes "responsible conduct" with respect to implementing a law, to use commentator Terry L. Cooper's phrase. In Cooper's view, responsible conduct is not merely a function of following rules prescribed beforehand. No set of rules crafted by man—no matter how carefully codified and explained—can govern every situation encountered by administrators. Thus, determining responsible conduct is not so much the explication of a set of rules as it is identifying general components that must be considered by an administrator as he or she struggles to act responsibly.[49]

In a sense, the ethical public administrator is a servant of two masters. On one hand, he or she must recognize the authority vested with the political branch of government—the Congress—and act accordingly. Protests that the administrative role merely is to carry out the will of Congress, of course, are naïve or disingenuous, for administrative discretion is a necessary component of any bureaucratic position, no matter how mundane. On the other hand, in addition to political considerations, administrators must consider legal standards and requirements, which may or may not be in line with a congressional delegation of authority. Societal expectations sometimes are important if an administrator is to reach decisions that will be supported and honored by the public.

In another sense, this explanation of administrative functions is far too simplistic. If the truth is known, administrators are servants of many masters. As administrators, they first and foremost work within a given organizational structure. Many factors affect how well an organization operates, including whether clear lines of accountability and communication exist, whether procedures exist for an administrator to participate in decision-making, and whether channels of dissent are clear and open. In an organization where one or more of these features are absent, an administrator will find it difficult to perform in a responsible manner.[50]

Organizational structure sometimes receives short shrift in the literature on administrative ethics, but it is an important issue. In no small measure, the structure of an organization determines its function. Large bureaucratic organizations with many workers and departments have a tendency to spread responsibility among many sources. As a result, the chain of command is extremely difficult to discern, especially for an outsider looking at an organization. The ethical administrator faces a daunting challenge in trying to behave in a responsible manner when he or she cannot identify what course of action is prudent in a given situation—and most especially so when no one authority can assist in such a determination.[51]

Moreover, it is well established that each agency develops its own identity and organizational culture. If an organization's structure is the formal plan for how the organization is supposed to operate, the organization's culture represents the informal reality of how the organization operates. This dichotomy is, in effect, the classic distinction between "ought" and "is." Administrators who hope to succeed in any agency must learn the norms of behavior and master the intricacies of working effectively within the confines of those norms in addition to understanding the structure and hierarchy of the organization. If the agency is long-standing and well run, the norms generally will reflect an appreciation of the political and legal roles assumed by administrators. In egregious cases, however, an agency's norms and procedures will be directly or indirectly at odds with bureaucratic norms.[52]

Societal expectations also influence one's understanding of responsible conduct. Prior to the rise of the administrative state with the advent of the New Deal in the 1930s, the public perception of administrative agencies was fairly limited. Agencies provided some services, but decisions routinely made today by regulatory agencies, for example, would have been far beyond the boundaries of societal expectations in the 1920s and earlier in American history. The dawn of the twenty-first century represents a far different era. Administrative agencies decide questions involving the natural environment, safe foods and drugs, housing standards, worker safety, and on and on. Societal expectations have changed, and the ethical administrator must change with them.[53]

In short, the ethical administrator must strive to understand appropriate laws and regulations affecting the agency, but this endeavor is not enough to ensure responsible conduct. Laws are seldom clear and unambiguous, and in some cases laws that are directly on point do not yet exist. Owing to the less-than-precise nature of administrative activities, sooner or later an administrator will be called upon to use discretion in handling a matter. After consulting appropriate legal sources—the statute in question as well as applicable rules and regulations in the *Code of Federal Regulations*—the administrator must decide what legal requirements are in place and how they can be met. Afterward, assuming that some interpretation and discretion are required, the administrator must develop a plan of action based on the organization's mission, structure, and culture. In this way, he or she is engaging in responsible conduct. In short, following the law is the preferred course of action when the law is clear. When the law is not clear, following the organization's mission and norms is desirable. When the organization's mission and norms are unclear, the ethical administrator must look to his or her own values for guidance. As discussed elsewhere in this work, those values should be developed with a deep understanding of the needs and interests inherent in the nation's republican form of government.

Exercises and Discussion Questions

1. Why does Congress sometimes delegate authority to administrative agencies? Does this delegation of authority present constitutional problems? What are the benefits of delegating authority from generalists to specialists? What are the costs?
2. What is rulemaking and why do administrative agencies argue that they need to make rules? How does an administrative rule work in tandem with a statute enacted by a legislative body?
3. What is adjudication? Commentators argue over whether administrative agencies can exercise adjudicatory authority without violating the Seventh Amendment of the U.S. Constitution. What is the central issue in this argument?
4. What is the purpose of the Administrative Procedure Act (APA)? In your opinion, has the APA increased or decreased the discretion of administrative agencies?

5. What are the duties of the ethical public administrator with respect to administrative law? Is there overlap between law and ethics? Can you think of instances in which law and ethics diverge?

6. You are working in an agency that periodically engages in rulemaking, and your job is to ensure that the agency collects all public comments and adequately responds. During one especially contentious round of rulemaking you realize that other administrators in the agency working on the rulemaking are not reading the hundreds of public comments they receive; they are merely listing them under the general heading "not applicable," which they will then briefly summarize in the *Federal Register* when they issue the final rule. The Administrative Procedure Act (APA) requires that the agency must respond to public comments, but it does not require an agency to respond in any particular way. You are concerned that the agency may be missing valuable insights contained in at least some of the comments. What should you do?

   a. "Go public" by blowing the whistle on your fellow administrators in a press conference.
   b. Do nothing because the agency is not required to read or respond to public comments in any particular way. By summarizing the comments as "not applicable," agency officials have complied with APA procedural requirements.
   c. Approach your fellow administrators, voice your concerns, and ask them to read the comments. You can even offer to read them.
   d. Approach your superiors within the agency, voice your concerns, and ask that someone intervene to ensure that the comments are adequately considered.
   e. You should perform more than one of the actions listed above (be specific.)

7. You are a public administrator in the Social Security Administration (SSA) and you possess the authority to approve or reject disability petitions from claimants applying for SSA benefits. You encounter a claimant who professes to be disabled because he suffers from agoraphobia, a fear of open spaces. The term "disability" is not adequately defined in the statute. The regulation lists several conditions that meet the definition, but "agoraphobia" is not listed. Part of the regulation states, "Any condition generally accepted by the medical community as disqualifying a per-

son from performing at least 75% of his or her customary duties shall be deemed a 'disability' for the purposes of this regulation." In your opinion, what should an ethical administrator do in this situation? Defend your decision.

a. You should reject the claimant's disability petition because the term "agoraphobia" is not clearly listed in the statute or regulation.

b. You should approve the claimant's disability petition because, as far as you can tell, "agoraphobia" is a very serious condition.

c. You should consult outside sources, possibly including one or more medical professionals, to determine whether "agoraphobia" is "generally accepted by the medical community as disqualifying a person from performing at least 75 percent of his or her customary duties."

d. You should review previous SSA petitions and/or ask more senior SSA staffers to determine whether a disability petition listing "agoraphobia" has been approved or rejected in past cases.

e. You should perform more than one of the actions listed above (be specific).

Notes

[1]   See, for example, *United States v. Lopez*, 115 S.Ct. 1624 (1995) and *Printz v. United States*, 117 S.Ct. 2365 (1997).

[2]   Alfred C. Aman, Jr. and William T. Mayton, *Administrative Law* (St. Paul, Minn.: West Publishing Company, 1993), 9-12; Roger H. Davidson and Walter J. Oleszek, *Congress and Its Members*, 3d. ed. (Washington, D.C.: Congressional Quarterly Press, 1990), 264-66.

[3]   Some commentators refer to this as the "corporation theory" of congressional-administrative relations. See, e.g., Dwight Waldo, *The Administrative State* (New York: Holmes & Meier, 1984), 139-40.

[4]   See, for example, Barry Cushman, "Rethinking the New Deal Court," *Virginia Law Review* 80 (February 1994): 201-61.

[5]   Aman and Mayton, *Administrative Law*, 12-14; William T. Mayton, "The Possibilities of Collective Choice: Arrow's Theorem, Article I, and the Delegation of Legislative Power to Administrative Agencies," *Duke Law Journal* (December 1986): 957-58.

[6]   David H. Rosenbloom, *Public Administration: Understanding Management, Politics, and Law in the Public Sector*, 3d. ed. (New York: Random House, 1993), 54, 56.

[7]   Aman and Mayton, *Administrative Law*, 15. Associate Supreme Court Justice Antonin Scalia famously raised this question in *Mistretta v. United States*, 488 U.S. 361, 415 (1989).

8 Walter Gellhorn, Clark Byse, Peter L. Strauss, Todd Rakoff, and Roy A. Schotland, *Administrative Law: Cases and Comments* (Mineola, N.Y.: The Foundation Press, Inc., 1987), 66-77.

9 293 U.S. 388 (1935).

10 295 U.S. 495 (1935).

11 Gellhorn, *et al.*, 74-76, 295 U.S. 495 at 495-539.

12 295 U.S. 495 at 553. A good discussion of the *Schechter* doctrine in subsequent years can be found in Lisa Schultz Bressman, "*Schechter Poultry* at the Millennium: A Delegation Doctrine for the Administrative State," *The Yale Law Journal* 109 (April 2000): 1399-1442.

13 531 U.S. 457 (2001).

14 Clean Air Act of 1970, 42 U.S.C. § 7410 (1990).

15 *American Trucking Association v. U.S. Environmental Protection Agency*, 175 F.3d 1027 (D.C. Cir. 1999) at 1034.

16 *Hearing of the Senate EPW Subcommittee on Clean Air*, 105th Cong. (1999) (Testimony of Carol M. Browner, Administrator, EPA), *at* http://www.epa.gov/ttn/oarpg/gen/cmbtest.html.

17 531 U.S. 457 at 458.

18 Kenneth Culp Davis, "A New Approach to Delegation," *The University of Chicago Law Review* 36 (Summer 1969): 713-33.

19 319 U.S. 190 (1943).

20 415 U.S. 336 (1974).

21 448 U.S. 607 (1980).

22 448 U.S. 607 at 681; Aman and Mayton, *Administrative Law*, 24.

23 426 U.S. 88 (1976).

24 Rosenbloom, *Public Administration*, 54, 56.

25 488 U.S. 361 (1989) at 416.

26 Aman and Mayton, *Administrative Law*, 40-66.

27 5 U.S.C.A. § 553(c).

28 Gellhorn, *et al.*, *Administrative Law*, 34-37; Thomas E. Patterson, *We The People: A Concise Introduction to American Politics*, 6th ed. (Boston: McGraw-Hill, 2006), 462-64.

29 States have their own administrative procedures acts as well. With some variations, state APAs tend to be modeled on the federal APA. Aman and Mayton, *Administrative Law*, 67-69.

30 Henry Campbell Black, *Black's Law Dictionary*, 5th ed. (St. Paul, Minn.: West Publishing Company, 1979), 1196; Alexander Hamilton, James Madison, and John Jay, "Federalist No. 37" in *The Federalist Papers*, ed. Clinton Rossiter (New York: The New American Library, 1961), 224-31.

31 Aman and Mayton, *Administrative Law*, 69-76.

32 467 U.S. 837 (1984).

33 *Natural Resources Defense Council v. Gorsuch*, 685 F.2d 718 (D.C. Cir. 1982).

34 467 U.S. 837 at 843.

35 467 U.S. 837 at 865-66.

[36]   529 U.S. 120 (2000) at 127-28, 138. For more detail on post-*Chevron* cases, see, for example, Linda R. Cohen and Matthew L. Spitzer, "Solving the *Chevron* Puzzle," *Law and Contemporary Problems* 57 (Spring 1994): 65-110.

[37]   535 U.S. 212 at 216, 220-21.

[38]   Aman and Mayton, *Administrative Law*, 76-78; Gellhorn, *et al.*, *Administrative Law*, pp. 38-40; Rosenbloom, *Public Administration*, 380-81, 465.

[39]   Aman and Mayton, *Administrative Law*, 128-30.

[40]   Aman and Mayton, *Administrative Law*, 138-42.

[41]   301 U.S. 1 (1937).

[42]   415 U.S. 189 (1974).

[43]   415 U.S. 189 at 194-95.

[44]   430 U.S. 442 (1977).

[45]   Rosenbloom, *Public Administration*, 46-47.

[46]   5 U.S.C.A. § 553, *et seq.*

[47]   Gellhorn, *et al.*, *Administrative Law*, 38-40.

[48]   Patrick J. Sheeran, *Ethics in Public Administration: A Philosophical Approach* (Westport, Conn.: Praeger, 1993), 8-11.

[49]   Terry L. Cooper, *The Responsible Administrator: An Approach to Ethics for the Administrative Role*, 3d. ed. (San Francisco: Jossey-Bass, 1990), 123-54.

[50]   James Q. Wilson, *Bureaucracy* (New York: Basic Books, 1989), 279-82.

[51]   Robert T. Golembiewski, *Ironies in Organizational Development*, 2d. ed. (New York: Marcel Dekker, 2003), 144-48.

[52]   John P. Burke, *Bureaucratic Responsibility* (Baltimore and London: Johns Hopkins University Press, 1986), 86-90.

[53]   Cooper, *The Responsible Administrator*, 178-83.

PART FOUR:
CORE FUNCTIONS *of the* ADMINISTRATIVE STATE

Chapter Seven
Ethical Issues in Personnel Management[1]

Public personnel administration seeks to ensure that the proper people are hired, trained, promoted, and retained within the public sector, but such a task is far easier said than done. To reflect changing expectations in public service, rules and regulations governing public personnel administration have changed over time. Occasionally a "proper" approach to the subject has involved strong executive leadership at the top of an organization. Neutral competence also has been stressed as the paramount feature of a public sector firm at some times in American history. In some cases, the trend has been to staff the public sector with employees who mirror the demographic composition of the national population. In any case, the "proper" people are the people who merit the public trust, however it might be defined.[1]

Merit and the Development of American Public Personnel Administration

The concept of "merit" is difficult to assess because there is no agreed upon, uncontested meaning of the term. Since antiquity, when Plato argued in *The Republic* that the philosopher- king, with his "soul of gold," must rule the city in speech because the philosopher-king is the wisest man in the regime, mankind has sought to identify the most meritorious individuals and ask them to govern. College admissions committees seek to admit the most "meritorious" students to their institutions of higher learning, but they have difficulty determining what measures—high school grades, performance on the SAT, participation in extracurricular activities, and so forth—constitute "merit." Similarly, in public employment, identifying "merit" is an enterprise fraught with peril because the concept changes over time, as this chapter will discuss. The only more-or-less agreed upon issue is that merit, whatever it is and however it is measured, should be the standard for public employment.[2]

Historians of the civil service generally trace the development of the merit principle through six periods since the inception of the American regime. During the first four decades after the U.S. Constitution was adopted, from 1789 to 1829, historians such as Paul P. Van Riper speak of Government by the Guardians. This was the period when the Founders and their immediate progeny still walked the earth. During the administrations of the first six presidents of the United States—George Washington (1789-97), John Adams (1797-1801), Thomas Jefferson (1801-09), James Madison

(1809-17), James Monroe (1817-25), and John Quincy Adams (1825-29)—the concept of merit in government service was predicated on a notion of a natural aristoi. Born into well-to-do families and raised to lead the Revolutionary generation, these leaders subscribed to the doctrine of *noblesse oblige*, an idea of civic virtue which suggested that someone who had been given much by the society was obliged to give back through public service. These men were either Founders or, in the case of John Quincy Adams, the son of a Founder.[3]

They were well-educated, contemplative men who believed they ruled because they were men of merit. No mere politicians, the leaders during this era saw themselves as statesmen. They would have been shocked at the suggestion that they were elites who rewarded their friends with positions in government, for such talk violated their conception of good character in a democratic regime. Nonetheless, in light of their privileged class, one cannot escape this judgment indefinitely. It is instructive to take note of Thomas Jefferson's first memory as a child. He was still a toddler when he recalled being transported around the grounds of his homestead on a pillow carried by a slave. One Jefferson scholar even titled his book *Jefferson's Pillow* to highlight the incongruity of Jefferson, the Sage of Monticello, the original American Sphinx, as an integral player in a democratic regime.[4]

A new era dawned with the passing of the Founders from the scene. Sometimes referred to as "Government by the Common Man," the period from 1829 to 1883 was the high tide of the spoils system. The idea of "to the victor belong the spoils" in government service is most closely associated with Andrew Jackson, and his administration (1829-37) marks a turning point in the history of the regime. Jackson was not well-educated; he was a rough, homespun, unrefined frontiersman. In *Anti-Intellectualism in American Life*, Pulitzer Prize-winning historian Richard Hofstadter wrote of an episode, perhaps apocryphal, when President Jackson was invited to receive an honorary degree from Harvard University, that bastion of Brahmin learning in Cambridge, Massachusetts. In those days, a recipient of such a high honor was expected to stand and recite a speech in Latin, from memory, demonstrating the breadth and depth of his learning. Imagine the delight of John Quincy Adams, Jackson's nemesis in the two bitterly-fought presidential contests of 1824 and 1828—the latter of which Adams lost—when he envisioned this Tennessee backwoodsman's embarrassment as he was unable to speak Latin with the requisite mastery. According to the story, Jackson accepted the award, stood, and said, simply, "*E Pluribus Unum*." True or not, the tale illustrates an important point in the Age of the Common Man—a ruler need not be highly educated to be meritorious. The only Latin he needed to know was the motto of the United States, which Jackson recited that day: "From many, one."[5]

Merit during this era was seen as loyalty. Jackson argued that he needed a government administration that was responsive to the executive who, in turn, was responsive to the citizenry. The most efficacious way of ensuring loyalty was to appoint people to government positions with the realization that they served at the pleasure of the president. What the president giveth, he could taketh away. Patronage appointments to lucrative public positions—especially in the customs house and the post office—ensured a strong measure of loyalty.[6]

Unfortunately, after Jackson left office, many of his successors were weak executives who did not share King Andrew's leadership abilities. As the nineteenth century progressed, the spoils system was itself spoiled. Lord Acton famously remarked that "power corrupts, and absolute power corrupts absolutely." So it was with patronage. Over time, loyalty as a merit principle was bastardized so that it became a question of who you knew, not what you knew. Abraham Lincoln found the process of doling out government jobs incredibly frustrating, especially since he was desperately trying to oversee the prosecution of the Civil War. According to legend, Lincoln once was lying in his bed, prostrate and sick with chicken pox. Told that people were still lined up outside his room, waiting to lobby him for government positions, he supposedly said, "Tell the office seekers to come in at once, for now I have something I can give to all of them!"[7]

A few years later, the patronage system had become so corrupted that it essentially destroyed the administration of President Ulysses S. Grant. Grant himself was apparently an honest man, but his supporters and cronies were so intent on self-gain that today the administration is ranked as one of the worst in American history. This sad state of affairs might have continued indefinitely—far outliving Grant's tenure in the Executive Mansion—had it not been for an unfortunate episode that occurred in July 1881 when Charles Guiteau, invariably described as a "disgruntled office seeker" upset with James A. Garfield because Garfield would not extend him an offer of public employment, assassinated the president. Although other factors led to its passage, the 1883 Pendleton Act was enacted by Congress and signed into law by the otherwise hapless Chester A. Arthur owing in no small measure to the public outrage over a disappointed officer seeker shooting his president.[8]

The Pendleton Act represented a sea change in the concept of merit in the public sector, and it ushered in what is sometimes called Government by the Good (1883-1906). Although it was not widely used until the 1920s and thereafter, the Pendleton Act established the federal civil service and the U.S. Civil Service Commission. The idea of "merit" was seen as a system of government administration based on neutral competence that rose above the dirty, machine-controlled, boss-oriented politics of the day. Federal administrative personnel in the executive branch would be selected on the basis of knowledge and skills as demonstrated through examination. Government jobs would no longer be dependent on who you knew, but what you knew.[9]

By 1906, the era of Progressivism had arrived. Progressives such as Wisconsin Senator Robert LaFollette and President Theodore Roosevelt believed that government could not stand on the sidelines and allow its citizens to be overtaken by vicious Robber Barons and corrupt elected officials. Government was either part of the problem or it was part of the solution. The classical liberal state of the Founders—"that government is best which governs least"—must give way to a government that recognized it had an affirmative obligation to its citizens After Roosevelt read the muckraking journalist Upton Sinclair's famous account of abuses in the U.S. meat-packing industry in *The Jungle* (1906), the president called for government regulation of various industries and industrial practices, including food, medicine, railroad freight rates, and other highly industrialized, complicated businesses enterprises.[10]

The concept of merit in public employment evolved as the nation entered into an age of Government by the Efficient. From 1906 to 1937, a meritorious public administrator was someone who relied on the principles of Scientific Management to administer government programs as efficiently as possible. Frederick Taylor was the quintessential proponent of Scientific Management. A motion efficiency expert, Taylor contended that there was a right way to perform any task. The job of an efficient administrator was to isolate the appropriate principles of a particular task and instruct others within an organization on the best way to perform it in accordance with the principles. Thus, merit was equivalent to efficiency.[11]

This "factory mentality" championed by Taylor and others in the Scientific Management School eventually evolved as the nation moved into the era of Government by Administration. From 1937 to 1955, the U.S. federal government was headed by two strong presidents—Franklin D. Roosevelt

(1933-45) and Harry S. Truman (1945-53). Although their personal styles were markedly different, Roosevelt and Truman were strong chief executives who believed in a vigorous federal government, especially in the executive branch. Roosevelt, in particular, did much to consolidate the power of the federal executive branch as he created a multitude of alphabet agencies—the Agricultural Adjustment Administration, the Civilian Conservation Corps, the Public Works Administration, and the Works Progress Administration, among others—during the New Deal of the 1930s. To some extent, Truman continued his predecessor's policies. Under President Dwight D. Eisenhower (1953-61), a man whose administration is sometimes referred to as the "invisible hand presidency" because he did not seem to be engaged in the details of governing, the executive branch remained an integral part of federal public policy, but change was on the horizon.[12]

Government by Administration meant that a meritorious public administrator was someone who tried to implement public programs that, to the extent possible, carried out the will of the chief executive. In essence, there was a strong state that developed policies and passed them down the hierarchy. This is what Donald F. Kettl referred to in *The Transformation of Governance* as the Hamiltonian Tradition of strong chief executives.[13]

After 1955, the United States entered a period that historians have labeled Government by Shared Powers. Congress and the U.S. Supreme Court have become more vigorous since the 1950s in ensuring that the president does not exercise too much power. Thus, the Twenty-Second Amendment to the U.S. Constitution, passed in 1951, limits the president to 10 years in office. The War Powers Resolution of 1973 allows the president to commit troops to combat for up to 90 days without congressional approval but, after that time, he must withdraw the troops if Congress does not agree to support continued hostilities. In the wake of the Vietnam War, the Watergate scandal, and the loss of confidence in many federal leaders, the president does not exercise the same amount of power that he did in previous years.[14]

The era of Government by Shared Powers also saw changes in public employment. The most important change in those years was passage of the Civil Service Reform Act of 1978, the first comprehensive amendment of the Pendleton Act in 95 years. During the 1976 presidential campaign, Democratic challenger Jimmy Carter called for sweeping reforms to improve the performance of the sluggish, unresponsive, bloated, expensive federal bureaucracy. After he was inaugurated in January 1977, Carter began pushing for a revision of the civil service laws. Under the CSRA, which passed during

Carter's second year in office, the old Civil Service Commission was divided into two separate offices—the Office of Personnel Management (OPM) and the Merit Systems Protection Board (MSPB). The CSRA also created the Senior Executive Service (SES). The SES was designed so that high-ranking officials in government service could switch around from one agency to another, as appropriate. In the private sector, if a corporation is experiencing difficulty performing up to expectations, a new manager—a "turnaround" expert—can be brought in to help shake up management and save the corporation. Why not apply a similar principle within the federal executive branch? This was the central insight behind the creation of the SES.[15]

Throughout the years, the idea of "merit" in public employment has changed as the public sector has changed. In times when loyalty was highly prized, those public employees who were loyal to the chief executive and his policies were deemed to be "meritorious" employees. In times when neutral competence or scientific management was valued, merit was reflected by those public employees who could act in accordance with the values of efficiency and economy that were so highly regarded at the time. "Merit," therefore, generally can be defined as a principle by which a public employee acts in accordance with the dominant values of the public sector at the time he or she is employed there. The more an employee faithfully adheres to those values, the more "merit" he or she displays.[16]

In recent years, however, the merit principle has faced its greatest challenge to date. The principle in public employment is predicated on the idea that the public sector has a certain legitimacy or rightfulness. During the past quarter century, however, a new movement has arisen that calls into question the legitimacy of the public sector, to some extent. Labeled "Reinventing Government" in the United States and "New Public Management" in countries such as England and New Zealand, this new movement denies the centrality of government. Its adherents contend that government, especially bureaucracies, cannot meet the needs of citizens as efficiently or effectively as the private sector can. Public Choice economists, for example, suggest that market forces should be relied on in all but the most egregious examples of market failure. To "reinvent government," therefore, means to privatize as many government functions as possible and allow power to "devolve" from the federal government to the states. When traditional government functions are subjected to market forces, or so the argument goes, there can be competition. With competition comes a push to make a better product for less money or supply a service as efficiently and as effectively as possible. "Citizens" become "customers" and government becomes either a hulking mono-lith to be avoided, if at all possible, or another competitor in the market-place.[17]

There have been numerous federal and state-level reforms as part of this sweeping new movement. Time considerations preclude an exhaustive review of all the reforms, but a synopsis of several recent ones is in order. At the federal level in 2005, there was a major reform within two large federal agen-cies, the Department of Homeland Security (DHS) and the Department of Defense (DOD). The reforms were aimed at making the two major agencies responsible for American security more flexible and subject to less rigid rules so that they could respond to national needs quickly and effectively. Thus, the general schedule that applies to federal agencies is not in place at DHS and DOD. Moreover, compensation is based on market forces to a greater extent than it is in most agencies so that DHS and DOD can compete with the private sector in recruiting the best personnel. Poor performers can be disciplined or fired by lower-level managers, though these administrators must meet a high burden of proof to show why they did what they did. Also, position assignments are not subject to collective bargaining, which means that DHS and DOD managers retain greater freedom and flexibility than most other federal agencies enjoy about where to position public employees.[18]

At the sub-federal level, several states have eliminated or severely cur-tailed civil service protections. After July 1, 1996, new employees in Georgia are considered at-will employees; consequently, they can be hired, trained, promoted, demoted, disciplined, or fired much more easily than employees hired prior to that date because their predecessors enjoy civil service protec-tions. Similarly, in Florida, a program called Service First allows public em-ployees to be managed with greater flexibility than was previously allowed.

These reforms—and this new movement away from government as a central feature in the lives of citizen—have enormous repercussions for the concept of merit in public employment. With greater decentralization of au-thority and the abrogation of civil service protection, the concept of public sector "merit" seems to be under attack. The general public has a stereotypi-cal view of "bureaucrats" as rule-bound paper-pushers who, not being able to make it in the private sector, snagged "cushy" government jobs that let them stay around forever. To argue that there is such a thing as a meritorious pub-lic servant seems silly and self-serving to large segments of the public. These trendy reforms and demeaning stereotypes may sound the death knell for the concept of "merit" in public sector employment.

However, despite this seemingly dire state of affairs, there are reasons not to be overly alarmed. Much of American history resembles a pendulum that swings back and forth as times change. Political power ebbs and flows between a desire for greater centralization followed by a desire for greater decentralization. Early in our history, we sought to have a more responsive bureaucracy under Andrew Jackson, so we established a strong patronage system. That system ultimately was corrupted, so we established a civil service system as a reform. Now, people are dissatisfied with the civil service system because it no longer meets the needs of citizens as we enter the twenty-first century. We seek to minimize the role of government through reforms that strengthen patronage again. (Or do we? In the aftermath of the 9/11 terrorist attacks, we have increased our defense apparatus and consolidated some federal powers. We still want a government that provides certain goods and services—or at least oversees those who directly provide those goods and services.)

Americans are distrustful of big government, and we always have been. But when reformers cut government services or call for privatization, the public eventually comes to see how much it needs government. Reformers then call for greater government control to rectify private abuses, and the pendulum starts to swing back. It is a never-ending cycle. And when the pendulum swings back toward improved government services, behind the scenes—perhaps hidden away in a cubicle or tucked into a small corner office—the dedicated public employee still labors away at his or her job demonstrating, whether noticed or not, that he or she is a meritorious public servant, however "merit" may be defined in that particular day and age.

Protecting Public Employees in Public Personnel Administration

As the concept of merit has evolved over time, one of the major concerns in public personnel administration is balancing the need for managerial flexibility with the constitutional rights of public employees. On one hand, public managers often express their frustration at legal impediments that prevent them from effectively and efficiently managing public employees who, in their view, fall below the appropriate standard of "merit." Hiring critical personnel quickly in times of great need, disciplining or firing poor performers, and rewarding stellar work are exceedingly difficult in the public sector because managers must navigate through a maze of laws, regulations, and personnel policies that severely constrain their ability to take appropriate action.

On the other hand, those same laws, regulations, and personnel policies provide public employees with a measure of protection that insulates them from tyrannical supervisors as well as direct political pressure. It also protects them from discrimination based on race, ethnicity, age, or gender. These protections are crucial in the public sector because employees there, unlike the private sector, are working in an area that affects the welfare of the general public. Thus, one person's view of frustrating legal impediments is another person's constitutionally protected due process rights. Balancing the needs of managers with the rights of employees in the public sector is never easy, but it is a necessary component of effective public personnel management.

The constitutional rights of public employees stem from the Fifth (1791) and Fourteenth (1868) Amendments to the U.S. Constitution, both of which guarantee, among other things, due process of law. "Due process" is a vague term that has been interpreted by courts numerous times over the years. For purposes of public personnel administration, "due process" refers to the protections that must be afforded to a public employee before action can be taken that adversely affects his or her interests.[19]

In *Bailey v. Richardson* (1951), the U.S. Supreme Court ruled that a public employee did not have a property right in a government job. Despite this ruling, subsequent courts, including the U.S. Supreme Court, have determined that public employees may have a property or liberty right in public employment if there is a reasonable expectation of such a right. A reasonable expectation of a property or liberty right is created when laws, regulations, and personnel policies establish, explicitly or implicitly, such a right. After a right is established, it is protected by the Fifth Amendment due process clause as that clause is incorporated through the Fourteenth Amendment and applied to states (and, by extension, local governments).[20]

This discussion is not to suggest that a public employee is therefore protected from being disciplined or fired under all circumstances. A public employee can be disciplined or fired after steps have been taken to ensure that due process has been provided. Generally, in employment law cases, "due process" refers to whether the public employee has been allowed to have a hearing and tell his or her side of the story. In most, although not all, cases, the hearing must be held prior to termination. In some cases, the hearing need not be in-person; it can be in writing as long as the public employee is afforded an opportunity to tell his or her side of the story and provide supporting documentation and/or relevant testimony from witnesses.

Many court cases have addressed the question of what process is due and when it is due; that is, the cases explicate what type of hearing is required and when it is to be held. In *Goldberg v. Kelly* (1970), for example, the U.S. Supreme Court held that recipients of welfare benefits—a government entitlement program—could not have their benefits reduced or denied absent a hearing prior to the time the adverse action was taken.[21] Six years later, in *Mathews v. Eldridge*, the Court considered whether Social Security recipients could have their benefits reduced or denied without a hearing. In refining the *Goldberg* holding, the *Mathews* Court articulated a three-pronged test for determining when a hearing is required: (1) When an individual right is affected by state action; (2) When the risk of "erroneous deprivation" is high; and (3) After the administrative and fiscal burden to the state has been weighed against the burden placed on the individuals affected by the reduction or denial of a benefit. In other words, after government generates an expectation of some kind of government largesse—a right, a benefit, a public program—it cannot unilaterally reduce or deny that largesse absent some kind of notice and hearing to the affected party or parties.[22]

An expectation of employment, or the lack thereof, is vividly illustrated in three landmark U.S. Supreme Court cases. In *Board of Regents v. Roth* (1972), an assistant professor at a state university spoke out against the Vietnam War during a turbulent era in the nation's history. He was not a tenured professor; instead, he had been hired through a series of annual contracts. After he spoke out on this controversial subject, the university administration decided not to renew his contract for the coming year. Roth sued, but the Supreme Court held that he had no expectation of being rehired. Had he been a tenured professor or had he been the signatory to a contract that specified his rehiring, that would have been a different issue. In this case, however, a reasonable expectation of continued state employment was absent.[23]

By contrast, in *Perry v. Sinderman*, a second 1972 case, the Court found that the plaintiff, another faculty member who aggravated the university administration by expressing unpopular views, did have a reasonable expectation of continued employment. *Perry* was distinguished from *Roth* because in the former case a faculty handbook created the expectation of continued employment, while there was no such handbook in the latter case. The handbook in *Perry* contained a statement indicating that faculty members hired from year-to-year could normally expect to be rehired as long as the faculty member's performance in the classroom was satisfactory. There was nothing in the case suggesting that the plaintiff's classroom performance was sub-standard. Instead, his personal and political views were at issue.[24]

The two cases seem identical because they involve faculty members espousing unpopular views, but they differ because, in one case, the faculty member could reasonably expect to be rehired and, in the other case, he could not reasonably expect to be rehired. This distinction is crucial, and it extends not only to faculty members but to any public employee who is given an expectation of continued public employment absent a performance issue. Thus, in *Cleveland v. Loudermill* (1985), a security guard who had been deemed a "classified" employee protected by the civil service could not be discharged without a hearing even though he was found to have falsified part of his employment application when he claimed not to have a criminal history.[25]

In the private sector, which generally (although not always) operates in a free market system, employees work at-will; that is, they can be disciplined or fired for almost any reason apart from legally actionable discrimination. As long as the private employee does not have an employment contract or separate agreement affecting the terms and conditions of employment, the employee can be subjected to managerial controls that allow private managers to decide how the employee can best be used to fulfill an organization's mission and goals. In the public sector, however, it is necessary to protect employees because of the "public" nature of their position.

An employee at the Social Security Administration (SSA), for example, is working in an agency that enjoys a government-created monopoly. Persons petitioning for their Social Security benefits cannot seek the same good or service from a competing firm if their application for benefits is denied. Consequently, the SSA employee potentially can affect hundreds or even thousands of people's lives. Even if he or she is a "street-level bureaucrat," to borrow Michael Lipsky's phrase, the SSA employee has enormous bureaucratic discretion. How that employee interprets applicable laws and regulations may determine who is denied benefits and who is not.

Suppose that a political appointee high up in the SSA echelon saw himself as a partisan Republican who believed strongly that Social Security benefits should be reduced, whenever possible, because this action meshed with his personal political philosophy of a smaller government. He might instruct SSA employees to deny benefits in all but the most clear-cut cases. In the private sector, the employee would be compelled to comply with this instruction or face disciplinary action and perhaps termination. In the public sector, however, such political pressure on a public employee is viewed as far more serious because, generally speaking, the public employee has more authority to wreak havoc on the public. A supervisor's partisan political predilection should not interfere with a public employee's abilities to perform his or her job. If the supervisor wants to affect the public in this way, he or she should act through appropriate channels—such as trying to initiate rulemaking and adjudication that changes existing regulations to make it more difficult to receive Social Security benefits. In short, browbeating employees is not an approved method for effecting change.

Due process protections are designed to differentiate between the roles served by public and private employees. Public employees require constitutional protections because they are especially vulnerable to partisan political pressure that potentially serves as a "backdoor" means of altering and amending public policies. An ideological political appointee is one example of someone who might impose his will on lower-level employees were it not for due process considerations. With due process protections, the public employee who refuses to comply with instructions that violate previously established rules and regulations can be secure in the knowledge that, before any adverse action can be instituted against him or her, a hearing must be held. At that point, the public employee can explain what the political appointee was doing. Knowing that this exposure might occur, the political appointee probably will be more reluctant to apply the political pressure in the first place.[26]

Insulating public employees from direct political pressure is the subject of many court cases. One leading case, *Branti v. Finkel* (1980), arose when an assistant public defender (PD) was discharged because the PD did not share the party affiliation of persons higher up in the office. The court held that the discharge violated the PD's due process rights because a hearing was not provided.[27] Similarly, a decade later in *Rutan v. Republican Party of Illinois*, the court held that partisan politics could not be grounds for refusing to hire public employees. In *Rutan*, Illinois Governor James Thompson, a Republican, allowed hiring decisions to be made at a state personnel agency where positions routinely were assigned to people who had supported the Republican Party. The court determined that this kind of channeling of employment through a partisan organization was, in effect, the creation of an agency devoted to patronage. Accordingly, the use of patronage to make employment decisions was deemed unconstitutional.[28]

Discrimination, Affirmative Action, and "Merit"

Cases protecting public employees have expanded over the years to include protections against invidious discrimination based on a person's status—primarily race, ethnicity, or gender. This shift in emphasis is hardly surprising. Until the advent of the modern civil rights and women's movements, public employment, like so much in American life and culture, was limited predominantly to white males. As laws and societal norms shifted, especially after the 1960s, increasing numbers of ethnic minorities and women entered the workforce. With their inclusion in mainstream American society, the old ways of selecting personnel for public agencies could not endure. In short, when the values of the United States changed, the concept of "merit" changed.

A word of caution is in order. The definition of "merit" and the ideal of "equal employment and opportunity" are contentious issues. Opponents of affirmative action programs to assist blacks, ethnic minorities and, to some extent, women in securing public employment argue that these programs are far removed from the goal of a "colorblind Constitution." By focusing on the race, ethnicity or gender of an applicant, affirmative action programs accentuate the very qualities—the status of individuals, not their actions—that were deemed unconscionable reasons for discrimination by civil rights activists. Instead of hiring, retaining, and promoting workers based on their status, affirmative action opponents contend that selecting employees based on "objective qualifications" should be the paramount objective. They define these qualifications as years of education and experience, performance on employment examinations, and other tangible indicators of competence and potential to perform well in public service.

For supporters of affirmative action programs, "merit" must be judged not only on supposedly "objective" standards, but also on a quintessentially American appreciation of inclusion, tolerance, and equality of opportunity. In this way of thinking, the desire is to open up public sector employment to a wide variety of people, especially those who historically have been underrepresented. This conclusion does not suggest that offers of public employment should be extended to patently unqualified employees. Instead, it indicates that people can be considered "meritorious" for a variety of reasons, not simply because they present an illustrious pedigree, prestigious college degrees, or high scores on a standardized employment examination.

Affirmative action supporters argue that before historically disenfranchised people can advance in public employment, they must overcome the vestiges of past discrimination. Thus, the courts have responded with a series of standards to determine whether discrimination has occurred. In cases involving gender, the courts have applied "intermediate" or "moderate scrutiny," which means that a defendant still faces an onerous burden in justifying his actions, but occasionally the burden can be met. Some cases of gender discrimination are constitutionally permissible if the defendant can demonstrate valid reasons why women were treated differently than men. In most gender discrimination cases in the area of public personnel administration, however, the central issue involves comparable worth or pay equity.

"Comparable worth" is the idea that women historically have been placed into position classifications or categories of jobs that pay less and carry lower prestige and opportunities for advancement than the position classifications or categories of jobs where men work. Our culture abounds with examples of this kind of subtle discrimination against women. If a young lady is asked what she wants to do when she grows up, she might respond, "I want to be a teacher or go into the health care profession." The traditional response is to say, "Oh, that's great. You will make a terrific kindergarten teacher or nurse." The response to a young man who expresses the same career goals is to say, "Oh, you will make a terrific college professor or physician." These different responses do not denigrate the work of kindergarten teachers or nurses, but those positions tend to pay less and carry lower prestige and opportunities for advancement than the positions of college professor or physician.[29]

In an employment context, it is not difficult to see the equity of "equal pay for equal work." If a woman works the same job and the same number of hours as a man, she should receive exactly the same compensation. The difficulty arises in determining comparable worth. Women in public employment often have been channeled into lower positions than men. For example, if Agency X has two positions—"Health Care Specialist I" (HCS I) and "Health Care Specialist II" (HCS II)—they may carry different levels of compensation and prestige even though the work is more or less equivalent. HCS I might be the entry level position for physicians with 0-10 years of experience, and it pays $90,000-$125,000 a year. HCS II, the upper-level position, is designed for physicians with eight or more years of experience and it pays $115,000-$175,000 a year. Because women have only entered the ranks of physicians in large numbers during the past quarter century, there are generally fewer women who meet the qualifications of HCS II than there are who meet the qualifications of HCS I. Therefore, the human resources personnel at Agency X—perhaps without specifically intending to discriminate against women—may channel female physicians who join the agency into HCS I positions while they channel male physicians into HCS II positions. If someone were to examine the HCS I and HCS II positions, however, it would be readily apparent that employees in both positions engage in essentially the same work. If so, this is an example of a "comparable worth" problem. Women make up a disproportionately high number of employees in the lower position, but they perform the same work as men in the higher position. Their "worth," compared to men working in Agency X, seems to be lower when, in reality, they are performing the same jobs.

The courts recognized gender discrimination in public employment much later than they recognized racial discrimination, but by the 1980s they had begun to respond. Two important cases from that decade demonstrated the courts' commitment to extending constitutional protections to women. In *AFSCME v. Washington* (1985), the court recognized that women had been discriminated against in public employment and specifically required state agencies to afford women the same opportunities as men.[30] Two years later, in *Johnson v. Transportation Agency, Santa Clara County*, the court allowed gender to be one among many considerations in evaluating women for public employment positions.[31] Following on the heels of the much-publicized case of *Regents of California v. Bakke* (1978), which allowed race to be a factor in admission to public universities as long as a quota system was not employed, *Johnson* allowed gender to be a factor, but gender quotas were not found to be constitutionally permissible.[32]

Race is another troubling area where past discrimination arguably has led to present inequities. The long, tragic history of race and discrimination in the United States is far beyond the scope of this chapter, but some of the more important twentieth-century U.S. Supreme Court cases included the two famous cases that desegregated the public schools, *Brown v. Board of Education I and II*.[33] In *Bailey v. Patterson*, the Court prohibited racial segregation in interstate and intrastate transportation facilities.[34] *Loving v. Virginia* invalidated state laws prohibiting interracial marriages.[35] In *Jones v. Mayer Company*, the Court held that federal laws prohibit all racial discrimination, public or private, in the sale or rental of real property.[36] *Lau v. Nichols* held that a city school system's failure to provide English language instruction for Chinese students was unconstitutional.[37] In *Batson v. Kentucky*, the Supreme Court decided that a black defendant was denied the equal protection of the laws when members of his race were purposefully excluded from the jury.[38] *Grutter v. Bollinger*, a 2003 case, held that the University of Michigan's law school could rely on a limited affirmative action program to determine which applicants would be admitted.[39] In these and many other cases, modern courts have applied "strict scrutiny," which means that the burden on a defendant to show why such actions were not tantamount to discrimination is extremely onerous. It is almost impossible to demonstrate a valid reason why a person of one race was treated differently from a person of another race.

The leading U.S. Supreme Court case involving racial discrimination in public employment is *Griggs v. Duke Power Company* (1971). In *Griggs*, an intelligence test was administered to black employees to determine whether they could perform certain jobs. The Court held that testing must be related to the requirements of a specific job. Therefore, a driving test could be administered to a person seeking employment as a truck driver. In this case, however, the intelligence test was not reasonably related to jobs at the power plant. In reality, the intelligence test was administered to blacks in hopes of showing they were incapable of working at the plant and did not have to be hired. The Court saw the intelligence test for what it was: A means of practicing racial discrimination against blacks.[40]

The federal courts' willingness to hear cases involving constitutional rights during the latter half of the twentieth century did much to ensure that public employees were not disciplined or fired without a justifiable cause. The courts also have successfully prohibited most racial or gender discrimination in the public sector. For persons who otherwise might have been excluded from public employment, the results overwhelmingly have been positive. A question arises, however, whether extensive federal requirements have improved or hindered the overall quality of the public service. From an employee's standpoint, legal protections shield them from the vagaries of bad bosses and partisan politics. From a manager's perspective, the difficulties inherent in punishing poor performers and rewarding good performers make it virtually impossible to manage public agencies effectively. It is simply too difficult to navigate through the maze of applicable laws and regulations to punish poorly performing employees, especially those who fall into a protected class. Constitutional protections are a double-edged sword, allowing some measure of protection for employees who need it while also handcuffing managers who may wish to improve the performance of their employees and their agencies but who believe that they do not have the authority to do so.

Understanding Civil Service Operations: Is Reform Needed?

One method of answering the question whether constitutionally protected rights against discrimination and unfair employment practices hinder or improve the performance of public employees is to investigate the effect of removing such protections, to the extent possible. Two states, Georgia and Florida, revamped their public personnel systems in the 1990s by essentially removing civil service protections. Under GeorgiaGain, state employees hired after July 1, 1996 are at-will employees. Among other things, they do not have the right to a hearing before they are terminated.[41] In Florida, under Service First, public employees are subjected to a "private-sector model." They are treated as though they are at-will employees.[42]

Several academics have examined these reforms to determine the effect, if any, of reform. The conclusion is that very little change has occurred at a micro-level. Georgia Governor Zell Miller, who championed GeorgiaGain, and Florida Governor Jeb Bush, who championed Service First, promised that the state bureaucracy would be more efficient, less expensive, and perform demonstrably better after the changes were in place. These promises presuppose that the state bureaucracies in question were performing poorly in the first place. Dramatic gains have not been realized.[43]

As for the absence of the constitutional protections previously afforded to public employees, the old state civil service systems in Georgia and Florida have been replaced by patronage systems. The problem now is one of human capital. People who might otherwise have gone into public service may seek employment elsewhere because, while once they would have enjoyed civil service protection, now they are vulnerable to being disciplined or fired. There used to be a tradeoff between less pay and more job security. Now, there is less pay and less job security. Why not just work in the private sector instead? With a large number of retirements in the public sector in coming years, these reforms may actually make the public sector less effective as public managers scramble to meet their human resource needs.[44]

For proponents of diversity in the public workforce, constitutional protections for public employees can create problems for managers, but on the whole they are valuable. They are put into place to recognize the "public" nature of government employment. Without them, a patronage system becomes the order of the day. Patronage has it place, but civil service protections ensure that people who make decisions affecting the general public are somewhat immune to the vagaries that influence the private sector.

Aside from the issue of whether civil service protections are desirable, in most jurisdictions some form of civil service exists. The national government, the states, and some local governments have created their own independent, autonomous personnel systems—some of which retain civil service protections and some of which believe that patronage systems are preferable—but, for illustrative purposes, the national system provides a general framework for understanding public-sector personnel management and how it works. Just over 90 percent of all national executive-branch employees are covered by some kind of merit system, and most systems are administered by the Office of Personnel Management (OPM), which replaced the Civil Service Commission in 1979. OPM is responsible for managing the national government's personnel system consistent with presidential personnel policy. The task involves recruiting, examining, selecting, and compensating the many thousands of non-partisan employees that comprise the public workforce.[45]

One of OPM's most complicated and controversial duties is to engage in position classification, an integral component of the civil service system. Because a multitude of agencies may have a multitude of positions that perform essentially the same function despite different titles, position classification ensures equity and efficiency by providing a written job description that outlines job duties and responsibilities. Ideally, a position classification allows commonality across all federal agencies so that a person who performs a similar job in one agency is treated and compensated substantially the same as someone performing a similar job in another agency.

In the United States, the national government classifies jobs according to ten levels, or grades, called the General Schedule (GS). Each grade of service contains steps based on an employee's years of service. At the top of the personnel structure is a "super grade" known as the Executive Schedule. Promotion within the Executive Schedule is not automatic, and the scale was established specifically to recognize high performance that might not otherwise be recognized or adequately rewarded.[46]

Position classification remains one of the most contentious issues in public personnel management in part because it depends on two fundamentally different concepts. On one hand, public administrators seek to incorporate notions of equity into personnel systems so that "like cases are treated alike." If Person A is performing the same or substantially similar tasks as Person B in another agency, it makes sense to ensure that both persons are compensated at roughly equivalent levels. To some extent, therefore, personnel systems seek to minimize the distinctions among and between people. On the other hand, trends in personnel management have been moving toward recognizing performance that exceeds the expectations normally associated with a particular position. One of the major criticisms of the "one size fits all" approach to public personnel management is that treating persons within the same position the same undermines the incentive for a person to excel in his or her job.

Moreover, the task of examining the many types of positions across agencies is difficult owing to the variety of jobs, many of which do not necessarily equate well with positions in other agencies. To combat this problem, some OPM officials have turned to "broadbanding," a concept that refers to the process of consolidating existing position classifications into fewer broad classifications. By consolidating categories, position classification is much less complicated and, presumably, more equitable.[47]

The question of equity in positions classifications is especially troubling in the wake of charges of bias. Probably the most salient question of bias in recent decades arose around the Professional and Administrative Careers Examination (PACE). The issue began in 1954 when the Civil Service Commission (CSC) established the Federal Service Entrance Examination (FSEE) for most federal jobs. The exam was designed "as a 'universal' instrument for selecting college graduates in entry level positions."[48] The FSEE later was criticized as "overly general" because it did not adequately pose questions reasonably related to job performance. Recognizing this problem, in 1974 the commission developed PACE as the primary tool for selecting entry-level applicants in 118 professional and administrative occupations at the General Schedule (GS)-5 and GS-7 level. PACE would allow the CSC to create a large, centralized applicant pool from which specific federal agencies could select qualified candidates; however, most candidates who received passing scores could not realistically expect to secure federal employment. The statistics graphically illustrated this conclusion. Between Fiscal years 1976 and 1980, only 35,419 of 723,563 candidates who sat for the exam actually were selected for federal jobs.[49]

PACE was designed to improve on the FSEE by testing "knowledge, skills and abilities" necessary for candidates to assume professional and administrative responsibilities in government service. CSC specifically developed the new exam in response to a landmark 1971 U.S. Supreme Court case, *Griggs, et al. v. Duke Power Company.* In *Griggs,* the Court prohibited the use of selection methods for federal civil service employment that "cannot be shown to be related to job performance." Moreover, the Court outlawed selection methods that discriminate on the basis of race.[50]

To compete for an entry-level PACE job, an applicant had to possess a four-year college degree, three years of professional experience, or the equivalent combination of education and experience. The applicant was required to complete an application and sit for the examination. Test scores were converted into numerical scores, with 40 being the lowest possible score and 100 being the highest. A score of 70 or above was considered passing. Veterans were awarded five or ten additional points depending on their length of service and whether they had incurred a disability during their time in uniform.[51]

After identifying eligible candidates with a score of 70 or higher, OPM, the successor to CSC, prepared a rank-ordered list of applicants known as the "PACE Register." Federal agencies seeking to fill open positions within the 118 PACE occupations had discretion either to consult the PACE Register or elect to fill the positions by promoting, reassigning, or transferring current employees. When an agency chose to use the register, it would request a list of eligible candidates from the local OPM area office. The requested list—called a "certificate" in agency parlance—was forwarded to the requesting agency, which then used the "rule of three." Under this rule, the agency could select any of the top three candidates, with preference given to veterans by statute.[52]

The OPM certificate was not the sole factor by which requesting agencies would fill positions. Depending on the request of the agency involved, the OPM could institute additional job-related requirements such as knowledge of a foreign language, certain types of computer skills, or other specialized training, education, or certifications. The willingness and ability to relocate or to travel extensively was a factor in some instances. As a result of additional requirements, even candidates with PACE scores significantly higher than 70 were not guaranteed a position in a federal agency. In fact, according to OPM data from Fiscal Year 1976 through Fiscal Year 1980, only 4.9 percent of applicants who sat for PACE were selected for PACE occupations. Clearly, an applicant who sat for PACE could not reasonably expect to be employed in a federal administrative agency.[53]

Four years after PACE was developed, OPM joined with the Equal Employment Opportunity Commission, the U.S. Department of Labor, and the U.S. Department of Justice to issue a series of guidelines that became known collectively as the *Uniform Guidelines on Employee Selection Procedures* (hereinafter the *Guidelines*). The *Guidelines* attempted to establish a rule to determine whether a particular examination had an "adverse impact" on a particular racial or ethnic group. Under the "4/5 rule," any examination that resulted in a selection rate of less than 4/5 (80 percent) for members of a particular racial, ethnic or gender group was deemed to have an adverse impact, regardless of the intent behind the development of the examination. The *Guidelines* did not absolutely prohibit the use of an examination that failed the 4/5th rule, but it did specify that such examinations must be validated through a series of fairly stringent validation standards.[54]

During the late 1970s, an increasingly large group of detractors began to criticize PACE owing to the significant differences between the proportions of white, black, and Hispanic job applicants who received a 70 or higher in the examination. Before these complaints were raised, OPM generally did not collect data on the race and national origin of PACE applicants. Owing to increasing questions about the potentially adverse impact on certain races, however, the agency collected sample data during the January 1978, April 1978, and April 1980 administrations of the exam. The 4/5 rule certainly supported the arguments voiced by PACE critics. The data indicated that in the January 1978 and April 1978 administrations of the exam sampled by OPM, approximately 42 percent of white test-takers earned 70 or higher, while only 12.9 percent of Hispanics and 5 percent of blacks achieved comparable scores. With a glut of highly qualified applicants competing for some positions, in many cases the threshold score necessary to procure employment was closer to 90.[55]

In light of the clear disparities in PACE results by race—the legal definition of "adverse impact"—it was only a matter of time before the examination was challenged. The challenge came on January 29, 1979, when Angel G. Luevano and a group of plaintiffs representing a nationwide class of blacks and Hispanics filed suit against Alan Campbell, director of OPM, alleging that PACE discriminated against class members in violation of Title VII of the Civil Rights Act of 1964. Based on the number of PACE applicants who were black and Hispanic, the class included well over 100,000 members. Scrambling to answer the suit, OPM asked for, and was granted, four time extensions for filing an answer, which it finally did on December 14, 1979.[56]

For almost two years, the parties litigated the case, exchanging requests for admissions, interrogatories, and the production of documents. At the end of several rounds of settlement negotiations, on January 9, 1981, the parties jointly moved for a court order granting preliminary approval to a consent decree to settle the case. After a minor amendment, the District of Columbia Circuit Court of Appeals granted the order for a consent decree on February 26, 1981, and the final decree was approved on November 19 of that year.[57]

Under the terms of the consent decree, OPM agreed to phase out PACE no later than three years after the settlement. One year after the effective date of the decree, 50 percent of applicable appointments had to be made using alternative examination procedures. Within two years, the goal was 80 percent. Three years after the decree went into effect, all applicants would have to be examined using alternative procedures. During the phase-out period, OPM would be required to undertake "all practicable efforts" to minimize the adverse impact of the examination. One such method was to provide financial assistance to applicants by offering the PACE test free of charge. The OPM assistance program was to be administered in selected areas where a high black or Hispanic population lived. Although the program was primarily designed to assist members of the identified class, it was not limited to the class.[58]

In its place, OPM or a particular agency seeking to hire personnel was directed to develop an examination as well as examination procedures specifically related to the job or a group of job categories where the vacancy existed. To ensure that the new system did not also result in an adverse impact, the consent decree required that OPM establish a monitoring committee comprised of representatives from both plaintiffs and defendants in the lawsuit to oversee the development of testing content and validation procedures, and to oversee all steps associated with implementation. The committee was directed to report back to the court on a regular basis.[59]

The court ordered that, after the examination and appropriate procedures were developed, the results would have to be disseminated to OPM and agency offices around the country. Moreover, OPM and affected agencies would have to provide for training so that agency testing personnel would be informed of the requirements contained in the consent decree. Over the objection of some class members—who insisted on the immediate elimination of the PACE requirement—the court concluded that the terms of the consent decree required a three-year implementation period to ensure that OPM and the appropriate agencies had adequate time to replace PACE.[60]

The PACE imbroglio demonstrates the difficulty that public personnel managers have faced, and in some measure continue to face, as they seek to identify "meritorious" job candidates. Identifying the merit principle and determining "proper" job candidates who meet the principle remain problematic. Nonetheless, despite the difficulty, a core function of public personnel managers is to select appropriately qualified people for appropriate positions.

Collective Bargaining in the Public Sector

Identifying meritorious job candidates remains a highly contested endeavor as managers sift through individual applicants on a "micro" level. Similarly, the process of determining working conditions for public sector employees on a "macro" level also remains controversial. Collective bargaining, a relatively new process in the public sector, began during the 1950s as an alternative to traditional management-controlled personnel practices. The process involves a formalized negotiation between management and labor and involves steps aimed at producing an agreement on working conditions. Unlike the private sector, however, collective bargaining in the public sector is complicated by preexisting civil service laws and regulations as well as the unique nature of government employment. Generally, if employees in a private firm refuse to work, a competing firm will step into the breach and a customer, while perhaps inconvenienced, can nonetheless acquire the requisite goods and services. By contrast, if a government employee in a federal agency strikes and refuses to work, the resultant damage to a citizen may be irreparable. For that reason, collective bargaining in the public sector is subject to controls that are not present in the private sector. An independent federal agency, the Federal Labor Relations Authority (FLRA), oversees public sector collective bargaining. The three-member panel serves as a moderator for negotiations by raising issues, pushing the parties to find consensus, and ensuring that an orderly process occurs.[61]

The collective bargaining process is relatively simple to describe, but in practice the negotiations can be complex and time-consuming. Efforts generally commence when labor begins organizing workers with the expectation that a union will be recognized. Afterward, labor and management specify bargaining teams to meet and discuss proposals and counterproposals. Assuming that the teams eventually draft an agreement, the proposed contract is submitted to appropriate parties within management and to labor for ratification. If an agreement cannot be reached, the parties must resort to a variety of impasse procedures, including mediation and arbitration.[62]

Collective bargaining in the public sector remains a contentious subject. Public employees argue that they need the same opportunities for compensation, promotion, and improved working conditions that are enjoyed by their counterparts in the private sector. Critics argue that the higher personnel costs associated with collective bargaining reduce the flexibility of government budget officials who struggle with a variety of constraints, including legislative mandates and budgetary restrictions. Many public sector managers already have a difficult time effectively using their personnel, and collective bargaining agreements provide an additional layer of constraints.[63]

Conclusion: Ethical Challenges in Personnel Management

An ethical administrator must assess the goals of the agency in which he or she works and strive to meet those goals in accordance with the administrator's assigned role within the agency. Sometimes an agency's goals are vague or ambiguous, in which case the administrator is called upon to use discretion and judgment. In rare cases, when the agency's goals contravene the public interest, the administrator must determine an appropriate course of action that may conflict with agency goals.

Be that as it may, the difficulty for developing an ethical grounding in public personnel management is that the concept of "merit" has changed over time and, consequently, the goals in managing personnel are not always clear. It is axiomatic that the ethical administrator in the role of a personnel administrator would seek to advance merit in fulfilling his or her duties. In some instances, however, loyalty to the administration has been seen as meritorious; in other instances, merit has been defined as objectively pursuing the goals of a particular agency as efficiently and effectively as possible without regard to loyalty.

In public personnel management, the ethical administrator seeks to identify appropriate standards of merit for public employees and then recruit, examine, select, train, retain, discipline and reward personnel, as appropriate. These activities require an administrator to possess a working knowledge of the laws and regulations affecting the workplace. Hiring and retaining good employees in the public sector is a complex task, but necessary to the success of a public-sector agency.

The ethical personnel administrator seeks to know the goals and standards of the agency in personnel matters before initiating the hiring process. He or she must then attempt to assess the skills and qualifications of applicants in a manner that is equitable and meets the needs of the agency while also complying with the law. Ideally, the process will identify candidates who are best suited to the position without attention to their demographic attributes except in cases where certain races of people have been disadvantaged. Even then, the level and extent of the preferences provided to some candidates remain contested issues. In any case, personnel managers seek to follow the merit principle as that is understood in their particular time and circumstances.

Exercises and Discussion Questions

1. Why is the concept of "merit" difficult to define and discuss? Can you think of instances in which "merit" is, or should be, timeless? Explain.
2. Describe the evolution of the merit principle throughout American history. Do you see this evolutionary process as inexorably moving toward a more refined, comprehensible understanding of merit or has the principle lost its meaning? Discuss.
3. What are the pros and cons of affirmative action programs in public personnel management? In your opinion, how might such programs be improved?
4. Why is the concept of "Reinventing Government" or the "New Public Management" potentially detrimental to the enterprise of public personnel management? How might public personnel management be "rehabilitated"?
5. Discuss the advantages and disadvantages of patronage and civil service systems. Which system do you believe is preferable? Why?
6. Why is broadbanding a crucial issue in public personnel management? Do you think position classification is a crucial issue? Why or why not?
7. Discuss the controversy over the PACE examination. Do you agree that historically disadvantaged groups should be treated differently than other groups for purposes of public employment? What are the pros and cons of the issue?
8. Your new manager in a federal agency tells you that she plans to make "some personnel changes in the agency" and asks you to explain the concept of merit as it has evolved over time. You suggest, at a minimum,

that the manager consult the agency's personnel office or perhaps the Office of Personnel Management (OPM) because merit and promotion policies are extremely complicated. The manager tells you, "We don't need to bother HR or OPM with this stuff. I can handle it just fine myself." What should you do in this situation?

a.   You should do nothing. Your job is to be a loyal employee who performs his or her tasks in accordance with the agency's core mission. If the new manager wants to make changes, it is not your problem or your business.

b.   You should ask for another meeting with the new manager and again insist that she not proceed without first consulting the appropriate personnel officials.

c.   You should go ahead and contact the agency's personnel office and/or OPM regardless of whether the new manager thinks "we don't need to bother HR or OPM with this stuff."

d.   You should immediately "go public" by holding a press conference and exposing your new manager's schemes.

e.   You should alert one or more members of Congress because the new manager has "violated the spirit and purpose of the agency's personnel policies."

f.   You should perform more than one of the actions listed above (be specific.)

9.   Why is collective bargaining a controversial, time-consuming process in the public sector? How does public-sector collective bargaining differ from private-sector collective bargaining? In your view, can public employees "ethically" threaten to strike if they truly represent the public interest?

Notes

[1]   For a good general overview of the salient issues in public personnel management, see, for example, Herbert Kaufman, "Administrative Decentralization and Political Power," *Public Administration Review* 29 (January/February 1969): 3-15.

[2]   Michael E. Milakovich and George J. Gordon, *Public Administration in America* (Belmont, Calif.: Wadsworth/ Thomson, 2004), 156, 293-94

[3]   Norman C. Thomas, Joseph A. Pika, and Richard A. Watson, *The Politics of the Presidency* (Washington, D.C.: Congressional Quarterly Press, 1994), 23-25.

4   Henry Adams, *The United States in 1800* (Ithaca, N.Y.: Cornell University Press, 1955), 127-28; Joseph J. Ellis, *American Sphinx: The Character of Thomas Jefferson* (New York: Vintage, 1998), 41-42; Roger Wilkins, *Jefferson's Pillow: The Founding Fathers and the Dilemma of Black Patriotism* (Boston: Beacon Press, 2002).

5   Milakovich and Gordon, *Public Administration in America*, 299; David H. Rosenbloom, *Federal Service and the Constitution* (Ithaca, N.Y.: Cornell University Press, 1971), 38-41.

6   Jay M. Shafritz, *et al.*, *Personnel Management in Government* (New York: Marcel Dekker, 1978), 14-16.

7   David H. Rosenbloom, *Public Administration: Understanding Management, Politics, and Law in the Public Sector*, 3rd. ed. (New York: Random House, 1993), 204; Shafritz, *et al.*, *Personnel Management in Government*, 33.

8   Rosenbloom, *Federal Service and the Constitution*, 70-71; Richard Stillman II, *American Bureaucracy: The Core of Modern Government*, 3d. ed. (Belmont, Calif: Wadsworth/Thomson, 2004), 158-59.

9   Rosenbloom, *Public Administration: Understanding Management, Politics, and Law in the Public Sector*, 204-10.

10   Stillman, *American Bureaucracy: The Core of Modern Government*, 49-54; Leonard D. White, *The Republican Era, 1869-1901* (New York: MacMillan, 1958), 232-56.

11   Rosenbloom, *Public Administration: Understanding Management, Politics, and Law in the Public Sector*, 140-43; Frederick Winslow Taylor, "The Principles of Scientific Management," in *Classics of Organization Theory*, 2d. ed., Jay M. Shafritz and J. Steven Ott, eds. (Pacific Grove, Calif.: Brooks/Cole Publishing Company, 1987), 66-81.

12   Milakovich and Gordon, *Public Administration in America*, 301; Stillman, *American Bureaucracy: The Core of Modern Government*, 54-57.

13   Donald F. Kettl, *The Transformation of Governance: Public Administration for Twenty-First Century America* (Baltimore and London: Johns Hopkins University Press, 2002), 29-32.

14   Thomas, Pika, and Watson, *The Politics of the Presidency*, 415-22.

15   Milakovich and Gordon, *Public Administration in America*, 327-31; Stillman, *American Bureaucracy: The Core of Modern Government*, 173, 176.

16   Rosenbloom, *Federal Service and the Constitution*, 70-71; Stillman, *American Bureaucracy: The Core of Modern Government*, 160, 161.

17   David Osborne, and Ted Gaebler, *Reinventing Government: How the Entrepreneurial Spirit is Transforming the Public Sector* (New York: Penguin Books, 1993); Stephen Page, "What's New About the New Public Management? Administrative Change in the Human Services," *Public Administration Review* 65 (November 2005): 713-27; Michael Spicer, "Public Administration, the History of Ideas, and the Reinventing Government Movement," *Public Administration Review* 64 (May/June 2004): 353-62; Larry D. Terry, "From Greek Mythology to the Real World of the New Public Management and Democratic Governance (Terry Responds)," *Public Administration Review* 59 (May/June 1999): 272-77; and James R. Thompson, "Reinvention as Reform: Assessing the National Performance Review," *Public Administration Review* 60 (November/December 2000): 508-21.

18   Kettl, The Transformation of Governance: Public Administration for Twenty-First Century America, x-xi, 67.

19   The literature on due process is voluminous. See, for example, William Cohen and David J. Danelski, *Constitutional Law: Civil Liberty and Individual Rights*, 4th ed. (Westbury, NY: The Foundation Press, 1997), 1145.

20   341 U.S. 918 (1951).

21   397 U.S. 254 (1970).

22   424 U.S. 319 (1976).

23   408 U.S. 564 (1972).

24   408 U.S. 593 (1972).

25   470 U.S. 532 (1985).

26   Stefanie A. Lindquist and Stephen E. Condrey, "Public Employment Reforms and Constitutional Due Process," in *Civil Service Reform in the States*, J. Edward Kellough and Lloyd G. Nigro, eds. (Albany, N.Y.: SUNY Press, 2006), 95-116.

27   445 U.S. 507 (1980).

28   497 U.S. 62 (1990).

29   Christopher Cornwell and J. Edward Kellough, "Women and Minorities in Federal Government Agencies: Examining New Evidence from Panel Data," *Public Administration Review* 54 (May/June 1994): 265-70; Meredith Ann Newman, "Gender and Lowi's Thesis: Implications for Career Advancement," *Public Administration Review* 54 (May/June 1994): 277-84; Milakovich and Gordon, *Public Administration in America*, 334-38;

30   770 F.2d 1401 (9th Cir. 1985).

31   418 U.S. 616 (1987).

32   438 U.S. 265 (1978).

33   Brown v. Board of Education of Topeka I, 347 U.S. 483 (1954) and Brown v. Board of Education of Topeka II, 349 U.S. 294 (1955).

34   369 U.S. 31 (1962).

35   388 U.S. 1 (1967).

36   392 U.S. 409 (1968).

37   414 U.S. 563 (1974).

38   476 U.S. 79 (1986).

39   539 U.S. 306 (2003).

40   401 U.S. 424 (1971).

41   J. Edward Kellough and Lloyd G. Nigro, "Dramatic Reform in the Public Service: At-Will Employment and the Creation of a New Public Workforce," *Journal of Public Administration Research and Theory* 16 (July 2006): 447-66; J. Edward Kellough and Lloyd G. Nigro, "Pay for Performance in Georgia State Government: Employee Perspectives on GeorgiaGain after Five Years," *Review of Public Personnel Administration* 22 (June 2002): 146-66; Robert M. Sanders, "GeorgiaGain or Georgia Loss? The Great Experiment in Civil Service Reform," *Public Personnel Management* 33 (Summer 2004): 151-64.

42   James S. Bowman, Marc G. Gertz, Sally C. Gertz, and Russell L. Williams, "Civil Service Reform in Florida State Government," *Review of Public Personnel Administration* 23 (December 2003): 286-304; James S. Bowman and Jonathan P. West, "Ending Civil

Service Protections in Florida Government: Experiences in State Agencies," *Review of Public Personnel Administration* 26 (June 2006): 139-57.

[43] Bowman and West, "Ending Civil Service Protections in Florida Government," 153-54; Sanders, "GeorgiaGain or Georgia Loss?" 158-160.

[44] Weston H. Agor, "The Measurement, Use and Development of Intellectual Capital to Increase Public Sector Productivity," *Public Personnel Management* 26 (Summer 1997): 175-86; Gary S. Becker, "Investment in Human Capital: A Theoretical Analysis," *The Journal of Political Economy* 70 (October 1962): 9-49; David P, Lepak and Scott A. Snell, "The Human Resource Architecture: Toward a Theory of Human Capital Allocation and Development," *The Academy of Management Review* 24 (January 1999): 31-48.

[45] Milakovich and Gordon, *Public Administration in America*, 304-6.

[46] J. Edward Kellough and Haoran Lu, "The Paradox of Merit Pay in the Public Sector," *Review of Public Personnel Administration* 13 (April 1993): 45-64; Milakovich and Gordon, *Public Administration in America*, 305-6.

[47] Edwin W. Arnold and Clyde J. Scott, "Does Broad Banding Improve Pay System Effectiveness?" *Southern Business Review* (Spring 2002): 1-8; John P. Campbell, "Matching People and Jobs: An Introduction to Twelve Years of R & D," in *Exploring the Limits in Personnel Selection and Classification*, John P. Campbell and Deirdre J. Knapp (Mahwah, N.J.: Lawrence Erlbaum Associates, 2001), 3-20.

[48] Carolyn Ban and Patricia W. Ingraham, "Retaining Quality Employees: Life After PACE," *Public Administration Review* 48 (May-June 1988): 708.

[49] *Luevano v. Campbell*, 93 F.R.D. 68, 74-76 (1981).

[50] 401 U.S. 424, 430 (1971).

[51] William R. Nelson, "Employment Testing and the Demise of the PACE Examination," *Labor Law Journal* 33 (November 1982): 729.

[52] Ban and Ingraham, "Retaining Quality Federal Employees," 709.

[53] 93 F.R.D. 68, 74.

[54] 93 F.R.D. 68, 74-75; U.S. Merit Systems Protection Board, *Restoring Merit to Federal Hiring: Why Two Special Hiring Programs Should Be Ended* (Washington, D.C.: MSPB, January 2000), 37-38.

[55] 93 F.R.D. 68, 75.

[56] William J. Lanouette, "Reagan's Team Agrees with Carter's—The Government Can't Keep PACE," *National Journal* 13 (March 7, 1981): 394-96.

[57] 93 F.R.D. 68, 75-76; Nelson, "Employment Testing and the Demise of the PACE Examination," 729-50.

[58] 93 F.R.D. 68, 78-79.

[59] 93 F.R.D. 68, 92.

[60] "Agencies Can Use *Luevano* to Bolster Diversity," *Federal EEO Advisor* 6 (January 30, 2004): 1; Ban and Ingraham, "Retaining Quality Federal Employees," 709.

[61] See, for example, Janet Currie and Sheena McConnell, "Collective Bargaining in the Public Sector: The Effect of Legal Structure in Dispute Costs and Wages," *The American Economic Review* 81 (September 1991): 693-718; Geoffrey Garret and Christopher Way, "Public Sector Unions, Corporatism, and Microeconomic Performance," *Comparative Political Studies* 32 (June 1999): 411-34.

[62]   The process is described at length in Milakovich and Gordon, *Public Administration in America*, 322-23.

[63]   See, for example, Joel M. Douglas, "State Civil Service and Collective Bargaining: Systems in Conflict," *Public Administration Review* 52 (March/April 1992): 162-71; David Lewin and Raymond D. Horton, "The Impact of Collective Bargaining on the Merit System in Government," *The Arbitration Journal* 30 (September 1975): 199-211.

Chapter Eight
Governmental Budgeting:
Allocating Resources in an Age of Scarcity

Governmental budgeting is hardly a glamorous area of study for most students, but it is nonetheless an important subject. Abstract theories of democracy and models of bureaucratic behavior mean little in the practical world if government policies and programs cannot be implemented because they are not funded. From the inception of the American Republic, questions of fiscal responsibility and budgetary alternatives have influenced what policies would be enacted and how government would operate. The failure of the Articles of Confederation, the first national constitution put into place in the fledgling nation, was due in no small measure to the central government's inability to raise revenues and implement effective governmental programs. If the American experiment were to succeed, it must first be constructed on a firm financial foundation. In Publius's words, "A nation cannot long exist without revenue. Destitute of this essential support, it must resign its independence and sink into the degraded condition of a province."[1]

The U.S. Constitution provided that firm foundation. Among its major provisions, the Constitution vested the "power of the purse" with the U.S. Congress in the legislative branch. A variety of provisions ensure that Congress will exercise its authority with wide latitude. Article I, Section 8 directs that "the Congress shall have the power to lay and collect Taxes, Duties, Imports and Excises, to pay the Debts and provide for the common Defence and general Welfare of the United States." Earlier, in Article I, Section 7, the Constitution requires that all revenue bills "shall originate in the House of Representatives; but the Senate may propose or concur with Amendments as on other bills." Finally, Article I, Section 9, specifies that "No money shall be drawn from the Treasury but in consequence of Appropriations made by law."[2]

Before the Civil War, the federal budget was relatively small. Many lawmakers still subscribed to Thomas Jefferson's and the Founders' well-known adage, "that government is best which governs least." With changes in the role of the federal government—and the ever-increasing oversight responsibility of Congress and federal executive branch agencies—budgets, especially at the federal level, have become much more important than the Founders anticipated. Today many policies at all levels of government succeed or fail owing to budgetary issues. Accordingly, students of public administration must understand budgets if they hope to master the field.[3]

Revenues

Before they can fund policies and programs, governments must collect revenues from a variety of sources. The federal government cannot simply print as much money as it desires without destabilizing the currency and undermining the national economy. Similarly, although governments can borrow money from banks and foreign sources, they must repay it with interest. Consequently, governments must look to other sources of funding in addition to printing money or borrowing funds. Of the many ways that governments raise revenue, income taxes probably are the most familiar to Americans.[4]

For much of American history, the federal government raised revenues through customs charges and tariffs. From 1789, when the Constitution went into effect, until 1894, income taxes were not an option, at least at the federal level, except under extraordinary circumstances. As a budget deficit loomed over the nation during the Civil War of 1861-65, the Lincoln administration instituted an income tax to help pay war debts. Individuals with an annual income of between $600 and $5,000 paid an income tax of 10 percent. After the war, individuals balked at paying additional taxes since the great crisis of the nineteenth century had ended. Although the U.S. Supreme Court ruled in an 1881 case, *Springer v. United States*, that an individual income tax was constitutional, the debate persisted until 1894. Americans' antipathy toward government taking money from their pockets to pay for programs from which they might not get an individual benefit made income tax proposals politically unpopular.[5]

President Grover Cleveland brought the issue to a head in 1894 when he proposed to cut the tariff and, in its place, institute a flat 2 percent tax on all individual incomes over $4,000. A year later, the U.S. Supreme Court upheld the constitutionality of imposing income taxes on salaries and wages. The question of whether income tax on investment income was constitutional remained controversial, but the matter was clarified in 1913 when the Sixteenth Amendment was ratified. The amendment allowed Congress to "lay and collect taxes on incomes, from whatever source derived, without apportionment among the several States, and without regard to any census or enumeration."[6]

Tax policy has always been controversial, but, in the early days of the twentieth century, many Americans saw income taxes as preferable to the customs duties that had been levied on goods since colonial times. As long as a tax was progressive—that is, as long as the rates rose in proportion to income—and the tax was administered equitably, many citizens were satisfied to pay their share with little complaint. In addition, income taxes were not a major issue because, during the first half of the century, federal government revenues in large part came from tariffs and other sources, and so taxes were not a significant source of funding. By the mid-twentieth century, however, changes began to occur that fundamentally altered the importance of income taxes in federal policy.[7]

Shortly after the Sixteenth Amendment was adopted, federal government revenues from income taxes were minuscule, but they increased throughout subsequent years. By 1954, approximately 44 percent of the federal government's revenues were financed by personal income taxes, 30 percent from corporate income taxes, and 11 percent from payroll taxes deducted from employees' wages. As this change occurred, citizens began to focus on income taxes and questions arose, especially as income taxes became a fundamental source of government revenue.[8]

Government revenues also are derived from sales and use taxes levied on goods and services at the time of purchase. Unlike personal income taxes, which often are considered politically controversial, sales and use taxes in modest amounts—typically between 3 and 8 percent in states that impose them—are relatively non-controversial and easy to collect. Retailers configure their cash registers and accounting systems to calculate the tax and add it into the amount that must be remitted by the consumer at the point of purchase. In times of fiscal crisis, lawmakers can increase sales taxes to collect more revenues or, in some instances, decrease taxes, although some states and counties require that such decisions be submitted to a referendum. Some states also deliberately exempt certain goods from sales tax as a method of encouraging sales or as a means of ensuring that vulnerable populations—children, the elderly, the infirm—do not spend limited resources on sales and use taxes for food or medicine essential to their well-being.[9]

Although many states have enacted sales and use taxes, by the 1990s only 2 percent of state operations came from such taxes. By contrast, property taxes funded about 75 percent of local government activities, especially the operation of public schools, sewer systems, and fire departments. To develop the property tax base, government officials generally create a list of all land and dwellings in a given jurisdiction, determine a millage rate as the basis for the tax, and apply the tax accordingly. Tax assessments often are controversial as property owners dispute the tax collector's assessment of the real property value, especially as property is assessed over time. Because it takes considerable time to reassess older property to ensure an equitable calculation in comparison with new property assessments, property taxes sometimes are inequitable. A $500,000 house may be assessed at one value in 1990 and the same type of house assessed at a higher value two years later.[10]

Government at all levels constantly is challenged to increase the amount and sources of revenue, particularly in times of fiscal shortfall. Other potential sources of revenue include motor fuel taxes, excise taxes, capital-gain taxes, and the issuance of government bonds. In the 1990s, the adoption of state-run lotteries, intangible taxes, and sales taxes on Internet purchases also have been touted in some quarters as solutions to problems of government finance. Each plan presents its own set of benefits and challenges.[11]

Expenditures

Governments use money collected from taxes and fees to fund a variety of programs and provide many goods and services. As government agencies have grown in size and number since World War II, programs and activities have expanded as well. Some expenditures—national defense, agriculture, transportation, veterans' benefits and services, and research into important science and technology issues—have been areas of governmental concern for most of the nation's history. Other areas where governments, especially the federal government, have increased spending include education, training, social service payments, health benefits, and income security. With increases in spending, deficits have grown as well.[12]

In some sense, deficit spending is encouraged by the American economic system, which readily supplies a variety of goods and services for consumers. Elected officials also have a strong incentive for spending outside the confines of a government budget; legislative careers often rise or fall according to how well congressmen or senators can "bring home the bacon" through pork barrel projects for their constituents. Thus, federal legislation enacted by Congress and signed by the president may contain numerous spending provisions that benefit a particular legislator's district but heavily contribute to overspending in the federal budget. As a consequence, much of the story of government budgets and finance has involved the tug-of-war between legislators and executives on the appropriate level of government expenditures.[13]

The philosophical appeal of deficit spending sometimes is referred to as Keynesian economics, although this description is often an oversimplification. During the 1930s, John Maynard Keynes, an English economist, posited a theory that is well established today, but it was considered radical at the time. Most government planners and officials at the time viewed the federal budget much as individuals view their personal finances. The prevailing idea was that, just as an individual should not spend more money than he can cover with his assets, so, too, are governments limited by their ability to raise revenues. Keynes argued that this view of government budgeting was too restrictive.[14]

In Keynes's view, only government—in the United States, specifically the federal government—can intervene in the regular boom-and-bust business cycle. By spending a large amount of money, even money beyond what it receives in revenues, the federal government can increase its share of the Gross Domestic Product (GDP), which means that the government can influence how well the economy operates. If government spends billions of dollars to employ workers, this form of massive job creation has a ripple effect on the economy. A man who now works for a federal agency cleaning up a national park, for example, suddenly has money in his pocket, thanks to his federal salary. He can afford to buy shoes for his children or a new washing machine or an automobile. This spending circulates money to shoemakers, washing machine manufacturers, and automobile manufacturers who, in turn, purchase raw materials from their suppliers, and so forth. Each of the beneficiaries in this supply chain will earn more money and therefore pay more taxes in the next fiscal year. In short, according to this theory, the federal government has "jumpstarted" or "primed" the economy.

This insight held great appeal for President Franklin D. Roosevelt when he became president in March 1933. Seeking a way to mitigate the effects of the Great Depression, Roosevelt found Keynesian economics to be persuasive. By creating government programs and agencies to employ people, Roosevelt's New Deal engaged in deficit spending in an effort to help the economy recover from the downturn. If one person were employed by the Civilian Conservation Corps (CCC), for example, he would then have money to spend, which would then help the economy by allowing producers of goods and services to cater to his needs. Thus, a single CCC job would produce a ripple effect, just as Keynes had foreseen. Thousands of CCC and other government jobs thereby allowed the federal government to influence the economy in a way that was unprecedented in American history. Although Keynesian economic principles were not entirely responsible for the end of the Great Depression—World War II mobilization and production would play an integral role as well—certainly it helped to ease the suffering of displaced workers in the 1930s.[15]

The problem with deficit spending in the long run is that sooner or later the overspending must be reined in and the government must replace the revenues that have been used. Although Keynes contended that deficit spending by a government eventually would produce higher tax revenues as more people went to work and therefore paid taxes, he did not envision an economic system where spending would continue to rise without an end in sight. Continued deficit spending exacerbates the national debt, a calculation of how much money a nation owes because of its pattern of overspending. The more debt a nation carries, the more difficult it becomes for a government to continue providing the goods and services its citizens have come to expect. Money can be borrowed and "revenue-enhancing" measures, including tax increases, can be employed, but eventually the budget must be balanced. In the twentieth century, a number of budgeting processes and procedures have been proposed to address these kinds of financial issues.[16]

The Budgetary Process

Budget questions ultimately are questions about how power is exercised. Like the old cliché about the "Golden Rule"—"he who has the gold, rules"—the story of the federal budgetary process is the story of who controls power and exerts influence within the federal government. Developing the federal budget is not like developing a household budget and then struggling to live within its means. Rather, the federal budgetary process is iterative, ongoing, and constantly being revised as policy-makers grapple with unexpected problems that arise, cost overruns, new technologies, and the ever-shifting terrain of politics. In fact, the difficulty in understanding the federal budgetary process is that there is not one budget but multiple ones.[17]

The story begins, for all intents and purposes, in 1921, when the Bureau of the Budget was created within the U.S. Treasury Department. Before that time, Congress generally had developed the budget each year, although the president could provide input when details of the budget plan were publicized. With the establishment of a new bureau, the executive branch would be more involved in the budgetary process than it ever had been in the past. This movement toward an invigorated executive was further strengthened during Franklin Roosevelt's presidency when the Bureau of the Budget moved into the Executive Office of the President in 1939. In 1970, the authority of the bureau was expanded and the office was renamed the Office of Management and Budget (OMB). Today, the president has become much more involved in federal budgeting than were presidents prior to the 1920s and 1930s owing, in no small part, to the OMB's influence.[18]

Congress is actively involved in developing the budget as well, especially through the work of the Congressional Budget Office (CBO). In many ways, the CBO is the legislative analogue to the OMB. Staffed by accountants, economists, and other policy experts on budget and financial issues, the CBO provides members of Congress with independent data and calculations so that congressmen and senators can assess the president's spending proposals and perhaps offer alternative approaches and recommendations.[19]

The process of bargaining and negotiation is substantial, and an exhaustive discussion of the process is beyond the scope of this book. In the simplest form, however, the formation of the federal budget begins at least eighteen months before the start of a fiscal year, which runs from October 1 to the following September 30. Budget officers in the various departments and agencies ask their bureau chiefs to review their programs and submit a preliminary budget estimate for review. In response, bureau chiefs review their activities during the preceding year and calculate their projected needs for the new fiscal year. The appropriate budget officer reviews the data he collects from the bureau chiefs and coordinates the development of the department's budget with the department head.

When a tentative budget has been developed, the department head submits it to OMB for review. OMB staff has discretion to approve the budget as it is submitted; alternatively, the bureau can increase or reduce the budget. Generally, OMB reduces budgets with an eye toward developing proposals that will not be too far out of line with CBO projections and which will pass easily through the legislative appropriations process. In any event, after OMB passes the budget back to the various agencies and departments, the budget officer reviews the changes with the department head before preparing a "final" estimate. Everyone recognizes that the budget can be modified many more times as it travels through Congress.

OMB sometimes holds budget hearings and asks department heads to defend their proposals. As a result of the hearings, OMB staffers make a budget recommendation to the president. After the president and his economic advisers review the recommendations and either accept or modify them, OMB prepares a final budget proposal for transmission to Congress. The CBO then reviews the budget and provides Congress with an analysis that will serve as the basis for congressional budget hearings. The Appropriations committees in both the House of Representatives and the Senate also hold hearings to determine how the executive and legislative proposals can be reconciled. The process is governed by the Balanced Budget and Emergency Deficit Control Act of 1985—better known by the last name of its principal sponsors, Gramm-Rudman-Hollings—which requires that certain measures be employed to reduce deficit spending.[20]

Implementation presents another challenge in the budgetary process. In this stage, the "rubber meets the road," in the words of the old cliché. As department heads and bureau chiefs receive their allocated funds, they must match the available appropriations to their high priority programs. In the time since agency officials submitted their budget requests, changes may have taken place within the agency. A crisis may have developed which requires the agency to use funds in a manner that could not have been anticipated beforehand. In addition, changes in personnel, the imposition of new legal requirements, or other external events may force a reevaluation of departmental budgets. Perhaps actual costs have exceeded estimated costs, in which case the agency must try to adapt to the current staffing and funding realities. In short, the process of implementing a department's programs may depend in no small measure on the budget that actually is put into place many months after the initial proposals were developed.[21]

Types of Federal Budgets

With the advent of the modern federal budget, policy-makers have tried to refine methods for using the budget as a policy tool, not merely as a laundry list of prices and funding requests. To that end, scholars and practitioners have developed several theories of budgeting. Early in the twentieth century, agencies experimented with line-item budgets, which represented a managerial advance over the lump-sum budget. A lump-sum budget simply appropriates a particular amount to an agency and leaves considerable discretion for agency personnel to determine how the money is used. A line-item budget, by contrast, requires the agency to specify how the money will be used. This allows budget planners and policy-makers to access more detailed information on an agency's needs. It also identifies areas that might be cut, which makes an agency's budget personnel nervous. By limiting discretion, the line-item budget shifts some of the discretionary authority for budgeting from the agency to OMB and other budget officials in the hierarchy.[22]

The Performance Budget is a prime example of a mechanism for using budgeting as a policy-making tool. When budget requests are sent up from bureau chiefs to the department heads, they must be accompanied by a performance report; that is, they must contain an explanation of how the money will be spent and why the expenditure is deemed necessary. This explanation is an integral part of the budget request. The report ensures, at least in theory, that performance can be evaluated later to determine whether the allocated funds were used in an efficient and effective manner. Thus, if a budget request for producing a new type of stealth aircraft came from the Department of Defense, the question a year, or several years, later is whether the new aircraft was produced. If it was not produced, why not? If it was produced, did it perform as expected for the costs that the bureau chief estimated?[23]

Closely related to the performance budget is the program budget. In the former case, budget planners examine the reasons that a budget is developed within a specific department or organizational unit. With a program budget, the emphasis shifts to the implementation of a particular program, which sometimes spans across more than a single agency. By observing a program and not limiting the analysis to a single department, budget officials hope to understand how cost effective a program is rather than focus on a specific agency. Probably the most famous program budget was the Planning Programming Budgeting System (PPBS) introduced into the federal government during the 1960s.[24]

At the time that Defense Secretary Robert McNamara championed the program, PPBS was viewed as a revolutionary new approach to federal budgeting. Instead of announcing general goals for a particular program, as traditional budgeting required, PPBS would place goals into a framework that could be tested using empirical tools. Thus, a Defense Department program would not be listed as "providing reserve parachutes to prevent deaths during parachute training." Instead, the program goal would be listed as "reducing training deaths during parachute drops by 50 percent, from 10 deaths last year to five deaths in the coming year." Moreover, the number of deaths reduced owing to the inclusion of a particular type of reserve parachute would be tested over multiple years to discern a trend that could be matched to the budget. Did allocating x amount of dollars for reserve chutes markedly reduce deaths? Did a reduction continue when y dollars were allocated? In other words, what causal effect, if any, resulted from the budget allocation? This kind of budgeting allows planners to systematize the budgeting process and compare alternatives using the budget as an analytical tool. In McNamara's words, PPBS allows researchers and budget planners to determine whether they are getting more "bang for the buck" than when they use alternatives.[25]

The problem with PPBS was that it assumed that most, if not all, major administrative decisions could be made with costs as the overriding concern. Unfortunately, such an assumption is not always accurate. Implementing and evaluating government programs are not like purchasing a commodity; costs are only one among many considerations. Moreover, innumerable forces may affect outcomes. Training deaths during parachute exercises may decrease owing to changes in the rigor of the training program, the caliber of the troops or the officers training them, the conditions of the jump, or other external forces. Government programs sometimes are so vague that defining the problem in operational terms that can be measured in monetary units is difficult. If the U.S. military is called into service to rebuild war-torn Iraq, how exactly does a budget planner put a price tag on that endeavor? Is a stable, pro-American government in a Middle Eastern country worth $25 million, $50 million, or $100 million? Any allocation of costs is purely arbitrary because the values and political objectives in the equation are so difficult to assess in terms of dollars.[26]

The PPBS approach to budgeting was an attempt to manage the bureaucracy using financial resources, but its complexity and implementation difficulties did much to undermine the effort. For some observers, the paramount concern was ensuring an efficient use of funds, and the PPBS did not accomplish that objective. Instead, an alternative approach called Zero Base Budgeting (ZBB) was developed. The approach proved to be popular in the 1970s, especially in the Carter administration.[27]

ZBB is based on the premise that a government agency or organizational unit must justify its budget anew each year. Simply because an agency received a particular budget the preceding year, this historical outlay does not guarantee that the same or even a similar budget will be in place the following year. To begin developing the budget under ZBB, planners divide the agency into decision units, which are the lowest level at which a budget is developed within an organization. The units develop decision packages, which are based on each unit's purposes and functions and include information on types of programs and their projected costs. Top managers then rank order the decision packages before submitting the budgets to OMB for review. In the traditional budget, the fact that a unit received funding at a certain level in prior years would serve as the base for the next year's budget, but ZBB presumes a zero base in each year, hence the name.[28]

On its face, ZBB sounds like a reasonable approach to budgeting, especially if budget planners are concerned about wasted resources and inefficient spending in government agencies. Unfortunately, it imposes enormous burdens on budget planners. Starting from zero each year in the budgeting process, ironically, becomes a poor use of resources as budget planners are forced to evaluate long-standing programs from scratch. Moreover, many government programs are ongoing, and they stretch from year to year. Cutting a multi-year program before it is fully implemented owing to budget concerns frustrates years of budgetary planning, to say nothing of the political repercussions of budget reductions for programs favored by powerful and influential elected officials.[29]

In the perspective of some budget analysts, the various managerial approaches fail to appreciate the incremental nature of modern budgeting. Rather than preparing budgets based on a broad, overarching program, most bureau chiefs rely on spending patterns from previous years as an indicator of current and future needs. They assume a given base and work from there to implement policies and programs in accordance with their historical budgets. The theoretical basis of using budgets as the starting point for evaluating the success or failure of government programs sounds promising, but incrementalists contend that these types of theories are far too idealistic and unrealistic to serve as adequate descriptions of the budgetary process. The idea of bureau chiefs carefully and meticulously developing spending proposals and adjusting budgets based on last year's needs and this year's crises is a more realistic assessment of the process of developing the federal budget. In addition, elected officials often intervene into the budgetary process—even at the agency level—through oversight hearings, requests for information, and so forth. Such interference ensures that carefully crafted budgets are modified at virtually every stage of the implementation process. Accordingly, the incremental view of budgeting captures the often chaotic and fluid nature of federal budgeting. It also recognizes that political issues will alter even the most sophisticated and elegant budget theories.[30]

Impoundment and Gramm-Rudman-Hollings

As government budgets—especially the federal budget under the Great Society in the 1960s—have skyrocketed, policy-makers have searched for a means of curtailing large deficits. For most elected officials, it is far easier to vote for budget increases, along with the accompanying pork barrel projects, than it is to cut spending. Constituents seem to appreciate federal largesse aimed in their direction, and they reward their elected representatives with votes. Even elected officials philosophically committed to fiscal responsibility are hard-pressed to cut projects that benefit citizens in their home districts.

If legislators lack the political will to cut spending, impoundment is a strategy employed by a strong executive to accomplish the task. President Nixon most famously used this tactic in 1971 and 1972 to prevent funds from being used for programs he deemed unnecessary. Congress had authorized and appropriated funding for various federal programs, but Nixon refused to convey the funds. In an action that particularly enraged representatives from the Midwest, Nixon used the congressional recess over the Christmas holiday in 1972 to impound funds allocated for several farm programs. Nixon argued that the chief executive, as the head of the branch empowered to implement federal policy, possessed the inherent power to withhold funding from programs the president deemed contrary to the public interest. Congress threatened to pass legislation to limit the president's impoundment authority, but, ultimately, the U.S. Supreme Court ruled in a series of cases that impoundment was not a constitutionally permissible executive power, thereby forestalling congressional action. The leading case in this area remains *Immigration and Naturalization Service v. Chadha*, a 1983 U.S. Supreme Court opinion that struck down an attempt to allow the president to impound funds subject to congressional approval. The Court ruled that such a "one house veto" was contradictory to the checks and balances enshrined in the U.S. Constitution.[31]

As controversial as Nixon's use of impoundment was during the 1970s, his actions were not the first time that a chief executive claimed such power, nor were they the last. As early as the nineteenth century, Thomas Jefferson exercised impoundment authority. However, it was used sparingly. It was not until the end of the twentieth century that impoundment became an important legal and political issue. Gerald Ford also relied on impoundment, but he used the power judiciously and avoided many of the clashes with Congress that plagued his predecessor.[32]

Political scientists have classified impoundment into two categories. The first category, a rescission, terminates funds for a particular agency or a specific program. In that respect, it seems to be a rejection of a legislative measure by the executive after the measure already has been signed into law. By contrast, a deferral amounts to a delay in disbursing appropriated funds. In both cases, however, the action remains the same—an activist executive is seeking to circumvent the congressional authorization and appropriations process.[33]

Despite its suspect constitutionality, the concern expressed by executives that employ impoundment as a tactic is based on the desire to curtail excessive expenditures. In an age of spiraling budgets and an ever-increasing national debt, policy-makers at all levels of government have searched for a means of cutting costs without committing political suicide in the process. One influential method was part and parcel of a legislative measure known as the Gramm-Rudman-Hollings Emergency Deficit Control Act, named for the Senators who sponsored the law in 1985.[34]

Gramm-Rudman-Hollings has been characterized as a "dress rehearsal for a balanced budget amendment" to the U.S. Constitution. The law originally required Congress to balance the federal budget by Fiscal Year 1991. In each year leading up to the target date, Congress was supposed to present budgets with smaller deficits in each successive year. By reducing the deficit in incremental steps, the law was designed to minimize the economic impact of smaller federal budgets on the rest of the economy as well as allow elected officials time to wean themselves and their constituents from pork-barrel projects of the past.[35]

Gramm-Rudman-Hollings succeeded in some ways, but failed in others. If nothing else, the act certainly propelled the concern about deficits and the mushrooming federal budget to the attention of mainstream America, no small feat in itself. By forcing Congress to set budget reduction goals, the statute also pushed legislators to consider the fiscal consequences of legislation in ways that they previously had not considered. Nonetheless, the law also highlighted the complexities in the budget process and the difficulty in setting meaningful goals. Budget analysts must make projections about expenditures several years ahead of time, which means that invariably events and unforeseen developments will intervene to render the projections faulty. Moreover, it seeks to put the budget process on a kind of "automatic pilot" mode without regard for the needs and interests of citizens.[36]

Despite the best efforts of lawmakers and budget analysts, the tough decisions surrounding government budgeting cannot be avoided if the process is to be realistic and achievable. Whatever else can be said about Gramm-Rudman-Hollings, it failed in this regard: Congress did not meet the budget priorities during the 1980s. Even when policy-makers began to balance the budget and occasionally present budgets with surpluses during the 1990s, the efforts had more to do with economic prosperity and external economic forces than with congressional policies. Perhaps the best that can be said is that the budget process is a complex numbers game that is influenced by a multitude of complicated, interrelated factors.[37]

Conclusion: Ethics in the Budgetary Process

Because budgeting involves financial matters that are fraught with peril when it comes to questions of right conduct, it is little wonder that ethical issues arise in the budgetary process. Bureaucrats often administer programs that cost millions, sometimes billions, of dollars. Although it is unlikely that budget officials could line their own pockets while escaping detection, it certainly raises ethical questions in light of the discretion many public managers exercise when implementing financial policies and programs.

If "street-level" bureaucrats were automatons who had no discretion about the policies that they implemented, ethical issues in budgeting would only apply to top policy-makers. As with so much in the modern understanding of public administration, however, the question of a particular bureaucrat's role in an organization is a crucial issue. Depending on the authority that a budget official exercises, he or she must take moral responsibility for using discretion. Researchers recognize that few, if any, bureaucrats can avoid moral dilemmas or escape responsibility since few, if any, bureaucrats exercise absolutely no discretion.[38]

A bureaucrat may be tempted to play games with the budgetary process by inserting his or her values into funding issues. For example, if an administrator in the Social Security Administration decided that some of the funds used to administer the office could be more effectively employed elsewhere, he or she might be tempted to channel funds into other programs, especially programs in which a shortfall existed. While an argument can be advanced that the administrator is using discretion appropriately to help a program in need of assistance, the same situation might be interpreted as an unconscionable substitution of the administrator's ideological values for the values expressed by policy-makers higher in the department, to say nothing of the values of legislators. The difficulty, of course, is that discretion, absent adequate guidelines, can be used in myriad ways. Is an administrator who uses budgetary slack—that is, funding not specifically committed to other programs or projects—to find creative means of accomplishing an agency's goals deserving of praise for his or her laudable actions or is this kind of behavior the quintessential example of an abuse of discretion?[39]

An issue related to the administrator's use of discretion is whether he or she must consider other factors outside of his or her role within the agency. In an age of government spending and budget deficits, how should the ethical administrator behave? Should he or she insist that monies not spent by the agency be returned to the federal treasury? Or is it naïve to expect—or, for that matter, desire—that an agency official will voluntarily relinquish part of the budget, hence the official's power, in the name of some vague goal, such as reducing the federal deficit?[40]

When bureau chiefs calculate their budgets for the coming year, no doubt they are tempted to inflate the numbers in an effort to maximize the agency's appropriation. In fact, a certain amount of puffery is expected as part of the normal give-and-take of budget negotiations. If a bureau chief does not build some fat into the figures, he or she has nothing with which to compromise when the OMB, CBO, or other appropriate sources mandate the inevitable cost reductions. Still, a difference exists between inflating numbers in anticipation of budget negotiations and outright falsifying records on costs associated with administering government programs. In the former case, the administrator can cite cost projections and historic data on program expenditures to tie the budget request into tangible evidence of the need. In the latter case, the administrator has developed proposals out of whole cloth, not knowing or caring whether the figures bear any resemblance to the real costs of a program. The ethical administrator must strive to know the difference between bargaining and fabricating if public administrators are to remain accountable for their actions.[41] As discussed elsewhere in this book, an agency's culture and traditions go a long way toward informing an administrator of the necessary distinctions.

Ultimately, ethical questions in the budgetary process boil down to two broad, related issues: scarcity and fairness. If enough money existed to meet the desires and needs of every party represented in the budgetary process, hard choices would not have to be made. Anyone who requested federal funding would receive the necessary monies. Setting aside the admittedly controversial question of whether government should fund all programs as a philosophical matter even if plentiful funds are available, ongoing and continuous surplus funding would resolve the vast majority of budget problems because everyone would get what he or she wanted or needed.

In an age of scarcity, however, difficult decisions must be made; some programs must be cut while others may be only partially funded. As a result, tradeoffs occur. For every dollar spent to bail out federal savings and loan institutions in the 1980s, money was not available to invest in government-sponsored AIDS research, housing for the poor, or school lunch programs. Money spent on the Iraqi War during the second Bush administration was money not spent to enhance a host of social welfare programs. When the U.S. Department of Agriculture cuts funding for meat inspectors, the possibility of *e coli* contamination increases, which could conceivably trigger a national health epidemic and lead to grave illness and perhaps unnecessary deaths. When government fails to inspect roads and bridges and a catastrophic collapse occurs because the funding was used elsewhere, the problem of scarcity in budgeting becomes all too real.[42]

Yet is the failure to provide funds for these worthwhile projects the result of an ethical breach? In all likelihood, a public administrator had no knowledge that a bridge would collapse at the time he or she chose to move funding away from bridge repairs into another program. If the other program was worthwhile as well, the question becomes almost insoluble: Which is a more critical concern—bridges that might (or might not) collapse or lunch programs for hungry children who might (or might not) have no other reliable source of nutrition or government bailout programs that might (or might not) shore up the U.S. economy? Programs are ranked and funds allocated based on perceived needs at the time. Retrospective "Monday morning quarterbacking" does not change the reality that budget officials make the best decisions they can based on limited information and resources. Assuming the official is not misappropriating the money for his or her own interests, it is difficult to say that targeting one worthwhile program for funding at the expense of another worthwhile program is tantamount to an ethical breach.

Add to the equation the reality of bureaucratic competition for scarce funding and resources. A career civil servant in, for example, the U.S. Department of State views the world differently than a career civil servant in the U.S. Department of Transportation. In both cases, the public administrator means well and genuinely wants to see that the public good is protected. They simply see the world through their own rose-colored glasses. If asked to define the number one priority in the United States today, the State Department official probably will respond that protecting the security of American embassies and American citizens traveling abroad is crucial. If the Transportation Department official is asked the same question, he or she will respond that fixing the nation's crumbling transportation infrastructure and bringing the air traffic control system into the twenty-first century are the paramount considerations. How are these competing values to be judged based on ethical standards? Which agency is more deserving of scarce funding?

The short answer is that no objective measure exists to rank the multitude of competing government programs and priorities except in rare cases when the nation is under attack or an epidemic of disease breaks outs or a new study incontrovertibly points to an urgent, time-sensitive need that must be met. In most other instances, the reality is that each agency competes with other agencies for the limited pot of federal funds, and any objective measure of the worthiness of a project is not the key inquiry. In the world of scarce government funding, the ethical budget official recognizes a need to practice bureaucratic politics. (For more on the subject of bureaucratic politics and power, see Chapter 3.)

Political concerns are never far from the forefront when public agencies battle with each other, and with Congress, for funding. Researcher D. D. Riley contends that public administrators must possess political skills and not merely serve as policy specialists or technocrats, especially in the scramble for funding in a world of scarcity. "If bureaucrats are going to enter the political arena they will need to bring some coin of the realm—that is, they will need power," Riley notes. "Knowledge provides some, but not enough, so bureaucrats must find an expressly political base of power."[43] Public organizations are staffed by personnel who compete with other agency personnel to establish a domain, distinguish the agency from its competition, and develop effective political strategies for maintaining the agency's domain. In short, ideology and political consciousness are never absent from an agency's agenda.[44]

The ethical public administrator recognizes that budgetary decisions will be made in an age of scarcity, which requires budget officials to practice bureaucratic politics both outside and inside the agency. Outside the agency, the administrator makes the best case he or she can to legislators to protect the agency's domain and increase funding for the agency's programs. Inside the agency, the administrator recognizes that efficiency and fairness are necessary in ranking programs. As H. George Frederickson has observed, "[f]airness is not a concept or idea that fits into the logic of either perfect or imperfect markets. But fairness, both procedurally (as in due process) and in outcomes, is often the core issue in government." Instead of facing budgetary issues by solely asking whether an outcome is efficient or inefficient— although questions of efficiency can never be completely divorced from public sector calculations—the public sector budget official asks whether the outcome is both efficient and fair.[45]

An ethical budget official must list all possible programs and policies that may be funded within the agency and assign values to those programs and policies. This is the kind of analysis a PPBS was designed to accomplish back in the 1960s. Rather than performing a strict cost-benefit analysis focusing solely on economic efficiency, the budget official must decide which programs take a higher priority over others based on the depth of the need, the political salience of the issue, the controversial or non-controversial nature of the program, the probability of garnering multiple funding commitments and other factors beyond strictly "objective" short-term cost-benefit calculations.

External factors will play a role in this calculation as well. As some elected officials push for smaller government and the public indicates its mistrust of a big, fat, bloated federal bureaucracy, some programs may be moved to the private sector through privatization or deregulation. In this political climate, a budget official must recognize that the available funding for government programs that might have been approved in past years is likely to be limited. He or she must act accordingly. In other instances, external forces will propel programs back into government. After the terrorist attacks of September 11, 2001, for instance, the public became concerned about homeland security and military preparedness in a way it had not been concerned with previously. Because government is the entity best capable of providing these services, the realities of the budgetary process changed. Funding was much more forthcoming for the U.S. Department of Defense while other agencies such as the U.S. Environmental Protection Agency lost funding as priorities and monies were shifted.[46]

Thus, the ethical budget official recognizes that he or she will constantly grapple with scarcity and fairness. Depending on the internal and external forces affecting the agency as well as his or her internal priorities, the task of the official is to procure adequate funding, to the extent possible, to meet the agency's programmatic goals. Achieving the goals of other agencies—some perhaps more deserving, some perhaps less deserving—will depend on the ability of officials in those agencies to compete for funding. In the end, the budget official hopes to achieve at least some of his or her goals (at least the most important ones from the perspective of efficiency and fairness) and push for greater funding to achieve additional goals, and thereby fund more programs, in the years ahead.

Exercises and Discussion Questions

1. Danny Boyd is a budget official in a large state welfare agency. In recent years, the agency has suffered through one budget crisis after another as declining state revenues have forced the governor to call for several across-the-board budget decreases—some for as much as 5 percent. In Danny's opinion, the agency has been cut so much that he believes the staff can no longer fulfill many of its core functions without violating a variety of state and federal mandates.

    Fortunately, state revenues have rebounded this year for the first time since the recession began three years earlier. The rising revenues are hardly what Danny would call dramatic, but at least the agency does not have to cut more money from next year's budget proposals. If all goes well, Danny may be able to propose modest increases in some of the more chronically underfunded programs administered by the agency.

    One evening after work, Danny is leafing through a copy of the local newspaper when he stumbles across a story in the back pages of the Metro section. In a speech at the Chamber of Commerce the previous day, the governor, a conservative Republican, promised that he would re-store fiscal responsibility to state government. Recognizing the gover-nor's remarks as typical political rhetoric, Danny was not especially alarmed at the tenor of the article. It was only at the end that he read a comment that caused him concern.

In response to a reporter's question about budget priorities, the governor remarked that some agencies were more efficient and worked better than others. "Those agencies that have a proven track record for providing cost-effective service have nothing to fear. We intend to restore their budgets to the pre-recession levels," he promised. "For other agencies—like those that hand out welfare checks to Cadillac-driving welfare mothers—the times will continue to be lean, and they may get a whole lot leaner."

The next morning, with the article highlighted, Danny approaches his supervisor, Gary Goodguy, to ask about the agency's budget request. "Gary," he says, "this article on the governor's new priorities has got me worried. Are we gonna get even more money cut from the agency's budget?"

Gary had seen the article and he, too, shared Danny's concern. "The only thing I can say is that we have to do something to make sure we don't get the axe. Let's take the figures we projected for core programs and multiple them by 1.5. That should give us enough money to work with so we can resist any further cuts. A little padding is prudent in this case."

Danny initially agrees, but as he goes through the calculations in ensuing weeks, he realizes that inflating budget numbers to such an extent will result in inaccurate budget projections far beyond what the agency has requested in the past. "Won't this send up a red flag if the figures are so far above what we requested last year?" he asks.

Gary smiles. "That's the beauty of this new Zero Base Budgeting," he explains. "We have to start from scratch this year. As long as we can justify our requests as part of a necessary expenditure, we won't have to base our requests on historic budget projections. So let's jack the numbers up as much as we can."

a. Discuss the ethical implications of Gary Goodguy's decision to inflate the agency's budget figures. Should Danny comply with his boss's suggestion or should he take a different stance? Explain your answer.

b. If the agency has lost funding in previous years—and, in fact, if it is neglecting its legal requirements owing to budget considerations—

shouldn't Danny do whatever he can to restore the funding to suitable levels? Why or why not? Explain your answer.

c. What is the difference from an ethical standpoint between inflating budget figures for bargaining purposes and inflating them to hide the true cost of programs? Does the distinction matter? Should ethical questions be evaluated based on their ends, their means, or both? Discuss.

d. Should Danny consider background information he has read in the newspaper in making recommendations or decisions with respect to the budget? Does he have an ethical obligation to consider such information? Can an ethical administrator ever take into account outside sources of information in decision-making? Why or why not?

2. William Carter has been a budget analyst in the state's Community Development Agency (CDA) for more than two decades. He has seen it all—boom and bust cycles in state government, calls for budget reductions, lawsuits against agencies that failed to fulfill their statutory requirements—and he has become proficient at playing political games with the budget.

One of Carter's tried and true methods for handling budget requests is to "build in fat" so that CDA administrators will have money for new equipment, out-of-state travel, and other expenses that arise during the course of the year. In the past, he has tried to submit budget requests properly labeled as "equipment expenses" or "travel expenses," but often these funds are cut from the final budget. By hiding the money in other budget requests, especially those required by federal mandates and existing state and federal regulations, he is able to procure the necessary equipment and travel funds.

When you, as one of Carter's peers in the CDA, learn of this practice, you engage in a conversation with him. "Isn't this fraud, pure and simple?" you ask.

"No," he argues. "Fraud is when you use money for your own benefit. You embezzle funds to feed your cocaine habit or impress your mistress or pay for your kids' college tuition. Me? I'm still using the funds for CDA business. I'm just playing the political game. Budgeting is never 100 percent accurate, anyway. It's all just a numbers game. Everybody embraces certain assumptions—most of which are wrong or poorly prepared—and just hopes for the best. It's not like I'm stealing money from anybody, for Pete's sake."

   a. Discuss the merits of Carter's argument. If he uses the money to pay for CDA business, has he acted fraudulently? Why or why not?

   b. Assuming that you can persuade Carter not to hide equipment and travel monies in other budget requests, what should he do in the future to behave ethically? Should he come clean about his past practices? Discuss.

   c. If budgeting is a "numbers game" and is not really "stealing money from anybody else," does Carter have a point here? Why or why not? If projections are educated guesses only—as many budget analysts contend—why not alter the guesses in a manner that benefits the agency? After all, the legislature probably will cut the request, anyway. Is this a sound ethical argument?

   d. Is there a difference between abstract ethical concepts and practical ethical concepts, as in this example? Can you make a case for Carter's perspective? Discuss.

3. David Lane is in charge of a massive federal program administered by the U.S. Department of Energy (DOE). As part of the program, DOE provides grants to a variety of regional groups as well as state and local governments. The statute authorizing the funds provides the program administrator with a great deal of discretion in distributing the grants. As a result, David generally can pick and choose who receives funding, and who does not.

     At a meeting of the Regional Energy Commission (REC) in Atlanta one September afternoon, the commission's executive director, J. Kentwood Nimrod, corners Lane and makes a case for increasing the REC budget. "Look," Nimrod says, "every year you give more and more money to states and other regional groups, but REC is constantly underfunded. Something's gotta give."

     Lane shrugs. "What are you saying to me?"

     "I'm saying that REC will do whatever it takes to get the money. How about a solar energy project?"

     Lane is a well-known proponent of solar energy research. In his opinion, America's continued dependence on foreign sources of oil and petroleum is the weakest link in the country's national security chain.

Because nuclear power is too controversial and the use of fossil fuels such as coal degrade the natural environment, the only alternative is to invest in renewable energy sources such as hydroelectric dams, biomass, and solar energy. Nimrod's suggestion that REC undertake a solar energy project is appealing.

For his part, Nimrod has worked with REC for more than a quarter of a century. In his experience, solar energy becomes a pet project every few years when a new budget administrator at DOE decides to spend money on a project. Nonetheless, the projects always fail owing to a lack of interest on the part of researchers and the general public. In Nimrod's opinion, solar energy is a pipe dream and no one in his right mind would ever explore this area unless the federal government first spent billions of dollars to develop the infrastructure and refocused federal energy policy in this area. Nimrod has been an outspoken critic of solar energy, as David Lane well knows.

Still, Nimrod's agency is desperate for funding and Lane is interested in promoting solar energy using REC's prestige as a regional group. Even if the project never pans out, both men can gain something from working together. They shake hands and agree to develop a multi-million dollar project whereby DOE will funnel research funding to REC to explore the state of solar energy production in the United States and develop recommendations for improvement. It is unlikely that the project will ever yield effective results, but each man is happy with the agreement.

a. Has David Lane behaved unethically in promoting solar energy and rewarding groups that agree to study the issue even though he knows that the likelihood of success is small? Should the outcome, or consequences, matter in evaluating ethical issues or is intent the key consideration? Discuss.

b. If Lane has discretion in awarding grants, does it matter that he awards funding to favored groups or projects? Isn't it only an ethical issue if he makes a decision that goes beyond the scope of his authority? Why or why not?

c. Is J. Kentwood Nimrod behaving ethically if he takes money for a project that he believes to be doomed at the outset? Regardless of his personal feelings, as long as he fulfills the requirements of the grant award, isn't he behaving ethically? Why or why not?

d. If you were redesigning the DOE grant program, would you limit the discretion of the program administrator after reviewing the David Lane-J. Kentwood Nimrod scenario? Should the program administrator be held to a particular standard for awarding grants? Assuming there is no fraud, is the issue of a standard for awarding grants, or the lack thereof, even a question of ethics? Why or why not?

4. Why were income taxes controversial early in the history of the United States? How did government raise revenues before income taxes were instituted? In your opinion, are income taxes an effective means of raising government revenues? Can you think of appropriate alternatives to income taxes? Discuss.

5. Discuss the pros and cons of Keynesian economics. How has this concept influenced government budgeting in the United States? In your opinion, are Keynesian economics a positive or negative development?

6. Discuss the budgetary process in the United States. What is the role of the Office of Management and Budget (OMB)? Can you think of ways to improve the budgetary process?

7. Discuss the types of budgets throughout the history of the United States. In your opinion, which type is preferable? Why?

8. Why is it difficult to control government expenditures? Discuss the role of recent developments such as impoundment and Gramm-Rudman-Hollings. Why were these innovations used to help control expenditures? Have they been successful? Why or why not?

9. Discuss the role of administrative ethics in the budgetary process. What role, if any, does an ethical administrator play?

Notes

[1] The quote is from Alexander Hamilton, James Madison, and John Jay, "Federalist No. 12" in *The Federalist Papers*, ed. Clinton Rossiter (New York: The New American Library, 1961), 96. See also Daniel P. Franklin, *Making Ends Meet: Congressional Budgeting in the Age of Deficits* (Washington, D.C.: Congressional Quarterly Press, 1993), 10-11.

[2] See especially Christine Barbour and Gerald C. Wright, *Keeping the Republic: Power and Citizenship in American Politics* (Boston: Houghton Mifflin Company, 2001), 720-24; Richard F. Fenno, *The Power of the Purse* (Boston: Little, Brown & Company, 1966),

esp. Chapter 1; Roger H. Davidson and Walter J. Oleszek, *Congress and Its Members*, 3d. ed. (Washington, D.C.: CQ Press, 1990), 377-89.

3   Steven E. Rhoads, *The Economist's View of the World: Government, Markets, and Public Policy* (Cambridge: Cambridge University Press, 1989), 61-81; David H. Rosenbloom, *Public Administration: Understanding Management, Politics, and Law in the Public Sector*, 3rd. ed. (New York: Random House, 1993), 273-317.

4   Bruce Miroff, Raymond Seidelman, and Todd Swanstrom, *The Democratic Debate: An Introduction to American Politics* (Boston: Houghton Mifflin, 1995), 490-95.

5   *Springer v. United States*, 102 U.S. 586 (1881).

6   *Pollock v. The Farmers' Loan and Trust Company*, 157 U.S. 429 (1895). See also Franklin, *Making Ends Meet*, 22.

7   Thomas A. Barthold, Thomas Koerner, and John F. Navratil, "Effective Marginal Tax Rates Under the Federal Individual Income Tax: Death By One Thousand Pin Pricks," *National Tax Journal* 51 (September 1998): 553-64; Franklin, *Making Ends Meet*, 22-23; David H. Rosenbloom, *Public Administration: Understanding Management, Politics, and Law in the Public Sector*, 3rd. ed. (New York: Random House, 1993), 279-83.

8   Elizabeth Garrett, "Harnessing Politics: The Dynamics of Offset Requirements in the Tax Legislative Process," *The University of Chicago Law Review* 65 (Spring 1998): 501-69; Diane Lim Rogers and Alan Weil, "Welfare Reform and the Role of Tax Policy," *National Tax Journal* 53 (September 2000): 385-402; Joseph White, "Making 'Common Sense' of Federal Budgeting," *Public Administration Review* 58 (March/April 1998): 101-8.

9   David Futrelle, "Tax for the Memories," *Money* 32 (April 2003): 40; Deborah Rigsby, "Legislation Would Simplify Sales, Use Taxes," *Nation's Cities Weekly* 26 (September 29, 2003): 3; Rosenbloom, *Public Administration*, 281.

10   Ann O'M. Bowman and Richard C. Kearney, *State and Local Government*, 3d. ed. (Boston: Houghton Mifflin Company, 1996), 356-59, 415-19.

11   Futrelle, "Tax for the Memories," 40; Rigsby, "Legislation Would Simplify Sales, Uses Taxes," 3; Rosenbloom, *Public Administration*, 282-83.

12   Hashem Dezhbakhsh, Soumaya M. Tohamy, and Peter H. Aranson, "A New Approach for Testing Budgetary Incrementalism," *Journal of Politics* 65 (May 2003): 532-58; Franklin, *Making Ends Meet*, 24-26.

13   James L. Blum, "The Congressional Budget Process," *The Bureaucrat* 12 (Winter 1983/84): 14-16.

14   John Maynard Keynes, *The General Theory of Employment, Interest, and Money* (London: Macmillan & Company, 1936).

15   Franklin, *Making Ends Meet*, 11; Rosenbloom, *Public Administration*, 283-87.

16   Steven E. Rhoads, *The Economist's View of the World: Government, Markets, & Public Policy* (Cambridge: Cambridge University Press, 1985), 94-97; Rosenbloom, *Public Administration*, 286-87.

17   White, "Making 'Common Sense' of Federal Budgeting," 101-8.

18   Elizabeth Sanders, "The Presidency and the Bureaucratic State," in *The Presidency and the Political System*, 3d. ed., Michael Nelson, ed. (Washington, D.C.: Congressional Quarterly Press, 1990), 416-17.

19   Davidson and Oleszek, *Congress and Its Members*, 377-84.

20   Joseph Cooper and William F. West, "Presidential Power and Republican Government: The Theory and Practice of OMB Review of Agency Rules," *Journal of Politics* 50 (November 1988): 864-95; Franklin, *Making Ends Meet*, 39-47; Mark S. Kamlet and David C. Mowery, "The Budgetary Base in Federal Resource Allocation," *American Journal of Political Science* 24 (November 1980): 804-21; John Kitchen, "Observed Relationships Between Economic and Technical Receipts Revisions in Federal Budget Projections," *National Tax Journal* 56 (June 2003): 337-53.

21   Kamlet and Mowery, "The Budgetary Base in Federal Resource Allocation," 804-21; Rosenbloom, *Public Administration*, 295-98; White, "Making 'Common Sense' of Federal Budgeting," 101-8.

22   Geert Hofstede, "The Poverty of Management Control Philosophy," *The Academy of Management Review* 3 (July 1978): 450-61; Rosenbloom, *Public Administration*, 301.

23   Davidson and Oleszek, *Congress and Its Members*, 384-89; Rosenbloom, *Public Administration*, 302; Catheryn Seckler-Hudson, "Performance Budgeting in Government," in *Governmental Budgeting*, Albert Hyde and Jay M. Shafritz, eds. (Oak Park, Ill.: Moore Publishing, 1978), 80-93.

24   Hofstede, "The Poverty of Management Control Philosophy," 450-61; Vincent Puritano and Lawrence Korb, "Streamlining PPBS to Better Manage National Defense," *Public Administration Review* 41 (September/October 1981): 569-74.

25   Puritano and Korb, "Streamlining PPBS," 569-74; Rosenbloom, *Public Administration*, 302-6; Irene S. Rubin and Lana Stein, "Budget Reform in St. Louis: Why Does Budgeting Change," *Public Administration Review* 50 (July/August 1990): 420-26.

26   Hofstede, "The Poverty of Management Control Philosophy," 450-461; Rosenbloom, *Public Administration*, 304-6; Rubin and Stein, "Budget Reform in St. Louis," 420-26.

27   Mark W. Dirsmith and Stephen F. Jablonsky, "Zero-Base Budgeting as a Management Technique and Political Strategy," *The Academy of Management Review* 4 (October 1979): 555-65; Barry J. Ewell, "Planning Is the Key: To Budget, Start from Zero, "*Sales & Marketing Management* 134 (April 22, 1985): 46-48; V. Alaric Sample, "Resource Planning and Budgeting for National Forrest Management," *Public Administration Review* 52 (July/August 1992): 339-46.

28   Dirsmith and Jablonsky, "Zero-Base Budgeting as a Management Technique and Political Strategy," 555; Perry Moore, "Zero-Base Budgeting in American Cities," *Public Administration Review* 40 (May/June 1980): 253; Rosenbloom, *Public Administration*, 306-8.

29   Frank D. Draper and Bernard T. Pitsvada, "ZBB—Looking Back After Ten Years," *Public Administration Review* 41 (January/February 1981): 76-83; Donald F. Haider, "Zero Base—Federal Style," *Public Administration Review* 37 (July/August 1977): 400-7; Thomas P. Lauth, "Zero-Base Budgeting in Georgia State Government: Myth and Reality," *Public Administration Review* 38 (September/October 1978): 420-30; Daniel M. Ogden, Jr., "Beyond Zero Base Budgeting," *Public Administration Review* 38 (November/December 1978): 528; Allen Schick, "The Road from ZBB," *Public Administration Review* 38 (March/April 1978): 177; Mark J. Versel, "Zero-Base Budgeting: Setting Priorities Through the Ranking Process," *Public Administration Review* 38 (Novem-

ber/December 1978): 524-27; Aaron Wildavsky, "A Budget for All Seasons? Why the Tradition Budget Lasts," *Public Administration Review* 38 (November/December 1978): 501-9.

30 Dezhbakhsh, Tohamy, and Aranson, "A New Approach for Testing Budgetary Incrementalism," 532-58; Rosenbloom, *Public Administration*, 308-12; Aaron Wildavsky, "The Political Economy of Efficiency: Cost-Benefit Analysis, Systems Analysis, and Program Budgeting," *Public Administration Review* 26 (December 1966): 292-310.

31 *Immigration and Naturalization Service v. Chadha*, 462 U.S. 919 (1983); Franklin, *Making Ends Meet*, 32-34; Jerry L. Mashaw, Richard A. Merrill, and Peter M. Shane, *Administrative Law: The American Public Law System—Cases and Materials*, 5th ed. (St. Paul, Minn.: West Publishing Company, 2003), 95-115.

32 Michael E. Milakovich and George J. Gordon, *Public Administration in America* (Belmont, Calif.: Wadsworth, 2004), 375.

33 Ibid.; Rosenbloom, *Public Administration*, 296.

34 Franklin, *Making Ends Meet*, 34-35; Norman C. Thomas, Joseph A. Pika, and Richard A. Watson, *The Politics of the Presidency*, 3d. ed. (Washington, D.C.: Congressional Quarterly Press, 1994), 389-91.

35 Stanley E. Collender, *The Guide to the Federal Budget: Fiscal 1990* (Washington, D.C.: Urban Institute Press, 1989), 55; Franklin, *Making Ends Meet*, 34-35.

36 Franklin, *Making Ends Meet*, 34-35. For more on the budget process in the early '90s, see Aaron Wildavsky, *The New Politics of the Budgetary Process*, 2d ed. (New York: HarperCollins, 1992), esp. Chapter 2.

37 Franklin, *Making Ends Meet*, 34-35; Thomas, *et al.*, *The Politics of the Presidency*, 389-90.

38 Jennifer Alexander, "A New Ethics of the Budgetary Process," *Administration & Society* 31 (September 1999): 542-65.

39 Patricia Casey Douglas and Benson Wier, "Integrating Ethical Dimensions into a Model of Budgetary Slack Creation," *Journal of Business Ethics* 28 (December 2000): 267-77; Jacqueline L. Reck, "Ethics and Budget Allocation Decisions of Municipal Budget Officers," *Journal of Business Ethics* 27 (October 2000): 335-50.

40 James M. Buchanan, "The Moral Dimension of Debt Financing," *Economic Inquiry* 23 (January 1985): 1-6; Stephen G. Peitchinis, "Government Spending and the Budget Deficit," *Journal of Business Ethics* 9 (July 1990): 591-94.

41 Peitchinis, "Government Spending and the Budget Deficit," 591-94; Reck, "Ethics and Budget Allocation Decisions," 335-50; Rosenbloom, *Public Administration*, 525.

42 H. George Frederickson, "Ethics and the New Managerialism," *Public Administration & Management* 4 (2) (1999): 299-324.

43 Dennis D. Riley, *Controlling the Federal Bureaucracy* (Philadelphia, Pa.: Temple University Press, 1987), 60.

44 Constance A. Nathanson, "Social Movements as Catalysts for Policy Change: The Case of Smoking and Guns," *Journal of Health Politics, Policy and Law* 24 (June 1999): 421-88; Riley, *Controlling the Federal Bureaucracy*, 60-63.

45 Frederickson, "Ethics and the New Managerialism," 317.

[46]   Frederickson, "Ethics and the New Managerialism," 317-19; Jeroen Maesschalck, "The Impact of New Public Management Reforms on Public Servants' Ethics: Towards a Theory," *Public Administration* 82 (June 2004): 465-89.

Chapter Nine
Public Policy and Management in the Administrative State

To have a thorough understanding of how American government works, one must carefully study how public policy is formulated, implemented, and evaluated. The most elegant political philosophy ever conceived is nothing but a lofty theory without effective public policy. Plato's "city in speech," for all its elegance and influence on the western intellectual tradition, fails as public policy because it remains unrealized—and probably unrealizable.

If politics is defined as "who gets what, when, and how," policy-making is defined more specifically as a general plan of action to determine who gets what, when he or she gets it, and how he or she gets it.[1] In short, public policy is adopted by government to address an issue, solve problems, counter a threat, or achieve a relatively well-identified goal. Sometimes the goal is established beforehand and policy-makers then deliberately design a program to achieve it. At other times, the goal is loosely defined over time, and policymakers are forced to "muddle through" to address part of an intricate, possibly intractable, problem.[2]

Policy-making can be an extremely complicated process. Ideally, in a democratic nation, policies are developed when voters and stakeholders make their wishes known to policy-makers. A successful candidate for elective office often will insist that the electorate wanted a particular policy when it placed him in office; therefore, the new office-holder claims a mandate for certain reforms or even specific policy goals. This claim may or may not be true. Voters may cast ballots for a given candidate based on a variety of factors which may or may not be related to policy choices. Whatever the reason a particular office holder was successful, once in power the person proposes policies in line with his or her underlying philosophy of government. Ideally, if the electorate is displeased with the office holder's performance in articulating and actualizing these policies, the voters' disaffection can be communicated in the next election.[3]

The policy process raises a variety of ethical concerns, some of which involve individual issues and some of which involve structural issues. If the key questions revolve around "who gets what, when, and how" during each stage of the policy process, a public administrator invariably will be involved in addressing those questions. The "who" refers to the clients of the public agency. In some cases, the clients are specified by clear eligibility criteria, in which case an individual administrator has little or no input into the "who" question. This is the quintessential example of a structural issue. The structure of the agency determines whether a particular person falls into the "client" category. In other instances, the eligibility criteria allow for interpretation and discretion. In those instances, the ethical administrator is the person who consults the applicable agency guidelines and eligibility criteria, as well as previous examples, to determine whether a particular person should or should not be serviced by the agency. The lack of an agency eligibility requirement makes this an individual ethical issue because the individual administrator must decide on eligibility based on his or her practical judgment.

The "what" question generally is straightforward because it refers to the goods or services supplied by the agency. If the agency distributes transfer payments, food stamps or other tangible benefits, the "what" is a check or tangible benefit transferred from the agency to the recipient. The amount may be left to the discretion of an individual administrator but, more likely, the specific dollar figure is set by law, regulation, or guidelines governing the agency. In other words, the structure of the agency largely determines what goods or services are distributed. An individual administrator agonizing over the relative paucity of goods and services provided to clients can do little to influence the actions of the agency in such a situation because this is not an issue that can be resolved by an individual relying on administrative discretion. The appropriate recourse would be to address the legislature in the hopes of influencing the legislative process.

"When" and "how" are procedural questions closely related to each other. Again, in some instances an existing law, regulation or guideline specifies when and how an agency distributes goods and services. Even in those cases, however, an administrator may have some control over how well an agency client understands the process and whether he or she correctly completes the requisite paperwork and supporting documentation to ensure timely delivery. Cutting red tape and assisting clients in navigating the maze of government requirements—always a daunting enterprise for beleaguered citizens who may possess little or no understanding of how government works—certainly has an individual ethical component. As Herbert Kaufman noted in his classic study of bureaucratic red tape, a concern for fairness in the delivery of goods and services by government agencies "obliges officials to give people affected by governmental action a fair chance to get their views on official decisions registered so that their interests are not overlooked or arbitrarily overridden by those in power."[4]

Aside from relations with clients and the general public, administrators affect the policy process in many other ways. Employees at every level of an organization have at least some small measure of power to ensure that the agency performs its work efficiently and effectively. As discussed later in this chapter, efficiency and effectiveness are contentious concepts and generally involve tradeoffs. Setting aside those difficulties for the moment, as a general proposition the individuals who staff an organization can assist in ensuring a smooth transition from policy formulation to implementation to evaluation if they act in good faith to perform their roles as efficiently and effectively as possible. Persons with greater responsibility and discretionary authority will affect the policy process to a greater extent than employees at a lower level, but every public employee at every level can play a part.

Examining ethics in terms of the policy process is, in some sense, an Aristotelian approach to ethics because it assumes that administrators become ethical people by making ethical decisions. In other words, ethics is a practice that is carried out by the actions we undertake, not merely the words we speak. This approach is dynamic. Thus, throughout the stages of the policy process, an ethical administrator is called upon to assess his or her role within an organization. Based on this understanding, a conscientious public administrator will be well-suited to perceive an ethical problem, describe the problem, define the salient issues, identify alternatives, project consequences, select an appropriate course of action, and resolve the issue. An administrator who undertakes this series of steps while working diligently to fulfill an agency's mission and goals in a manner consistent with democratic values will improve the policy process immeasurably.[5]

Models of the Policy Process

Political scientists and policy analysts have developed a number of models of the policy process. In the words of one researcher, James E. Anderson, public policy is "a relatively stable, purposive course of action followed by government in dealing with some problem or matter of concern." Like many policy scientists, Anderson views policy-making as a series of closely related stages. First, policy-making is not simply the culmination of a series of more or less random events. Rather, it is a purposive undertaking designed by policy-makers, some elected, some appointed, to achieve certain goals. To place the activity in an academic framework, policy-making begins hypotheses-linking actions (the independent variable) with expected outcomes (the dependent variable). According to this conception, policy-makers hypothesize that if certain policies are adopted and certain programs are put into place, these policies and programs will proximately lead to this expected outcome.[6]

If the first stage in Anderson's model can be thought of as the planning stage, the second step can be thought of as an extension of planning. Not only must policy-makers develop hypotheses, but they must also develop implementation plans. Anderson quite rightly observes that "policies consist of courses or patterns of action taken over time by governmental officials rather than their separate, discrete decisions."[7] In other words, policy-making involves a series of interrelated, continuously flowing decisions that, taken together, should result in the development of a policy that meets the needs identified in the hypothesis. In academic parlance, the decisions invariably lead to the conclusion that the independent variable caused, in whole or in part, changes in the dependent variable, a phenomenon known as the treatment effect.

Public policies do not emerge in a vacuum. Anderson observes that policies are created specifically because of policy demands. Demands can be amorphous and diffuse, such as the general public's call for public officials to "do something." In other contexts, policy demands can be extremely specific, as when lobbyists try to persuade lawmakers to support or oppose particular bills or proposed regulations. However they are formed and in whatever context, policy demands require policy-makers to take action so that hypotheses developed early—and planning performed earlier in the process—will produce a tangible result.

According to Anderson, "Policy involves what governments actually do, not just what they intend to do or what officials say they are going to do." Policy researchers refer to this stage of the policy process as policy output, or the actions taken to ensure that policy statements and designs are implemented. Even the best policies will be deemed failures if they do not produce measurable results that address the problem at hand.[8]

After outputs have been catalogued, they must be evaluated to determine whether the treatment effect, if any, was positive or negative and to what extent it occurred. Evaluation is one of the most important and rigorous parts of the policy process. Researchers are constantly pressed to explain how much "bang for the buck" a particular policy or program delivered. The traditional means for determining the efficacy of a policy or program has been to employ cost-benefit analysis. In its simplest form, cost-benefit analysis requires researchers to perform an elementary calculation. They add up all the benefits of a policy or program and compare them with the costs incurred. If the costs are greater than the benefits, they advise policy-makers to modify or abandon the policy or program in the future. If the benefits outweigh the costs, however, the program is deemed a success and may be continued. The calculations can become extremely contentious as policy-makers debate what constitutes a benefit versus a cost, but at its core this kind of analysis provides guidance on whether the policy achieved the desired objectives.[9]

This leads to the last stage of the policy process, which Anderson calls the authoritative legal stage. Once a policy has been developed through the preceding stages, it must then be recognized as having the force and effect of law. If it is a statute, it is codified into the appropriate federal or state code. If it is a regulation, it, too, is codified where parties affected by the new policy or program can readily access it. As a part of positivist law, the new policy or program must be recognized as authoritative, even by individuals or groups that do not agree with the policy and think it misguided. Legitimate public policies almost never enjoy universal support, but they must be honored and obeyed if the policy process is to work effectively.[10]

Anderson's model is not the only one available, but many policy models follow a more or less linear approach, just as he does, although they introduce important variations on the theme of stages. The famous garbage can model developed by Cohen, March, and Olsen is a prime example of the effort to understand stages of the policy process through a different method of analysis. This model seeks to explain "organized anarchies," which are institutions with three characteristics: problematic preferences, unclear technology, and fluid participation.[11]

Another related model is known as the Advocacy Coalition Framework, or ACF. According to authors Paul A. Sabatier and Hank C. Jenkins-Smith, the ACF applies especially to highly technical, complex problems such as environmental issues where the actors involved in formulating and implementing a policy share a belief that they can accomplish important public policy goals. The ACF framework suggests that technical information is an important component in analyzing a problem. In addition, policy changes must occur over an extended time period—a decade or longer. This time period extends beyond the usual policy cycle of two to four years, which matches the U.S. election cycle. Within this time frame, the unit of analysis for understanding change is what Sabatier and Jenkins-Smith call the "policy subsystem." A policy subsystem consists of the policy actors from many public and private organizations who are actively involved in shaping and implementing the policy. The subsystem includes not only elected officials, bureaucrats, and interest group members, but media representatives, policy analysts, academics, and all persons concerned about the policy. According to ACF theory, four elements are involved with policies: relatively stable parameters, external events, constraints and resources of the subsystem actors, and the existence of a policy subsystem.[12]

ACF theory is important because it introduces a conceptual framework that is simple enough to explain why certain actions occur but it is sophisticated and complex enough to capture real-world complexities, which are always challenging for a model. Moreover, it allows for flexibility in adjusting part of the model as conditions change and as information becomes more complete. Socioeconomic conditions, public opinion, system-wide governing coalitions, or policy outcomes from other subsystems can be factored into the analysis.

The ACF has received much attention in the literature since it first appeared. Perhaps the most serious criticism involves the theory's assumption that coalitions share goals and beliefs, which lead them to work together to lower transaction costs, distributional conflicts, and the free rider problem. The free rider problem is when some group members are unwilling to bear the burdens involved with collective action but they still receive the benefits. Thus, non-union members of a manufacturing plant may enjoy the same benefits as their union counterparts but not have to pay the dues that funded the protracted negotiations which ultimately secured those benefits. ACF critics argue that these kinds of difficulties suggest limitations in the model.[13]

Stages in the Policy Process

Many models of policy-making exist, but at their core most feature a linear decision-making process. In the first stage, certain problems are defined as political issues and therefore placed on the political agenda. Before the September 11, 2001 terrorist attacks in New York and Washington, D.C., America's policy on terrorism, while an important issue for many decision-makers in government, was not at the top of the national agenda. Since those horrible events occurred, many Americans who previously would not have seen terrorism policy as a high national priority have clearly changed their opinions. Policy-makers have responded by proposing innumerable policies to identify terrorists, increase government surveillance techniques, and redesign key government agencies and institutions to coordinate information and data collection.[14]

Some policies are elevated to the national agenda owing to external events, as was the case with terrorism in the United States. On other occasions, policy-makers deliberately devise a campaign to call attention to an issue and propel it onto the agenda. When Candy Lightner's daughter was killed by a drunk driver, she set out to revise state laws so that intoxicated drivers, especially repeat offenders, were punished more severely, hopefully deterring some would-be motorists from acting irresponsibly. Her largely grassroots effort to form a group, Mothers Against Drunk Drivers (M.A.D.D.), did much to raise the national consciousness about drunk drivers and helped to reform laws in many states so that stiffer penalties were imposed.[15]

An integral component of agenda-setting is what some political scientists call "issue definition." Defining an issue initially sounds as though it would be a relatively simple enterprise. If people drive drunk and get caught, they should be punished harshly to prevent them from maiming or killing other people. In the case of M.A.D.D., defining the issue was fairly straightforward, but some public policy issues are extremely complicated and not necessarily amenable to easy definition.[16]

Consider the issue of poverty. During the 1960s, federal policy-makers in the Johnson Administration declared war on poverty. The problem is that poverty is not easily definable, much less resolvable, because reasonable minds can differ on interpreting the problem. Moreover, poverty is not caused by a single factor but by a series of interrelated factors that are complex and difficult to assess. The Johnson administration spent a great deal of time, money, and energy combating an issue that was only vaguely defined and poorly understood. As a result, the war on poverty, while making some progress, was generally perceived to be a failure, in no small measure owing to the inability to define the problem adequately.[17]

After a problem has been defined and placed on the agenda, policy-makers must formulate a policy to address the salient issues. The most obvious way that policy is formulated occurs through the legislative process. In response to a perceived need—raised by constituents, the mass media, or as a result of external events—legislators draft legislation defining a problem and offering a proposed solution.[18] Other parties can formulate policy as well. A governor or the president of the United States may propose legislation. Executive branch agencies may formulate policy through the regulatory process.[19] Even the judicial branch is involved in formulating policy through the interpretation of law.[20] The U.S. Supreme Court's requirement that all public schools must be integrated in *Brown v. Board of Education* (1954)[21] and *Brown v. Board of Education, II* (1955)[22] formulated a new policy for public education in the United States.

Most models of the policy-making process depict policy formulation as a single-stage process, but in reality it frequently takes many years and numerous steps to formulate public policy. Policy formulation tends to be incremental. It takes time for a problem to emerge and garner the public attention that results in issue definition, agenda placement, and policy-makers' attention. Afterward, affected parties often debate all sides of the issue as well as the relative merits of the proposed solutions. Such a process seldom occurs swiftly. In some cases, political opposition can defeat all proposals, and a policy is never formulated. Even in cases where the opposition fails to crystallize, the policy that finally is formulated represents a compromise among and between the various parties involved in the issue.[23]

Policy formulation undoubtedly is important, but so, too, is policy implementation. The challenges of implementing public policy have been highlighted in numerous academic studies and publications in recent years. Implementation research often focuses on one of two major approaches: "Top Down" or "Bottom Up." The former is the classical approach propounded by major public administration scholars. The Top Down literature—especially works such as Pressman and Wildavsky's book *Implementation: How Great Expectations in Washington Are Dashed in Oakland* and Mazmanian and Sabatier's *Implementation and Public Policy*—discusses the issue as though public policy is developed at the top of a traditional hierarchy by members of Congress and heads of agencies at the federal level. After the policy has been formulated, it must be communicated to those bureaucrats and other parties lower in the hierarchy. Sufficient guidance and resources also must be made available.[24]

By contrast, the Bottom Up approach considers the issue from the perspective of the "street-level bureaucrat." According to this school of thought, which is championed by many practitioners and scholars such as Michael Lipsky, Benny Hjern, and Peter and Linda deLeon, policies are often so vague or ambiguous that the specific details of implementation are left to those bureaucrats who must administer them. Because they must use their discretion to decide hard cases, street-level bureaucrats in many ways shape and even write policy. Members of Congress and political appointees in the agencies develop the vision and set the tone for the policy, but the program parameters are the work of people at lower levels.[25]

Despite problems that occur when different agencies and levels of government are involved in implementing a policy, the benefits of cooperation are enormous. Consider the example of environmental policy implementation. In *Pluralism by the Rules*, Edward P. Weber contends that despite the U.S. political system's fragmented, pluralistic heritage, where different parties compete for political power, a new model emerged at the end of the twentieth century. All parties involved in implementation—especially in a complex, ever-changing field such as environmental policy—have a strong incentive to engage in collaborative efforts. Weber calls this "pluralism by the rules" because the realization that collaboration holds mutual advantages pushes state and federal agencies to develop rules for implementation. Formal binding agreements, memoranda of understanding, and resource-sharing programs achieve efficiency and economies of scale that would be unavailable if the parties did not work together. Using case studies involving acid deposition, reformulated gasoline, and oil refinery pollution control regulations, Weber shows how efforts to improve environmental quality have been enhanced owing to collaboration. The results—lower transaction and compliance costs, more efficient and effective enforcement, and an atmosphere of trust—have been impressive.[26]

After a policy has been implemented, it must also be evaluated to assess its effectiveness and efficiency. At first blush, evaluating public policy would appear to be relatively simple and straightforward. If the original problem was clearly defined; the issue placed on the agenda; and a policy articulated, formulated and implemented in a reasonable and consistent manner, policy-makers should be able to review the outcomes and compare the results with the objectives stated at the outset. Unfortunately, evaluation is not as straightforward as it initially appears. The data and information necessary to reach a definitive conclusion or a defensible decision may not be available, or, if it is available, it may be ambiguous or contradictory. Biases presented by the wide variety of policy-makers involved in the process may lead to irreconcilable conflict. Unintended consequences or intervening acts may occur, which require a reassessment of the original policy. The goal of gaining feedback on the performance of the policy is an integral part of the process, but it presents a host of challenges.[27]

Policy-makers and planners often employ a range of tools to evaluate programs. Probably the most prevalent and intuitive evaluative techniques involve before-versus-after studies. As the name suggests, policy-makers examine a problem before the program was implemented and compare it with the period after implementation. This type of evaluation works well when only a few personnel are involved, the time period is short, and the program is well defined and narrow in scope. As the number of people grows, the time expands, and the program becomes larger and less well defined, it becomes difficult to determine whether changes occurred owing to the program or because of other factors or intervening variables.[28]

A similar evaluative measure is called time-trend projection. Researchers use preprogram data to project likely results after a particular program is implemented. Afterward, they implement a program and compare the actual results with the projected results. If the actual results are not in line with projections, researchers can then trace the deviations in an attempt to isolate and correct problem areas. As was the case with before-versus-after studies, however, it is not always a simple matter to determine which factors contributed to the actual results.

Ideally, policy-makers prefer to evaluate programs and policies by comparing two groups. Just as scientists conduct controlled experiments using two groups of subjects—one a control group that takes a placebo and one a group served by the thing being tested—so, too, do social scientists prefer to examine programs and policies side by side. Unfortunately for evaluators, controlled experiments may not be possible outside a laboratory setting. One reason is the previously discussed Hawthorne Effect, where results in an experiment change owing to the presence of the researcher.[29]

Perhaps a more important objection to controlled experimentation in evaluating public policies is an ethical issue. Because governments are using human subjects and may be implementing policies that affect people's lives—for example, administering a new series of AIDS drugs or providing job training to disadvantaged workers—researchers are obliged to inform subjects about the nature of the research. By virtue of providing information on the research, the evaluation is compromised because the subjects' knowledge alters their behavior. In the absence of informed consent, however, government research has the potential to expose people to all sorts of risks, or deny them treatments or programs deemed essential to their well-being. Unfortunately, some of the dark pages of American history reveal how researchers exposed unwitting Americans to radiation during testing in the 1940s and

1950s or used controversial chemicals such as Agent Orange near soldiers without informing them of the potential consequences of exposure.[30]

Aside from the individual steps in the policy process, policy and program formulation, implementation, and evaluation is rife with problems owing to what many scholars call multiplicity and fragmentation. The former term refers to the many centers of power involved in democratic decision-making. In the legislative process, for example, numerous participants contribute to the policy process and, in one sense, the multitude of participants is beneficial because it ensures that virtually every interest or party is represented. However, as the number of participants increases, the number of issues increases and the potential for controversy, argument, and delay increases as well.[31]

When many parties craft policy and attack a problem in different and sometimes competing ways, fragmentation occurs. No one is above the fray, but every participant competes for political power and for ultimate policy-making authority. In light of this war of interests against interests, no one is looking out for the "public interest"; everyone is pursuing private self-interest, thereby leading to a fragmentation in government. This phenomenon is hardly surprising; it is one of the hallmarks of the American political system owing to separation of powers and federalism. Separation of powers divides power horizontally into three branches: legislative, executive and judicial. Federalism divides power vertically into national, state, and local governments. Thus, the policy-making process in the United States is fragmented into one national government with three branches, 50 state governments with three branches, and approximately 87,000 local governments, many of which have three branches. About 500,000 elected policy-makers are involved in the process.[32]

The multiplicity and fragmentation of the policy process often results in competing policies, inconsistent policies, policies that are poorly understood by the public, or policies that are not adequately funded by legislators. It is little wonder that the policy process is therefore characterized as divisive and messy. Programs and projects are formulated, implemented, and evaluated through a haphazard series of fits and starts.

Types of Policies

Researchers have attempted to identify broad types of public policies in an effort to understand how they work. Distributive policies, for example, are policy actions that deliver widespread benefits to individuals or groups that do not directly bear the costs of the policy. Tax deductions on home interest mortgages, loan guarantees provided by the federal government, agricultural price supports, and federally insured loans for college students are a few instances in which government chooses to promote certain policy goals without requiring the participants to bear the full policy costs. Consider home mortgage interest deductions. Federal policy-makers have decided that it is in the best interests of the regime for Americans to own their own homes, as opposed to renting a house or an apartment, whenever possible. Home ownership gives the property owner a stake in the community and provides equity over time, both of which lead to improved neighborhoods, a greater standard of living for citizens, and reasons for being interested in the policies of government. By allowing homeowners to deduct the interest paid on mortgages, the federal government is creating an incentive for Americans to purchase homes. Government policy is therefore distributing a benefit to a large group of people in order to promote the public benefits of wide-spread private home ownership.[33]

By contrast, redistributive policies involve efforts by government to shift the allocation of valued goods from one group to another. This definition sounds unremarkable, but redistributive policies often are among the most contentious issues addressed by governments. For a government to collect resources from one group of citizens and transfer them to another strikes a substantial number of people as inherently inequitable. The standard objection is voiced something like this: "I worked hard for my money. Why should I be taxed by a government that takes the money I earned and gives it to people who did not work as hard as I did?" For critics, redistributive policies are tantamount to robbing Peter to pay Paul.[34]

The rejoinder to criticism of redistributive policies is to say that not all segments of the population are able to support themselves equally well. The quintessential example is attributable to poverty. Because they have few if any resources, people who grow up poor have fewer opportunities later in life. They have little or no access to affordable housing, adequate health care, or quality education. As a result, poverty is a seemingly never-ending cycle. In redistributing a measure of income to the poor, government ensures that a floor exists below which the affected population will not sink. Proponents of programs such as Temporary Assistance for Needy Families (TANF) contend that, without redistributive policies, many people, especially children born into poverty, would never have realistic hopes for a better future. With little to lose, they would turn to drugs, prostitution, and crime in a desperate attempt to survive. TANF and other redistributive policies at least offer some hope that the cycle of poverty can be broken.[35]

Redistributive policies are used not only to combat poverty, but also to target situations where a population has been historically disadvantaged or people cannot fend for themselves. Thus, affirmative action policies seek to provide redress for problems resulting from decades of past racial discrimination. Elderly Americans, many of whom subsist on fixed incomes, need assistance in paying spiraling medical costs, hence the federal government created programs such as Medicare and Medicaid to meet those needs.[36]

Self-regulatory, or constituent, policies, while perhaps not as controversial as redistributive policies, nonetheless are politically sensitive. Governments do not possess the personnel or resources to regulate every type of behavior that policy-makers believe must be regulated. Therefore, governments sometimes allow certain groups to regulate themselves, although such self-regulators are subject to government oversight. The most obvious example is the licensing of professions and occupations such as physicians, lawyers, and real estate agents. The legal profession, for example, develops standards for admission into the profession. In most states, this requires law school graduates to sit for a bar examination and attest to their good character. The bar also develops codes of professional ethics for practicing attorneys and prescribes sanctions for ethical lapses or noncompliance.[37]

Self-regulatory policies are controversial among some members of society because they find an inherent conflict of interest in allowing lawyers to police lawyers or physicians to police physicians. The mistrust of "too much power in too few hands" makes the public wary of entrusting the oversight of a profession to its own members because the incentive to assist one's fellow professionals at the expense of the public interest is too obvious. For their part, professionals contend that members of the public are not qualified to oversee professionals because the specialized knowledge and training necessary to understand and apply professional standards are not available to the laity. According to this perspective, professionals should be left alone to regulate themselves and governments or members of the public should become involved only in situations where malfeasance can be demonstrated.[38]

Efficiency versus Equity: The Big Tradeoff

Whatever policies are affected, invariably public policy raises issues about the goals propounded by government decision-makers. Should the goal be to develop and implement policies using the fewest resources in the shortest amount of time (one definition of efficiency) or should the goal be to treat like cases alike (one notion of equity) even if such treatment is inefficient? Scholars and academics have long debated whether a tradeoff exists between efficiency and equity and, if so, what implications such a tradeoff holds for public policy. Typically, the debate casts these concepts as antithetical values so that an increase in one value necessarily requires a corresponding decrease in the other. Although in many cases such a tradeoff exists, efficiency and equity need not be competing values in every instance. Efficiency and equity sometimes can be balanced.[39]

At the outset, it is helpful to consider a continuum between individual liberty and state authority. At one end of the spectrum is absolute liberty, which can be defined as a complete absence of constraints on individual behavior. In a state of absolute liberty, no government exists. A person can do whatever he or she wants. Although some extreme libertarians—William Godwin springs to mind—have argued that a state of complete liberty is tantamount to existing in a virtual Garden of Eden free from government interference, most mainstream western thinkers, at least since the Enlightenment, have viewed a state of absolute liberty with horror—the ultimate laboratory for licentiousness. The seventeenth-century English philosopher Thomas Hobbes, a strong supporter of the social contract theory of government, famously wrote in his 1651 tome *Leviathan* that life in what he called a "state of nature" was "nasty, brutish, and short."[40] Later theorists spoke of "nature red in tooth and claw." Clearly, then, rational men would gladly surrender a measure of their individual liberty in exchange for the authority of a state to protect them and to meet basic needs that were not met in a state of absolute liberty.

After people have agreed to surrender a measure of liberty to create a state, the question becomes how much individual liberty should be surrendered in exchange for how much state authority? (In Figure 1, people move from Step 1 to some other step.) Individual liberty and state authority are antithetical ideals: An increase in one, by definition, decreases the other. There is indeed a tradeoff.

At the extreme end of the spectrum, Step 5, a totalitarian state could be created so that there is no individual liberty whatsoever. In such a state, all political and economic decisions are made by the government. There is a kind of ruthless equality of outcomes enforced by the state. Everyone is treated exactly the same regardless of a person's individual talents or industry.

Figure 1:
The Liberty-Authority Continuum

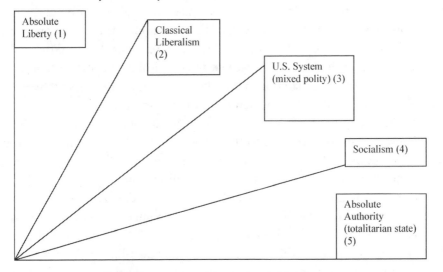

Unlike a state of absolute liberty, where people may starve to death because there is no one to provide for them and life becomes a Hobbesian war of all-against-all or a brutal test of natural selection where only the strong and/or cunning survive, a state with absolute authority can ensure that no one starves. The problem, of course, is that there is no check on the power of the state or the behavior of the people who administer its laws. Subjects of a totalitarian regime risk being exploited by its leaders and oppressing its citizens. This insight, if nothing else, was dramatically illustrated by the former Soviet Union and in many other totalitarian states throughout history.

Most mainstream theorists have rejected Step 5, a state possessing absolute authority, as too extreme. There must be room for individual liberty or life is not worth living. This conclusion is reminiscent of Patrick Henry's famous cry, "give me liberty or give me death." As Publius discusses in "Federalist Number 10," when a government chooses to quash liberty in an effort to control the mischief of factions, the cure is worse than the disease.[41] This leaves the realistic alternatives for developing a state as Steps 2, 3, and 4.

Step 2, which is a classical liberal state, was adopted by the American Founders in the Articles of Confederation in 1781. It proved to be seriously flawed. Their opinion was that they needed a state with very few powers so that they could enjoy maximum individual liberty. They subscribed to the libertarian creed: That government is best which governs least. Don't tread on me. Government should serve as a kind of night watchman but essentially not interfere in people's lives. Because a state that has very little authority must continually surrender to the will of the masses, and the masses are constantly in turmoil, the state simply cannot function effectively. After only eight years, American statesmen rejected the classical liberal state established by the Articles of Confederation and replaced it with a stronger system—the federal government found in the new U.S. Constitution.[42]

If Steps 1, 5, and 2 are rejected, is Step 4 a suitable alternative, namely Socialism? Socialism, according to the theorist Sidney Webb, is not a clearly developed set of doctrines or clearly delineated precepts. At its core, Socialism is the idea that people should enjoy a small measure of liberty, but with the state providing essential goods and services when they are necessary. Private enterprise is not prohibited, but it is strictly regulated, and large companies can be nationalized if it is in the public interest to do so. Different Socialist regimes provide different levels of individual liberty; in fact, some western European nations are labeled "democratic-socialist" states. In some cultures and traditions where individual liberty is not as highly valued as it is in the United States, a democratic-socialist state might be greeted with open arms. In this country, however, the idea that government controls most of the means of production and makes major economic decisions for the public and private sectors as part of a planned economy is simply anathema. Anything that smacks of Socialism, even if it inaccurately carries the Socialist label, will be met with scorn and derision in the American political landscape.[43]

This pushes democratic decision-makers into Step 3, the U.S. political system. In some ways, the deck was already stacked at the beginning. A mixed polity—that is, a regime where people, acting through elected representatives, make some political decisions but unelected experts also make decisions within their areas of expertise—is the preferred form of government for a people who profess to love individual liberty but also desire a strong state that meets many needs, especially for national defense, protect-

ing free markets, and ensuring equality of opportunity (although the definition of the latter term is highly contentious). The U.S. political system calls
to mind Winston Churchill's famous comment that a democracy is the worst
form of government—except, of course, for all the others.[44]

Having now set the stage, an exploration of theories of equity/fairness is
in order. One theory embraces free markets and the idea that individual liberty is a crucial component of life. Although this perspective is not exactly at
Step 2 on the continuum, it is not quite at Step 3. Call it 2.5. Free market
economists often accept this view. John Stuart Mill, author of the classic
1859 book *On Liberty*, argued that government should intervene to prevent
"other-regarding" actions if they are negative, but "self-regarding" actions
should be left alone.[45] Theorists such as Milton Friedman, the Nobel Laureate long associated with the University of Chicago, contended that, in most
cases involving essentially trivial choices, free markets are far more efficient
and effective than governments in meeting the needs and desires of citizens.[46]
Irving Kristol and Robert Nozick are two politically conservative theorists
who have also presented persuasive and influential arguments about the importance of private property and the liberty of the marketplace.[47]

In this framework, the standard notion of "efficiency" is conceptually
simple. It is the idea that a rational person seeks to achieve his or her goals
while also using as few resources as possible. To be "efficient," therefore,
means that the person achieves the greatest return on an investment of his or
her time and/or money. The colloquial expression is that a person gets "the
biggest bang for the buck." Presumably, an efficient course of action is also
effective, albeit effectiveness is a different concept. To be "effective," as that
term generally is understood, means that a person achieves the goal, but in
doing so may use more resources than necessary. In such a case, the person is
effective, but not efficient. (Conversely, a person could use very few resources—hence be efficient—but not be especially effective.)

"Equity," by contrast with traditional notions of "efficiency," refers to
fairness. Philosophers of jurisprudence talk about treating "like cases alike."
In other words, to be equitable means that distinctions, especially among and
between human beings, must be made according to a principle of fairness so
that people are not harmed or discriminated against based on factors such as
race, ethnicity, or gender that they cannot control. Much of modern American law involves efforts to ensure that legal standards and requirements are
equitable. But such efforts raise a key issue for mainstream economists: What
is the appropriate role of government in the marketplace? The traditional

model of capitalism—stretching back to Adam Smith's idea that an "invisible hand" guides the marketplace—champions free markets. According to this view, choosing efficacious public policy means basing decisions on the desires of consumers. The assumption is that people are self-interested rational maximizers. They may not always maximize their self-interest and they may not always act rationally because they may be mistaken in what they believe, they may have incomplete information (asymmetric information, in the economists' parlance), or transaction costs may be too high, but, to the extent possible, they attempt to maximize their self-interest in a rational manner.[48]

As long as markets do not fail owing to externalities, asymmetric information, or the presence of natural monopolies, the marketplace is seen as a more efficient barometer of what people want than any measure devised by governments. Public choice theorists such as Anthony Downs and Elinor Ostrom, for example, contend that the measures used by governments to gauge what the people want—voting results, feedback through political pluralism, public opinion polls, and so forth—are not nearly as precise as free markets for measuring what people want in public policies. People vote for many reasons, not all of which are clear. One certainly cannot determine from voting studies how people feel about specific policies, despite elected officials' claims to enjoy a mandate after they are elected to office. Pluralism—the idea that interest groups compete for political power and that this leads to compromises resulting in effective public policy—helps to discern a little of what people want, but not everyone participates in groups.[49] In fact, according to Robert Putnam's book *Bowling Alone*, group participation may be declining. People also do not follow political affairs closely, so public opinion polls are not an accurate indicator of how they feel about long-term policies. Moreover, because governments are so fragmented and policies are often complex and difficult to fathom, looking to government mechanisms for understanding the "will of the people" in the policy process is misguided.[50]

According to economists such as Weimer and Vining, the condition of markets can help determine when it is appropriate for government to intervene into the marketplace and when it is inappropriate. Weimer and Vining focus on "contestable markets," those markets where competition exists, but only among a few big, competing firms. A market is highly contestable when there is a large private supply of a good and ownership is vested in the private sector. In those cases, markets can function efficiently and government should stay out of the way. In cases where markets are not highly contestable—where supplies are low and ownership is almost wholly within the public sector—government intervention is appropriate. In other words, government should intervene when there is "market failure."[51]

According to Robert Haveman in *Economics of the Public Sector*, markets fail when there is a goal apart from efficiency in the smooth, orderly transfer of goods and services from one party to another. An example can be found in the Rural Electrification Act, a statute enacted by Congress during Franklin D. Roosevelt's administration in the 1930s. Congress and the president decided, as part of the New Deal policies, that every American should have access to electric service. The problem was that some impoverished peoples living in Appalachia could not afford to pay the market rate for electricity even if it were available. In this kind of situation, a private electric company would not have an economic incentive to invest in building an electric generation plant. This lack of a market response to a perceived need is what economists call a "market failure." In that case, the Roosevelt administration created a government corporation called the Tennessee Valley Authority (TVA). TVA built a plant that supplied electricity to poor people in that area at subsidized rates. The market failed, so government stepped in to fill the gap, as it were.[52]

Free market economists also see a role for government in leveling the playing field. Thus, Ronald Coase, a 1991 Nobel Laureate in Economics, developed a famous theorem bearing his name to explain the appropriate role of government, among other things. The Coase Theorem posits that property resources, absent transaction costs, will end up in the hands of the party that places the highest value on that resource. This phenomenon is one of the reasons that private enterprise is so efficient; people will cut a deal to acquire the resources they believe to be beneficial. When transaction costs are involved, however, this skews the process so that sometimes a party is dissuaded from acquiring a resource owing to the costs that have to be incurred in the acquisition. The role of government, according to Coase, is to intervene by adopting public policies that minimize transaction costs. For example, if railroad freight rates significantly impede the ability of buyers and sellers to transact business, government is justified in regulating freight rates through the Interstate Commerce Commission. Coase and free market economists harbor no love for the ICC or other government agencies, but they recognize that, if the agencies can help level the playing field, participants in the marketplace can be more efficient.[53]

Another problem in the marketplace occurs when externalities exist. Externalities are unintended or unforeseen consequences of individual behavior that are not factored into the decisions made by individual parties in a given transaction. Externalities can be positive, such as the benefits that accrue when someone is educated. It is difficult to know how much good will come out of a more-or-less straightforward transaction of a school instructing a pupil in exchange for tuition and/or tax monies, but the chances are good that the external benefits will extend in many ways well into the future since an educated person contributes to society in myriad ways. Externalities can be negative, too. The quintessential example is pollution. If a small amount of a hazardous air pollutant is below regulatory concern and is therefore allowed, the costs of generating the pollution do not have to be taken into consideration by an individual polluter; however, when hundreds or thousands of firms pollute, the aggregate level of pollution can lead to harmful health effects for everyone.

In cases where negative externalities exist, government generally steps in at some point and regulates those externalities. In some cases, government can impose a tax on the negative externality—a so-called "Pigouvian" tax, named for the influential Cambridge economist A. C. Pigou—or it can impose public programs to clean up the negative externality. The programs can be funded partially by private sector funds and partially through government funding. In any case, the goal is to ensure that the costs of externalities are accounted for so that the marginal social costs equal the marginal social benefits and a kind of balance is achieved.[54]

The traditional economic view of the efficiency-equity tradeoff associated with public policies and programs is certainly not a universally accepted perspective. One of the strongest critiques of this approach is offered by Deborah Stone in her book, *The Policy Paradox*. Stone views the traditional approach to public policy—which she derisively labels the "rationality project"—as seriously deficient because it assumes that a linear process exists, and this assumption is faulty. Mainstream economists and students of the policy process act as though people live independently of each other and make decisions as rational maximizers based on clearly defined goals and work through a clearly defined policy process. Stone argues that this conception of how policies are devised is simplistic.[55]

In her view, we actually live in a political community that is constantly evolving. To think that the policy process or the system of adopting public policies is somehow static and fixed with stable, ongoing issues and procedures is to mistake what happens in the policy process. As our world changes—new policies are adopted, new leaders come into power, new technologies emerge, people's interests and desires change—the process changes. The effect is that the process of adopting a policy today may or may not be the same as the process will be tomorrow. This insight is analogous to the concept of iron triangles. Political scientists used to talk about the triangular relationship among and between Congress, the bureaucracy, and outside interest groups as though this was a fixed framework. With Hugh Heclo's concept of issue networks—where relationships constantly change and alliances form and dissolve with lightning rapidity—iron triangles seem a bit antiquated.[56] Similarly, Stone's argument suggests that the notion that there is some kind of fixed, linear, unchanging relationship between efficiency and equity, on the one hand, and immutable economic principles, on the other. is simply outdated. There is an inherent paradox in any doctrine that assumes a fixed position, such as the standard economic position on efficiency and equity, because, as positions and relationships change, the idea of a fixed position must change as well.[57]

The import of Stone's thesis is that it is theoretically possible to adopt a public policy that has the potential to increase both efficiency and equity. In other words, unlike the standard economic viewpoint, which assumes that a tradeoff between efficiency and equity is unavoidable, a policy can embrace both values. To illustrate this point, consider the Clean Air Act (CAA), a major environmental law passed by Congress in 1990.[58]

CAA is one in a long line of statutes created to clean up the nation's polluted atmosphere, especially in "nonattainment" urban areas (such as Los Angeles, New York, Chicago, and Atlanta). Among its many provisions, CAA is designed as a "technology-forcing" statute, which means that it requires industries that are building new manufacturing facilities and emitting chemicals into the atmosphere to invest funds to install the latest, cutting-edge pollution control and abatement technology. Some industries have argued that a requirement forcing business to install pollution control devices is economically inefficient because it increases costs, but this argument is not necessarily true. A large percentage of Americans have indicated in a variety of public opinion polls and in many outlets that it is desirable to breathe clean, healthy air. When all pollution generating businesses are subject to the same requirement—they must meet the technology standards when they build a new plant or expand an existing facility—no one is at a competitive disadvantage when the standard is applied because it applies equally. The costs can be passed on to consumers who have already indicated a willingness to pay for cleaner air.[59]

The statute also recognizes the necessity of considering the needs of older facilities owned and operated by parties with a limited ability to pay for new pollution control devices. These facilities are subject to lesser standards. They are "grandfathered" into the law so that they need only use the technology already in place. This concept is equitable because it does not drive smaller owners out of business by making them potentially spend millions of dollars to upgrade marginal plants that probably won't be around much longer, anyway.

CAA is economically efficient because it creates a system of tradable allowances called "emissions reduction credits" (ERCs). Cleaner businesses can save up and "bank" their ERCs, selling them to businesses that cannot meet their pollution limits. This is economically efficient because it keeps the aggregate level of air pollution lower than it otherwise would have been while still allowing businesses room to operate. It also makes provision for the people and industries that have older plants and cannot afford to install the costly new pollution control devices.[60]

As Deborah Stone and the CAA illustrate, there need not be a tradeoff between efficiency and equity in every case. In an age of innovative public policy and smart technology, new approaches and concepts can be developed. There will always be tension between efficiency and equity, but there is a promise of rapprochement for those people who care to search for it.[61]

Conclusion: Evaluating Public Policy in an Ethical Manner

One of the long-standing criticisms of the policy process is that it is cumbersome, time-consuming, inefficient, and often fails to formulate and implement much-needed policies. Recognizing this deficiency, policy-makers have sought to improve the process in recent years. The focus has been on ensuring greater productivity; that is, researchers have tried to measure the relationship between the results produced and the resources required for production. With efficiency as a key measure of productivity, the concern arises as to whether equity will suffer.

In assessing his or her ethical responsibilities, a public administrator must consider three related factors: First, he or she must determine his or her role within an organization. Second, depending on the person's appropriate role—and the assumption here is that the public administrator is placed in a decision-making role near the top of the organization—he or she must decide whether the policy was formulated and implemented appropriately. Finally, the decision-maker must evaluate the policy to determine whether most or all of the policy goals were achieved. All three steps are essential to ensuring the effective use of administrative discretion in the public policy process.

A decision-maker at the top of an organization has greater responsibility for ensuring that a policy was appropriately formulated and implemented. Thus, a street-level bureaucrat cannot be expected to exercise a great deal of discretion in determining, for example, who meets eligibility criteria for governmental programs except in cases where such criteria are vague, ambiguous or non-existent. By contrast, a decision-maker near the top of the organization may have wide latitude for influencing the policy process. The ethical administrator recognizes that how he or she makes decisions and influences the policy process depends in no small measure on the nature and extent of his or her role within a public sector organization.

Assuming that the public administrator holds a position of authority within a public sector agency, the next step in the analysis is to ask whether the policy was formulated and implemented appropriately. To be judged "appropriate" means that a policy as it was formulated met the goals and objectives stated by the legislative body or other policy-making authority. Moreover, the policy must be implemented in accordance with the same goals and objectives, to the extent that the goals and objectives were reasonably clear and instructive.

If the policy was formulated and implemented pursuant to the organization's goals and objectives, the final step requires decision-makers to evaluate the effectiveness, or lack thereof, of the policy. One of the most difficult problems that public administrators face in evaluating a policy involves the problem of causality. In the context of public policy, the concern is that a policy, no matter how well-crafted and implemented, does not result in a desired effect. In short, how does a public administrator know that the policy caused a particular outcome? During the Fourth Century B.C.E., Aristotle wrote in his classic work *Metaphysics* that all things in the world have four "causes"—efficient, material, formal, and final causes, that is, the circumstances that produced it, the material of which it was composed, its structural or developmental principles, and its purpose or place in the natural scheme of things. Although Aristotle's conception of causality was abandoned long ago and most researchers would be reluctant to search antiquity for answers about causality, the ancient Greek philosopher's concern about such issues illustrates the centrality of causal questions to understanding the world.

Modern researchers have come to understand something that Aristotle did not, namely that causality is a complicated question and is not easily answered. In *Varieties of Social Explanation*, researcher Daniel Little observed that "[e]vidence of association gives us reason to believe that there is a causal relationship of some kind affecting the variables under scrutiny, but it does not establish the nature of that relation."[62] To conclude that event x "caused" event y assumes that no intervening events influenced this process or that those intervening events can be identified and controlled for in the research. In modern parlance, the researcher constructs a research design in an attempt to show that the independent variable "caused" variations in the dependent variable. This means that the researcher must try to account for all possible intervening or spurious variables so that the study has internal validity. Showing the existence of a causal relationship as well as its direction and extent are the researchers' paramount objectives.

The question of the adequacy of a research design really is the question of whether the research design is testing for the problem that the researchers think it is. A research design is a plan for answering the research question in a persuasive manner. Thus, the researcher needs to be able to conclude with a reasonable degree of certainty or authority that the hypothesis is supported or not supported by the results of the research. In a quasi-experiment involving a government program, for example, the researcher needs to show a comparison of what happened after implementing a program with what would have happened if the program had not been implemented (the counterfactual). The treatment effect would then be a measurement between the result with the program and the counterfactual.

Internal validity is the idea that the researcher can show that the independent variable "caused" changes in the dependent variable. A threat to internal validity occurs when a research design has been developed in such a way that the results of the research leave the central causality question unanswered; that is, the research does not demonstrate that the independent variable "caused" the change in the dependent variable. This is the quintessential example of an inadequate research design.

The principle of reduction to chance is one method that researchers use to resolve ambiguities about causality. The researcher needs to control for every possible cause so that only two reasonable explanations exist for the outcome: the treatment itself or chance. Because statistics can help account for chance, any researcher who can rely on the principle of reduction to chance makes a persuasive case for the treatment effect as an explanation of causality.

The principle has problems, though, including contamination or the introduction of a spurious variable, which occurs when something that has not been considered or controlled for intervenes in the research and seems to be a factor in the outcome. In other words, variation in the dependent variable may have occurred owing to variation in the independent variable or owing to variation in this uncontrolled for, spurious variable. The nature of the relationship is unclear. These factors tend to limit researchers' ability to assert causality in a research design, but they must be controlled or overcome if a researcher is to show a causal connection between the independent variable and the dependent variable.

Causality can be demonstrated, perhaps not to the satisfaction of everyone but usually to that of most people. A researcher can never guarantee certainty in demonstrating causality in a program evaluation, but he can still develop a persuasive research design. Researchers do not want to fall into the quagmire presented by the eighteenth-century Scottish philosopher David Hume. According to Hume, skepticism is the only logical response for man owing to the "narrow capacity of human understanding" in considering questions that go beyond his limited sense perception. Because man cannot objectively know concepts outside of himself with any reasonable degree of certainty, he cannot trust those concepts to guide human life. Except for mathematics and "experimental reasoning concerning matter[s] of fact and existence," everything else is "sophistry and illusion" and must be "committed to the flames," in Hume's view. Researchers need not meet such a high standard in demonstrating causality.[63]

The burden of proof for modern social science researchers is not the absolute certainty of the skeptic. Instead, it is a probability standard: All things considered and controlled for, the independent variable represented as a treatment effect probably caused the changes in the dependent variable. Such a conclusion may not be certain, but it avoids the pitfalls of solipsism and it allows the ethical decision-maker to conclude that the policy worked as intended. The ethical public administrator, therefore, is the person who seeks, based on his or her role, to understand the goals and objectives of a policy and whether the policy was formulated, implemented, and evaluated according to the original goals and objectives.

Exercises and Discussion Questions

1. Discuss one or more models of the policy process. What is the advantage of using a model to understand public policy? What concerns arise from the use of models?

2. Public policy sometimes is discussed as a process that begins with policy formulation, passes through policy implementation, and ends with policy evaluation. Explain how each stage of the process works. Do you see any problems with this "process" view of public policy? Explain.

3. Discuss the efficiency versus equity conundrum. In your opinion, can concerns about efficiency and equity be reconciled? Why or why not?

4. What steps should a public administrator take to behave in an ethical manner throughout the policy process? What role, if any, does administrative discretion play in ethics?

5. The figure in Chapter 9 labeled "The Liberty-Equality Conundrum," moves from absolute liberty on the left of the figure to absolute authority on the right of the figure. What is the purpose of the figure? That is, what information does it convey? How does the level of government control determine the ethical duties of someone working for government?

6. Discuss the three related factors that a public administrator must consider in determining his or her duties in a public agency. Can you think of other factors aside from these three? Why is an administrator's role in an organization a crucial factor in determining his or her ethical duties?

7. You are a researcher with the U.S. Food & Drug Administration (FDA). Under several provisions of federal law, drugs that are determined to cause, or contribute to, cancer cannot be used in the United States. One day your superior tells you that he has just read a journal article indicating that a popular drug used to treat diabetes already approved for sale in the United States has been found to cause tumors in certain laboratory mice in Europe. Accordingly, your superior decides that the FDA needs to pull the drug off the market. You read the journal article and believe that your superior is mistaken. The results of the study, as far as you can tell, are inconclusive. Because many European scientists use different testing standards and protocols than those used by U.S. scientists, you are not sure how valid or reliable the European testing was. In your opinion, the agency needs to undertake an exhaustive literature review on this drug to see what else has been published. Perhaps hiring a consultant to

replicate the study referenced in the journal article would be appropriate. In any case, you believe that any drastic action is premature. Your superior disagrees. "I believe in the precautionary principle," he says. "It's better to err on the side of caution. I prefer to be safe than sorry." You are worried that removing this drug from the market could seriously hurt diabetics and have no positive effect because your superior has misread the data on the drug's cancer-causing potential. What should you do if you wish to be an ethical public administrator?

a. You should do nothing. Your superior has made a decision, and you must obey your superior. Anyway, other people within the agency probably will prevent your superior from removing the drug from the market, so why make this issue your problem?

b. You should undertake an exhaustive literature review on your own. You can then present the information to your superior before the drug is removed from the market.

c. You should go above your superior's head and speak to top officials with the FDA to explain the situation.

d. You should approach key members of Congress and ask that they modify the FDA's congressional mandate by specifying in detail the steps that must be undertaken before a drug can be removed from the market.

e. You should contact U.S. scientists outside of the agency and ask them to contact the FDA with their objections to your superior's proposed course of action.

f. You should contact the pharmaceutical companies that manufacture the drug used for diabetes, alert them to the situation, and let them decide how best to proceed.

g. You should perform more than one of the actions listed above (be specific.)

Notes

[1] The phrase is taken from the title of a famous book: Harold D. Lasswell, *Politics: Who Gets What, When and How* (Gloucester, Mass.: Peter Smith, Publisher, 1990).

[2] Daniel A. Mazmanian and Paul A. Sabatier, *Implementation and Public Policy* (Lanham, Md.: University Press of America, 1989), 7-9.

3   R. Kenneth Godwin and John C. Wahlke, *Introduction to Political Science: Reason, Reflection, and Analysis* (Fort Worth, Tex.: Harcourt, Brace & Company, 1997), 242-44, 248-51.

4   Herbert Kaufman, *Red Tape: Its Origins, Uses and Abuses* (Washington, D.C.: The Brookings Institution, 1977), 43.

5   Kathryn G. Denhardt, *The Ethics of Public Service: Resolving Moral Dilemmas in Public Organizations* (Westport, Conn.: Greenwood Press, 1988), 23-27; Dennis P. Wittmer, "Ethical Decision-Making," in *Handbook of Administrative Ethics*, 2d. ed., Terry L. Cooper, ed. (New York: Marcel Dekker), 494-97.

6   James E. Anderson, *Public Policymaking: An Introduction*, 4th ed. (Boston: Houghton Mifflin, 2000), 4-5.

7   Anderson, *Public Policymaking*, 5.

8   Anderson, *Public Policymaking*, 6.

9   See, for example, Robert A. Pollak, "Imagined Risks and Cost-Benefit Analysis," *The American Economic Review* 88 (May 1998): 376-80; Barry R. Weingast, Kenneth A. Shepsle, and Christopher Johnsen, "The Political Economy of Benefits and Costs: A Neoclassical Approach to Distributive Politics," *The Journal of Political Economy* 89 (August 1981): 642-64.

10   Anderson, *Public Policymaking*, 6-7.

11   Michael D. Cohen, James G. March, and Johan P. Olsen, "A Garbage Can Model of Organizational Choice," *Administrative Science Quarterly* 17 (March 1972): 1-25; John F. Padgett, "Managing Garbage Can Hierarchies," *Administrative Science Quarterly* 25 (December 1980): 583-604.

12   Paul A. Sabatier and Hank C. Jenkins-Smith, "The Advocacy Coalition Framework," in *Theories of the Policy Process*, Paul A. Sabatier, ed. (Boulder, Colo.: Westview Press, 1999), 117-166.

13   Literature on the ACF theory is fairly extensive, and includes, for example: Brian A. Ellison, "Intergovernmental Relations and the Advocacy Coalition Framework: The Operation of Federalism in Denver Water Politics," *Publius* 28 (Fall 1998): 35-54; Menno Fenger and Pieter-Jan Klok, "Interdependency, Beliefs, and Coalition Behavior: A Contribution to the Advocacy Coalition Framework," *Policy Sciences* 34 (June 2001): 157-70; Paul A. Sabatier, "An Advocacy Coalition Framework of Policy Change and the Role of Policy-Oriented Learning Therein," *Policy Sciences* 21 (June 1988): 129-68.

14   Jon B. Gould, "Public Administration and Civil Liberties: Playing with Fire: The Civil Liberties Implications of September 11," *Public Administration Review* 62 (September 2002): 74-79; Daniel Philpott, "The Challenge of September 11 to Secularism in International Relations," *World Politics* 55 (October 2002): 66-95.

15   William DeJong and Ralph Hingson, "Strategies to Reduce Driving Under the Influence of Alcohol," *Annual Review of Public Health* 19 (May 1998): 359-78.

16   Robert M. Entman, "Framing: Toward Clarification of a Fractured Paradigm," *Journal of Communication* 43 (Fall 1993): 51-58; Deborah A. Stone, "Causal Stories and the Formation of Policy Agendas," *Political Science Quarterly* 104 (Summer 1989): 281-300; Janet A. Weiss, "The Powers of Problem Definition: The Case of Government Paperwork," *Policy Sciences* 22 (May 1989): 97-121.

[17]   Dale W. Jorgenson, "Did We Lose the War on Poverty?" *The Journal of Economic Perspectives* 12 (Winter 1998): 79-96; Randall B. Woods, *LBJ: Architect of American Ambition* (New York: The Free Press, 2006), 432-33, 587, 649-51.

[18]   Melissa P. Cole, "The Legislature and Distributive Policy Making in Formal Perspective," *Legislative Studies Quarterly* 13 (November 1988): 427-58; Morris P. Fiorina, "Legislative Choice of Regulatory Reforms: Legal Process or Administrative Process?" *Public Choice* 39 (January 1982): 33-66; Matthew C. McCubbins, Roger G. Noll, and Barry R. Weingast, "Structure and Process, Politics and Policy: Administrative Arrangements and the Political Control of Agencies," *Virginia Law Review* 75 (March 1989): 431-82.

[19]   Wallace S. Sayre, "Premises of Public Administration: Past and Emerging," *Public Administration Review* 18 (Spring 1958): 102-5; Bernard Steunenberg, "Congress, Bureaucracy, and Regulatory Policy-Making," *Journal of Law, Economics, & Organization* 8 (October 1992): 673-94.

[20]   Laurence Baum, *The Supreme Court*, 7th ed (Washington, D.C.: CQ Press, 2001), 4-6; Tracey E. George and Lee Epstein, "On the Nature of Supreme Court Decision Making," *The American Political Science Review* 86 (June 1992): 323-37; David M. O'Brien, *Storm Center: The Supreme Court in American Politics* (New York: W.W. Norton, 1986), 203-9.

[21]   347 U.S. 483 (1954).

[22]   349 U.S. 294 (1955).

[23]   Bryan D. Jones, James L. True, and Frank R. Baumgartner, "Does Incrementalism Stem from Political Consensus or from Institutional Gridlock?" *American Journal of Political Science* 41 (October 1997): 1319-39; Elizabeth Sanders, "The Contributions of Theodore Lowi to Political Analysis and Democratic Theory," *PS: Political Science & Politics* 23 (December 1990): 574-76.

[24]   See, for example, Richard Matland, "Synthesizing the Implementation Literature: The Ambiguity-Conflict Model of Policy Implementation," *Journal of Public Administration Research and Theory* 5 (April 1995): 145-74; Mazmanian and Sabatier, *Implementation and Public Policy*, 18-43; Jeffrey L. Pressman and Aaron Wildavsky, *Implementation* (Berkeley: University of California Press, 1973); Walter Williams, *The Implementation Perspective: A Guide for Managing Social Service Delivery Programs* (Los Angeles: University of California Press, 1980).

[25]   Peter de Leon and Linda de Leon, "What Ever Happened to Policy Implementation? An Alternative Approach," *Journal of Public Administration Research & Theory* 12 (October 2002): 467-92; Benny Hjern, "Implementation Research—The Link Gone Missing," *Journal of Public Policy* 2 (August 1982): 301-8; Michael Lipsky, "Standing the Study of Public Policy Implementation on Its Head," in *American Politics and Public Policy*, Walter Dean Burnham and Martha Weinberg, eds. (Cambridge, Mass.: MIT Press, 1978), 391-402.

[26]   Edward P. Weber, *Pluralism by the Rules: Conflict and Cooperation in Environmental Regulation* (Washington, D.C.: Georgetown University Press, 1998).

[27]   Paul Pierson, "When Effect Becomes Cause: Policy Feedback and Political Change," *World Politics* 45 (July 1993): 595-628; Peter Van der Knaap, "Policy Evaluation and

Learning: Feedback, Enlightenment, or Argumentation?" *Evaluation: The International Journal of Theory, Research and Practice* 1 (April 1995): 189-216.

28	Lawrence B. Mohr, *Impact Analysis for Program Evaluation*, 2d. ed. (Thousand Oaks, Calif.: Sage Publications, 1995), 65-74.

29	Mohr, *Impact Analysis for Program Evaluation*, 185-86; Carol H. Weiss, *Evaluation*, 2d. ed. (Upper Saddle River, N.J.: Prentice Hall, 1998), 196-99.

30	Lisa Eckenwiler, "Moral Reasoning and the Review of Research Involving Human Subjects," *Kennedy Institute of Ethics Journal* 11 (March 2001): 37-69; Harold Edgar and David J. Rothman, "The Institutional Review Board and Beyond: Future Challenges to the Ethics of Human Experimentation," *The Milbank Quarterly* 73, 4 (1995): 489-506.

31	Theodore J. Lowi, "Four Systems of Policy, Politics, and Choice," *Public Administration Review* 32 (July-August 1972): 298-310; W. E. Lyons and David Lowery, "Governmental Fragmentation versus Consolidation: Five Public-Choice Myths About How to Create Informed, Involved, and Happy Citizens," *Public Administration Review* 49 (November-December 1989): 533-43.

32	Beryl A. Radin and Joan Price Boase, "Federalism, Political Structure, and Public Policy in the United States and Canada," *Journal of Comparative Policy Analysis* 2 (April 2000): 65-89; Mark Schneider, "Fragmentation and the Growth of Local Government," *Public Choice* 48 (January 1986): 255-63.

33	Anne Schneider and Helen Ingram, "Social Construction of Target Populations: Implications for Politics and Policy," *American Political Science Review* 87 (June 1993): 334-47.

34	Richard Stillman II, *American Bureaucracy: The Core of Modern Government*, 3d. ed. (Belmont, Calif.: Wadsworth/Thomson, 2004), 71,73.

35	Steven G. Anderson and Brian M. Gryzlak, "Social Work Advocacy in the Post-TANF Environment: Lessons From Early TANF Research Studies," *Social Work* 47 (July 2002): 301-14.

36	Michael E. Milakovich and George J. Gordon, *Public Administration in America* (Belmont, Calif.: Wadsworth/ Thomson, 2004), 398-99.

37	J. Michael Martinez, "Law Versus Ethics: Reconciling Two Concepts of Public Service Ethics," *Administration & Society* 29 (January 1998), 690-722; Milakovich and Gordon, *Public Administration in America*, 399.

38	Milakovich and Gordon, *Public Administration in America*, 399.

39	Sudhir Anand and Kara Hanson, "DALYs: Efficiency Versus Equity," *World Development* 26 (February 1998): 307-10.

40	Thomas Hobbes, *Leviathan* (Indianapolis: Bobbs-Merrill, 1958), 107.

41	Alexander Hamilton, James Madison, and John Jay, *The Federalist Papers*, Clinton Rossiter, ed. (New York: New American Library, 1961), 78.

42	Frank Donovan, *Mr. Madison's Constitution: The Story Behind the Constitutional Convention* (New York: Dodd Mead & Company, 1965), 10-12; Merrill Jensen, *The Articles of Confederation: An Interpretation of the Social-Constitutional History of the American Revolution, 1774-1781* (Madison: The University of Wisconsin Press, 1940), 244.

43	G. D. H. Cole, *Fabian Socialism* (Oxford: Routledge, 1971); Jim Tomlinson, "The Limits of Tawney's Ethical Socialism: A Historical Perspective on the Labour Party and Market," *Contemporary British History* 16 (Winter 2002): 1-16.

44   Morton Grodzins, "The Federal System," in *Classic Readings in American Politics*, 2d. ed., Pietro S. Nivola and David H. Rosenbloom, eds. (New York: St. Martin's Press, 1990), 61-77; John P. Roche, "The Founding Fathers: A Reform Caucus in Action," in *American Government: Readings and Cases*, 3d. ed., Peter Woll, ed. (Boston: Little, Brown & Company, 1969), 55-78; Fred Rodell, *Fifty-Five Men* (New York: The Telegraph Press, 1936).

45   John Stuart Mill, *On Liberty* (Arlington Heights, Ill.: AHM Publishing, 1947), 9-11.

46   See, for example, Milton Friedman, *Capitalism and Freedom* (Chicago, IL: University of Chicago Press, 1962).

47   See, for example, Irving Kristol, *Reflections of a Neoconservative: Looking Back, Looking Ahead* (New York: Basic Books, 1983); Robert Nozick, *Anarchy, State, and Utopia* (New York: Basic Books, 1974).

48   Anand and Hanson, "DALYs: Efficiency Versus Equity," 307-10.

49   See, for example, Anthony Downs, *An Economic Theory of Democracy* (New York: Harper & Rowe, 1957); Elinor Ostrom, *Governing the Commons: The Evolution of Institutions for Collective Action* (New York: Cambridge University Press, 1991).

50   Robert Putnam, *Bowling Alone: The Collapse and Revival of American Community* (New York: Simon & Schuster, 2000).

51   David L. Weimer and Aidan R. Vining, *Policy Analysis: Concepts and Practice*, 2d. ed. (Englewood Cliffs, N.J.: 1992).

52   Robert H. Haveman, *Economics of the Public Sector* (Santa Barbara, Calif.: Wiley, 1976).

53   Ronald H. Coase, "The Institutional Structure of Production," *The American Economic Review* 82 (September 1992): 713-19; Joseph Farrell, "Information and the Coase Theorem," *The Journal of Economic Perspectives* 1 (Autumn 1987): 113-29.

54   James Andreoni, "Warm-Glow Versus Cold-Pickle: The Effects of Positive and Negative Framing on Cooperation in Experiments," *The Quarterly Journal of Economics* 110 (February 1995): 1-21; A. H. Barnett, "The Pigouvian Tax Rule Under Monopoly," *The American Economic Review* 70 (December 1980): 1037-41.

55   Deborah Stone, *Policy Paradox: The Art of Political Decision Making*, Revised Edition (New York: W. W. Norton, 2002): 376-83.

56   Hugh Heclo, "Issue Networks and the Executive Establishment," in *The New American Political System*, Anthony King, ed. (Washington, D.C.: American Enterprise Institute, 1978), chapter 3.

57   Stone, *Policy Paradox*, 412-14.

58   Dale W. Jorgenson, Peter J. Wilcoxen, "Environmental Regulation and U.S. Economic Growth," *The RAND Journal of Economics* 21 (Summer 1990): 314-40; United States Environmental Protection Agency, Office of Air & Radiation, *The Benefits and Costs of the Clean Air Act, 1970 to 1990* (Washington, D.C.: Government Printing Office, 1997).

59   Jorgenson and Wilcoxen, "Environmental Regulation and U.S. Economic Growth," 314-18.

60   Scott Lee Johnson and David M. Pekelney, "Economic Assessment of the Regional Clean Air Incentives Market: A New Emissions Trading Program for Los Angeles," *Land Economics* 72 (August 1996): 277-97.

61   Stone, *Policy Paradox*, 80-85.

[62]   Daniel Little, Varieties of Social Explanation: An Introduction to the Philosophy of Social Science (Boulder, Colo.: Westview Press, 1991), 22.

[63]   David Hume, *An Enquiry Concerning Human Understanding* (Indianapolis: Hackett Publishing, 1977), 112-14.

PART FIVE:
CONCLUSION

Chapter Ten
The Future of Public Administration and Ethical Implications

Ethics, or "right conduct," is an exceedingly difficult topic to explore owing to the many facets of the issue, as this text has attempted to make clear. Unlike other disciplines or courses of study, ethics, especially as it relates to the public sector in the United States, does not have an agreed-upon, uncontested set of propositions or theories that serve as the central tenets of the subject, although some general theories, concepts, and approaches can be suggested. Engineering, medicine, and law, by contrast, represent a more-or-less agreed-upon body of knowledge that can be researched and taught with a level of precision and specificity absent from, or at least not readily apparent in, the study of ethics.

Nonetheless, despite the inherent difficulties in identifying core ethical precepts and applying them, the purpose of this text has been to review and discuss ethical challenges confronting public sector employees and the tools that have been used to meet these challenges in the past. To that end, the authors have divided each of the preceding chapters into topics related to the study of American public administration. The text begins with overviews of ethical theory in the western intellectual tradition and the quest for administrative legitimacy and moves to specific topics such as the source and uses of bureaucratic power, bureaucratic decision-making processes and organizational theory as well as administrative law, public personnel management, governmental budgeting, and public policy and management.

The study of administrative ethics has been a separate subject of serious scholarly inquiry only since the 1970s, when many public administrators, as well as members of the public, were concerned about abuses of power in the wake of the Watergate scandal. Since that time, researchers have produced a large, richly-nuanced body of literature on administrative ethics. Although much of the literature has focused on "crude wrongdoing" and strategies for combating corruption—hardly surprising in light of well-publicized stories about public officials' malfeasance—in recent years the focus has shifted to a concern over the use of administrative discretion.[1]

At first blush, the use of administrative discretion would seem to be a relatively straightforward issue and a far cry from corruption and illegality. Assuming for the sake of argument that corruption is an exception to the rule that most public servants are well-meaning men and women who seek to follow the law and adhere to the core mission of their respective organizations, discretion becomes an important component of administrative ethics. Rather than focusing time and attention on discouraging corruption in the comparatively few instances in which public servants are corrupt, this new understanding of administrative ethics emphasizes the vast majority of situations in which a public servant, faced with a problem where no clear-cut law, rule, or organizational norm directly applies, desires assistance in making the "right" decision. This broadened perspective on administrative ethics does not discount the importance of combating corruption; instead, it highlights the need to furnish public servants with tools for performing their work in the "public interest," however that term is interpreted. Among other things, the study of administrative ethics requires researchers to explore the ideas and concepts that shape our understanding of the public interest.

Determining an appropriate use of discretion highlights a crucial issue, namely the tension between the philosophical abstractions, or values, underlying a regime and the need for public administrators to respond to concrete situations while equitably applying those values. In the words of H. George Frederickson and Jeremy David Walling, "Ethics will search for right and wrong while administration must get the job done. Ethics is abstract while the practices of administration are irremediably concrete"[2] Frederickson and Walling raise a key point; combining the theory and practice of policy implementation remains problematic because major differences exist between the world of the academic researcher and the world of the practitioner. To address this difficulty, to some extent, this text reviews a variety of substantive subfields within the larger field of public administration to determine how administrative ethics has been applied in a complex, fragmented political system comprised of many disparate public agencies. The text relies on examples mostly culled from public agencies at the federal level to avoid myriad differences among and between the 50 states and approximately 86,000 local governments currently operating in the United States, but a majority of the discussions and insights can, and do, apply across all levels of government.

To understand the richness and detail of ethics, broadly defined, the text begins in Chapter 1 with a review of ethical theory as it was understood by the ancient Greeks, who stressed the importance of character and virtue as cornerstones of an ethical regime. "Virtue" is a term pregnant with many meanings today, including a nuance, dating from the Victorian era, related to the term "pregnant." For the ancient Greeks, however, "virtue" referred to citizens' public spiritedness, which presumably will lead to the voluntary performance of actions beneficial to the regime. By "virtue," the Greeks referred to the "firmness, courage, endurance, industry, frugal living, strength, and, above all, unremitting devotion to the weal of the public's corporate self, the community of virtuous men."[3] Because a regime was only as good as the individuals who comprised it, the Greeks believed that government service, and the resultant ethical behavior of government servants, must be predicated on the inherently noble qualities of people, which could be nurtured through education and habituation.[4]

The Greek perspective seems hopelessly antiquated to us today. They were concerned with ethics as the concept related to individuals, with little or no regard for the structural component of ethics. Modern ethics, however, recognizes a moral distance between individuals and the institutions with which they interact. It seems axiomatic in the twenty-first century that a problem might arise between a public administrator's private ethical values and the organization or public agency that employs the individual. Not so for the ancient Greeks. In their view, the polity was not a separate, albeit fictional, entity existing in a separate moral universe from individuals. The polity was a collection of individuals that took on, collectively, the virtues and vices of the individuals inside the polity. As such, the Greeks believed that an ethical individual would join together with other ethical individuals and govern the regime accordingly. The reason why proper education and habituation were so crucial was because they pushed individuals to be virtuous, and virtuous individuals lead to, in essence, a virtuous government.

The Greeks provided a starting place for a discussion of public sector ethics, hence their inclusion in this text; however, over time this understanding evolved and broadened so that individual attributes and behaviors were not the only considerations in the study of ethics. In American public administration, especially, structural questions became as important as exploring individual ethical precepts. Institutional controls such as strict codes of ethics and legalized enforcement procedures combine concerns for individual ethical behavior with the realization that organizations have a dynamic separate and apart from individuals. In short, in the modern era, ethics involved not only individual behavior but also broader, structural issues. Twenty-first century theorists now seek to encourage ethical behavior by providing an institutional framework for exercising discretion in public service. Much of this text has been devoted to tracing this journey from early attempts to build individuals of good character to modern efforts at designing structural controls to encourage right conduct.

The framework of modern administrative ethics suggests that an ethical public administrator will confront a variety of issues requiring the use of administrative discretion in one or more areas of public administration. Unfortunately, administrative discretion may be antithetical to democracy because formal checks and balances do not always exist to ensure that decisions relying on discretion are made in accordance with the values of the republic. To use discretion in a responsible manner, a public administrator should understand his or her role in an organization, the goals and objectives of the organization, and the ethical dilemmas potentially arising in each area.[5]

Compounding the difficulties in determining administrative ethics is the state of the public administration field at the dawn of the twenty-first century. Public administration is a field that, in some sense, is in crisis. Because what constitutes "public administration" is far from a settled issue, discerning the appropriate nature and scope of administrative ethics is not always clear. Rather than directly addressing a contentious issue about the parameters of the field—which is itself the subject for a stand-alone book—*Administrative Ethics in the Twenty-first Century* focuses on the subfields generally recognized as integral to the study of American public administration. Scholars can, and do, disagree on which subfields should be studied or perhaps combined with other subfields—or whether public administration qualifies as a field in the first place—but distinctions had to be made and conclusions drawn. In this text, the authors address ethical issues in the subfields familiar to most students of American public administration, especially as it relates to the federal executive branch bureaucracy.[6]

Although the first chapter does not strictly apply to public administration, it is a general grounding in the concept of ethics as it has developed over hundreds of years. As the chapter suggests, ethics began as a philosophical inquiry with few practical rules or specific guidelines for practicing what ethical theorists taught. Moreover, the original assumptions were based on ethics as an absolute standard of right or wrong. Over time, this outlook was modified. Ethicists focused on providing specific examples of what constituted right and wrong even as the concept of an absolute standard came under attack. By the time the postmodernists took to the field, the question of whether ethical precepts existed apart from an artificial societal construct was an open question. In some sense, therefore, the crisis in modern American public administration mirrors the crisis in modern philosophy, namely, the loss of a clear, incontrovertible, immutable standard for deciding value-laden questions.[7]

Just as a trek through western ethical theory is a search for legitimacy, or "rightfulness," so, too, is the quest for bureaucratic justification. The text addresses the question of whether a bureaucracy can be grounded in something other than "might makes right" in the context of American government and the rise of the administrative state. In a direct democracy, legitimacy is bestowed by the people who come together to participate in decision-making. The give-and-take of debate ensures that all, or almost all, views are considered side-by-side. A republican form of government presents a separate set of problems because the participants in government decision-making are a step removed from the people they represent. Somewhere between determining the will of the electorate (to the extent that the will can be determined) and representing that will lies a measure of discretion. In the case of elected officials, they can be removed at the next election if the electorate believes that its will has been ignored, subverted, or misrepresented. This corrective action is not available when an unelected bureaucracy is involved. In some ways, the ethical challenge for public administrators is heightened by the lack of direct accountability to the electorate. American government clearly needs a class of public servants that functions based on technical competence and expertise, which allows decisions to be made based on sound, valid, reliable data. However, unelected experts potentially undermine a republican government because their use of discretion cannot be directly checked by citizens.[8]

Chapters 2, 3, and 4 move from the broad concept of ethics generally to administrative ethics as the concept is understood in the context of American public administration. Instead of addressing questions of individual character and virtue—although those questions remain important—these chapters examine the institutional context in which public servants act. Accordingly, much of Chapter 2 focuses on how the notion of administrative ethics in the United States has evolved over time and the related quest to ensure that the unelected bureaucracy is politically defensible and compatible with the democratic regime. Building on that knowledge base, Chapter 3 explores the political, legal, and managerial contexts in which public sector employees exercise power and are held accountable in U.S. public agencies. Chapter 4 addresses the ways in which public employees engage in decision-making inside their respective public agencies and the role of ethics in bureaucratic decision-making.

Taken broadly, these chapters illustrate the difficulties inherent in moving away from individual notions of ethics toward a broader emphasis on institutions. It is not difficult to understand how ethical precepts apply to private individuals acting in a private capacity since accountability is straightforward. Except in rare cases when an individual was acting under duress, mental illness, or diminished capacity, he or she will be held accountable for his or her actions. By contrast, an individual acting as a public employee in an official public capacity must consider a variety of factors apart from personal predilections in making choices. The potential conflict between an individual's desires and his or her duties to the agency and to the public can raise many ethical problems, and the nature of such a conflict complicates administrative ethics. To explicate the potential conflicts, chapters 5-9 delve into the differences between individual ethical considerations and a public servant's duties acting as a representative of a public organization in several subfields of American public administration.

It was not always clear that public administrators would face potentially intractable ethical questions. During the early years of public administration theory, the notion that bureaucrats exercised discretion was not deemed to be a serious problem; therefore, questions about the appropriate use of discretion were absent from public debate. Woodrow Wilson, in "The Study of Administration,"argues for the separation of politics and administration, contending that administrators should implement policy in accordance with rules that ensure a neutral competence with no regard for the individual administrator's private sense of ethics. In essence, according to Wilson, a public administrator is an automaton or technocrat whose duty is to fulfill the legislative mandate to the greatest extent possible. There is no room for discretion as long as elected officials clearly articulate the policy and exercise an oversight function.[9] This axiom was later challenged, but virtually every proponent of the Orthodox School of public administration took it on faith that the key issue in public administration was not a concern about how administrators might change policies through the use of bureaucratic discretion, but, rather, how the institutions of the bureaucracy—public agencies—could implement legislative policies efficiently and effectively.[10]

The problem, of course, is that elected officials do not always articulate clear policies or, for that matter, oversee public administrators effectively. In some cases, elected officials must bargain, negotiate, and compromise to shepherd a bill through the legislative process. To ensure the greatest possible support and buy-in from other legislators, an elected official has an incentive to push through vague, incomplete, or ambiguous policies that are open to multiple, often conflicting, interpretations. (No wonder Otto von Bismarck, a Prussian warrior not otherwise noted for his sense of humor, opined that people sleep better if they do not know how laws and sausage are made.) Later, if a particular policy proves to be popular after it has been implemented, the elected official can insist that the credit is his; the public administrators who put the policy into place were merely carrying out legislative intent. Conversely, if the policy proves to be unpopular, the elected official can argue that his great idea was changed by out-of-control, unelected officials whose budgets must be slashed. This is the dreaded phenomenon of "bureaucrat bashing." One reason decision-making receives such attention in Chapter 4—indeed, throughout the public administration literature—is because researchers today realize how important the decision-making process is for the ethical public administrator.[11]

Agencies themselves do not always have clear, well-developed goals, as Chapter 5 suggests; this lack of an adequate goal presents a crucial problem for administrative ethics. If the legislative body that theoretically oversees an agency does not articulate well-developed goals and if the agency itself fails to provide suitable guidance from the upper echelon, it falls to administrators at other levels of the agency to determine how the agency operates. It is true that administrators do not act in a vacuum—they can look to agency traditions, organizational culture, and other behavioral norms—but the key insight is that they must rely on informal processes in exercising authority and making decisions. Harold Seidman pointed out in *Politics, Position, and Power* in 1970 that certain public programs may be the result of several overlapping, perhaps conflicting, goals. He cited programs in the U.S. Department of Agriculture—especially the Food Stamp program—as examples. What, exactly, is the goal of, say, a program providing agricultural subsidies for farmers? Is it to help farmers, the economy as a whole, or consumers who want prices stabilized? Maybe the powerful legislator who championed the program simply wants to be politically popular and win reelection. Probably it is a combination of all these goals.[12] In any case, whatever the original legislative goal may have been, it falls to public administrators to interpret the goal and act appropriately.

Aside from the issue of discretion, public administrators sometimes look to the law for guidance in exercising discretion. As the book details in Chapter 6, since Congress, a law-making body, enacts statutes that provide authority to administrative agencies, statutory law may provide guidance. One of the hallmarks of a positivist legal system, as opposed to a system of ethics, is its rigorous search for specific instances in which the law applies as well as instances in which it does not. Unlike abstract philosophical principles that need not consider the vagaries of the world, law as it is promulgated by an authoritative governmental body is designed to apply to real-world situations. If a public servant facing an ethical conundrum could search the law and locate similar situations in which an analogous situation had been resolved, it would be relatively easy to decide the case by referring to the legal precedent, whether or not such a reference was required. In some cases, this reference to legal standards may be useful but in other cases the law may be too vague or ambiguous to provide much assistance. The law may assist public servants in clarifying a possible range of desirable outcomes, but probably the ethical conundrum will still exist in many instances. Legal standards categorize behaviors into classes that may or may not lend themselves to resolving ethical questions, which often are context-specific, vague, and not necessarily amenable to legal categorization.

Law, for all of its precision, is not a substitute for a privately developed system of ethics, nor can laws or lawmakers anticipate all context-specific issues that will occur at some later time. For example, Article I, Section 1, of the U.S. Constitution provides, among other things, that "All legislative Powers herein granted shall be vested in a Congress of the United States." This section vests extensive (though, tellingly, not all) legislative authority in the Congress of the United States. Congress legislates on so many issues that affect American life that such a small institution cannot possibly expect to develop expertise in every substantive area. Accordingly, Congress has legitimate policy reasons for delegating authority to federal agencies—if it provides sufficient guidance and retains oversight authority, that is, an "intelligible principle."[13]

To ensure that the technical issues under congressional control are resolved effectively, Congress has developed a doctrine—the Delegation Doctrine—that allows administrative agencies to handle the details necessary to implement a particular policy. The difficulty arises when the congressional delegation of authority is overly broad, vague, or ambiguous. For a variety of reasons—inattention, a crowded agenda, a lack of the necessary expertise, reluctance to take action on unpopular issues in an election year, and so forth—Congress may not provide the necessary guidance.[14]

The Delegation Doctrine has not been much of an issue in recent years because the Supreme Court generally is reluctant to substitute its judgment for the judgment of agency officials except in egregious cases when public administrators are authorized to use discretion with little congressional guidance or oversight. Even when elected officials desire to exercise a meaningful oversight role over the bureaucracy and the goals of the agency are generally clear, the task can prove to be difficult, especially in substantive areas where the issues are technical or extremely complex. It can become tantamount to the tail wagging the dog when a generalist (the legislator) must oversee and direct the specialist (the public administrator). Elected officials often serve as jacks-of-all-trades, masters of none. They are confronted with hundreds, perhaps thousands, of issues. Thus, they tend to know a little bit about a lot of issues, but their expertise in any one issue is limited. In the meantime, public administrators tend to be experts in one or two specialized areas, an enormous advantage when dealing with less-informed legislators.[15]

It should come as no surprise that when a legislator is called upon to question why an administrator reached a certain conclusion, the legislator can quickly become lost in a complex maze of facts, figures, and expert opinion. Moreover, there is generally little political benefit for the legislator to spend a great deal of time overseeing technical matters when he needs to be raising money for the campaign and trying to maintain his visibility to voters through media appearances and interviews. As a result, in many cases, public administrators are left with little or no guidance or oversight by legislators. Political scientist Theodore Lowi once labeled the propensity of legislative bodies to turn over more and more authority for what are essentially political decisions to unelected officials as "legiscide." The legislature guts itself and places a great deal of political power out of the hands of elected officials who are directly accountable to the people through the electoral process and into the hands of unelected experts who are protected by the civil service.[16]

Assuming that bureaucratic discretion is a reality—and most mainstream public administration theorists in the twenty-first century accept this premise as accurate—the question of accountability is pushed front and center. Orthodox theorists did not have to worry about discretion because discretion was not an issue. An elected official in the world of Orthodox public administration did not worry that a public administrator would exercise discretion when the bureaucracy was functioning correctly.[17]

With the death of Orthodoxy comes the unheralded birth of bureaucratic discretion, and this is an area where ethical considerations are crucial. In this brave new world, public administration researchers must explain how and why a public administrator exercises bureaucratic discretion. Absent such an explanation, bureaucracy appears to contravene democracy because it removes political power from the *demoi* (people) and places it with "experts." The legitimacy of public administration becomes suspect.

The question of legitimacy has two components: First, how does a public servant act to uphold the standards of a democratic regime? Second, assuming a public servant attempts to act pursuant to the legislative will, what is the relationship between elected and unelected public servants? As to the first point, the ethical use of bureaucratic discretion requires that a public administrator separate personal feelings from his or her role within a public organization when and if a conflict exists. This bifurcation of the administrator's personal opinions and professional duties theoretically ensures that rules and regulations promulgated within the agency or through instructions from a legislative body are not subject to the whims of individuals. While a particular individual may feel uncomfortable divorcing his or her individual feelings from the role he or she plays as a public servant, society benefits from this division. Social institutions within a democratic regime are designed so that individuals who interact with those institutions promote social values. If an individual working within an institutional setting decides to promote his or her personal values above the values of the institution, this circumvents the democratic process.

Recognizing that private opinions and public duties may conflict is not tantamount to saying that an ethical public administrator must blindly follow the rules. Because rational human beings frequently make decisions based on a variety of factors, including a sense of morality which they might be hard-pressed to articulate, it is questionable whether public servants can satisfactorily and consistently divorce their private and public selves, even if this act is considered a desirable component of their role morality. By creating a "moral distance" between "ordinary morality" and a person's professional duties, the "moral universe" of a public administrator is diminished unless the administrator recognizes that his or her role requires strict adherence to rules *except* in rare, egregious cases where the rules are obsolete, clearly mistaken, inapplicable, or irrelevant.

A concern for democratic theory means that in most cases a public servant will not substitute his or her judgment for the judgment of others who developed a rule. Assuming that a public administrator conscientiously seeks to implement a rule in accordance with, for example, the expressed desires of an elected official, the nature of the relationship between elected and unelected public servants does not become problematic. One obvious attempt to explain the relationship is to analyze the nexus between elected officials and unelected public administrators using principal-agent theory, which posits that the principal—that is, the elected official, the decision-maker—develops the goal and communicates that goal to the agent, the public administrator. The details of implementation are left to the discretion of the agent, but that individual must not exceed his authority or countermand the principal. This explanation initially sounds promising, but on reflection it smacks of exactly the sort of politics-administration dichotomy embraced by the Orthodox School.

The problem with principal-agent theory, according to an article published by Richard Waterman and Kenneth J. Meier in the *Journal of Public Administration Research & Theory* in 1998, is that the particular features of the principal-agent relationship are not well-explicated.[18] Some theorists, such as Charles Perrow, have tried to compare it to a market model so that the principal (the elected official) is a seller and the agent (the public administrator) is a buyer.[19] Other theorists, generally lawyers and legal scholars, have likened the relationship to the fiduciary obligation that a trustee has to protect the money of a person who cannot make decisions on his or her own behalf. Although all of these efforts are admirable, they still leave many unanswered questions in principal-agent theory.[20] Terry Moe has termed this the "black box" problem. Somehow, the process between policy formulation at the legislative level and policy implementation at the executive-branch agency level travels into in a black box where it magically emerges as a fully realized and implemented policy. The question of how the black box works is never fully explained.[21]

Related to the connection between elected and unelected officials is the question of how unelected officials come to hold their positions of authority in the first place. Chapter 7 of this text examines ethical issues that arise when public administrators seek to hire, train, promote, and retain employees. The primary difficulty in public personnel management occurs in defining "merit." Throughout the ages, the merit principle has evolved. In some instances, the principle refers to loyalty to the regime currently in power and at other times it refers to a system of government administration based on neutral competence. The definition of "merit" holds enormous repercussions for ethics because a public administrator who seeks to uphold the merit principle in personnel management must understand what merit requires. Is "merit" first and foremost loyalty? If so, to whom or what is loyalty owed—a person, an institution, or an abstract concept such as "truth," "justice," or "democracy"? If loyalty is not the paramount consideration, is "merit" defined as "competence"? Again, what does "competence" mean and how is it recognized and tested? The problem of merit is a fundamental component of public personnel management and, as the chapter makes clear, a frequently contested, highly contentious concept.[22]

Chapter 8 is devoted to a discussion of public budgeting. Finance is certainly an area where malfeasance can occur and obviously the temptation to engage in fraud or financial improprieties is great when access to funding is provided. Even more to the point is the question of how discretion is used in financial matters. Few areas of public agency management are as potentially problematic as public budgeting. Budgeting professionals may encounter episodes when they can choose how to allocate funds for a variety of public projects. They may be restricted by statutory or programmatic requirements, but in those instances in which discretion allows for choices among allocations the ethical public administrator is well-advised to spend wisely and in accordance with the public interest. Determining the public interest may be a matter of judgment, but an administrator who appreciates the objectives of the agency and its mission to serve the public should be able to discern, to some extent, an appropriate allocation formula.[23]

As discussed in Chapter 9, theorists in the area of public policy studies have contributed an enormous amount of literature during the last quarter of a century. One classic in this field is the study of the Economic Development Administration (EDA) in Oakland, California, published by Jeffrey Pressman and Aaron Wildavsky in 1973. The book traces the problems that occurred when a policy for revitalizing Oakland's sagging economy was developed from the top (in Washington, D.C.) and passed down the hierarchy to Oakland (the bottom). EDA failed, according to Pressman and Wildavsky, because such Top-Down policies often fail to account for changes along the way as public administrators use their discretion.[24] Many other scholars of the Top-Down approach to policy implementation—chief among them Daniel Mazmanian and Paul Sabatier as well as Stephen Linder and B. Guy Peters—have reached similar conclusions. A new and growing branch of implementation studies has arisen in response to the failures of Top-Down management.[25] Labeled the Bottom-Up approach and championed by theorists such as Benny Hjern and Michael Lipsky, these studies look at the ways in which public administrators at the lowest levels within an agency—which Lipsky famously calls "street-level" bureaucrats—influence public policy.[26]

All of these efforts are well and good, but they tend to beg the question of how and why public administrators exercise discretion. Should administrators be policed through external mechanisms, just as Herman Finer argued, or do internal controls provide the best check on behavior, as Carl J. Friedrich suggested?[27] In his classic book *The Responsible Administrator*, Terry L. Cooper writes that a combination of approaches works best. Cooper argues that, to the extent possible, public administrators must look to the guidelines set forth by their respective agencies to determine an appropriate course of action. In all but a handful of cases, the existing rules and procedures already in place—external controls—within an agency will guide the administrator in an appropriate exercise of discretion. In those rare occasions when the rules are silent or ambiguous, Cooper suggests, the individual administrator must fall back on his or her sense of propriety. This is what Friedrich meant by "internal controls." Public administrators behave the way they do because they have bought into an agency's goals and mission, for the most part, but if the agency has no clearly stated goals or mission or, worse, if the agency is violating those goals and mission, the ultimate internal check on bureaucratic power is the individual "responsible administrator" who speaks out. In egregious cases, the administrator must go public and become a whistleblower (though such cases are rare).[28]

Another possible means by which bureaucratic discretion can be reconciled with democratic accountability is advocated by proponents of refounding public administration. They seek to ground public administration in the U.S. Constitution. In other words, administrators must become familiar with the history and tradition of the Constitution and the presuppositions of the American Founders. After they are educated in these matters, they can use their discretion wisely because they will know what a democratic society requires, and act accordingly. In *Big Democracy*, Paul Appleby cautioned that the key issue for public administration ethics does not involve the question of corruption. While that is obviously important, it is overshadowed by the far greater question of determining a public administrator's duty in a democratic regime—a duty that clearly requires the use of discretion in order for it to be fulfilled. John Rohr raised a similar point in *Ethics for Bureaucrats.*[29]

Some theorists point to the idea of representative bureaucracy and suggest that because elites tend to make up the ranks of elected officials while "average, everyday people" are employed in public agencies, especially in the lower levels of sub-federal agencies, the bureaucracy actually is more representative of the demographics of the general population than legislative bodies. The assumption is that when the demographic characteristics of an organization reflect the demographic characteristics of society as a whole, the people who work within the organization will better reflect the will of the people—their constituents, if you will. One note of caution is in order. Although it may be true that bureaucracy resembles the makeup of the general population, this fact does not necessarily translate into more efficacious public policy. Even if it did translate, there is some question as to whether public agencies should provide services based on demographic characteristics.[30]

How, then, can the reality of bureaucratic discretion be reconciled with the need for democratic accountability? How can we avoid Lowi's "legiscide" and ensure that public administrators exercise discretion in accordance with the values of a democratic regime? The Founders believed that citizens of a democratic polity must be eternally vigilant. Vigilance requires education. As virtually all of the theorists referenced in this book have discussed, educating citizens about civic virtue is crucial. Informed citizens may not only select better elected officials, they may also make better public administrators as they become better consumers of government services.

The issue of bureaucratic discretion and its potential damage to democratic accountability will remain a problem for public administration. It is a perennial issue that is unlikely to be fully resolved. For that reason, it must be continually addressed by practitioners, scholars, and students of public administration. To the extent that generalizations can be made, an ethical public administrator seeks to understand the goals of the organization and its place within a republican form of government. In most cases a public sector organization will adopt goals compatible with the goals of the republic but, in those cases where the goals are antithetical, the public administrator must recognize that accountability, due process, and the need for a participatory government are the appropriate goals around which the practice of public administration should be formed. The ultimate objective is to transcend the base needs and desires of private and special interests to embrace higher and broader public interests.

As this book discusses throughout various chapters, the practice of ethical public administration is complicated by various factors inherent in the American political system. The fragmented nature of power at all levels of government, the virtual autonomy of many government agencies, the substitution of specialist authority over generalist authority, and the encroachment of professional norms of behavior on administrative discretion make it difficult even to recognize a public administrator's duty, much less act on it. John Rohr recommends that public administrators discern "regime values" by reading cases decided by the U.S. Supreme Court. Although Rohr's approach is not the only source for determining an appropriate standard of conduct for the ethical public administrator, it represents a crucial insight, namely, the need to educate public administrators in the appropriate ethical values for public service.[31]

In light of the difficulties identified in this text, the task for the ethical public administrator today is seen as two-fold: An individual ethical role and an organizational, or structural, ethical role. In the former, a public administrator must independently examine and question the standards by which administrative decisions are made. The administrator must be ready to adapt to the decisions made within an organization with the understanding that the core values of a democratic society supercede the rules or norms of a particular agency. Moreover, the public administrator must recognize that he or she will be held personally and professionally accountable for the decisions made in accordance with ethical standards that apply to his or her situation.

As for an organizational role, the thought process is similar except that the public administrator's organizational boundaries are deemed important indicators of what constitutes "ethical" action. In other words, obeying the organization's rules and norms generally is viewed as ethical except in instances where the organization violates its own rules and norms. In short, administrators, because they act as individuals as well as members of an organization, must consider their individual and professional roles in deciding how to act.

Acting ethically is, and remains, a vague, context-specific endeavor. Guidance is seldom available in all instances. Nonetheless, a well-educated, civic-minded public administrator who understands his or her roles and seeks to comprehend the values of the regime generally will acquire what Aristotle once labeled "practical wisdom."

Exercises and Discussion Questions

1. What makes public administration ethics such a difficult field to study? In your view, how can the study of ethics be improved?
2. How and why did the study of ethics change from the time of the ancient Greeks to the present? Do you believe the change generally has been positive? Why or why not?
3. Of the various aspects of ethics discussed in the chapters, which area of public administration do you find the most troubling? Explain.
4. Can ethics be taught? What are the benefits, if any, of teaching ethics? What are the drawbacks, if any?
5. If ethics can be taught, what is the most effective way of doing this? What kinds of subjects and approaches should be included?

Notes

[1] Terry L. Cooper, "Big Questions in Administrative Ethics: A Need for Focused, Collaborative Effort." *Public Administration Review* 64 (July/August 2004): 395-407.

[2] H. George Frederickson and Jeremy David Walling, "Research and Knowledge in Administrative Ethics," in *Handbook of Administrative Ethics*, 2d. ed., Terry L. Cooper, ed. (New York: Marcel Dekker), 37.

[3] Forrest McDonald, *Novus Ordo Seclorum: The Intellectual Origins of the Constitution* (Lawrence: The University Press of Kansas, 1985), 70.

[4] Aristotle, *The Nicomachean Ethics*, translated by David Ross (New York: Oxford University Press, 1980), 24-25; David E. Cooper, *World Philosophies: An Historical Introduction* (Cambridge, Mass.: Blackwell, 1996), 123; Mark T. Lilla, "Ethos, 'Ethics,' and Public Service," *The Public Interest* 63 (Spring 1981), 14; Alasdair MacIntyre, *After Virtue: A Study in Moral Theory* (London: Duckworth, 1982); Plato, *The Republic of Plato*, translated by Allan Bloom (New York: Basic Books, 1968), 184-92; James D. Wallace, *Virtues & Vices* (Ithaca, N.Y.: Cornell University Press, 1978), 10.

[5] Terry L. Cooper, *The Responsible Administrator: An Approach to Ethics for the Administrative Role*, 3d. ed. (San Francisco, Calif.: Jossey-Bass, 1990), 223-32; Niccolo Machiavelli, *The Prince*, translated and edited by Thomas G. Bergin (Arlington Heights, Ill.: AHM Publishing, 1947), 34.

[6] M. Shamsul Haque, "The Intellectual Crisis in Public Administration in the Current Epoch of Privatization," *Administration & Society* 27 (February 1996): 510-36; Zhiyong Lan and David H. Rosenbloom, "Public Administration in Transition?" *Public Administration Review* 52 (November/December 1992): 535-37; Rowan Miranda and Allan

Lerner, "Bureaucracy, Organizational Redundancy, and the Privatization of Services," *Public Administration Review* 55 (March/April 1995): 193-200; Vincent Ostrom, *The Intellectual Crisis in American Public Administration*, 2d. ed. (Tuscaloosa,, AL: The University of Alabama Press, 1989).

[7] Lawrence J. Biskowski, "Political Theory in the 1990s: Antifoundationalist Critics and Democratic Prospects," *Southeastern Political Review* 20 (Spring 1992), 62; Cooper, *World Philosophies*, 465-68.

[8] Michael E. Milakovich and George J. Gordon, *Public Administration in America* (Belmont, Calif.: Wadsworth/Thomson, 2004), 23-26; William D. Richardson, *Democracy, Bureaucracy, and Character: Founding Thought* (Lawrence: University Press of Kansas, 1997), 43-47.

[9] Woodrow Wilson, "The Study of Administration," *Political Science Quarterly* 56 (December 1941): 494 (originally published in *Political Science Quarterly* 2 [June 1887]: 209-17).

[10] Luther Gulick, "Science, Values, and Public Administration," in *Papers on the Science of Administration*, Luther Gulick and Lyndall Urwick, eds. (New York: Augustus M. Kelley, 1937), esp. 191-95; Wayne A. R. Leys, "Ethics and Administrative Discretion," *Public Administration Review* 3 (Winter 1943): 10-23.

[11] Donald F. Kettl, "The Perils—and Prospects—of Public Administration," *Public Administration Review* 50 (July/August 1990): 413; Douglas T. Yates, Jr., "Hard Choices: Justifying Bureaucratic Decisions," in *Public Duties: The Moral Obligations of Government Officials*, Joel L. Fleishmann, Lance Liebman, and Mark H. Moore, eds. (Cambridge, Mass.: Harvard University Press, 1981): 32-51.

[12] Harold Seidman, *Politics, Position, and Power* (New York and Oxford: Oxford University Press, 1970).

[13] Roger H. Davidson and Walter J. Oleszek, *Congress and Its Members*, 3d. ed. (Washington, D.C.: CQ Press, 1990), 258-66.

[14] Alfred C. Aman, Jr. and William T. Mayton, *Administrative Law* (St. Paul, Minn.: West Publishing Company, 1993), 15.

[15] David H. Rosenbloom, Public Administration: Understanding Management, Politics, and Law in the Public Sector, 3rd. ed. (New York: Random House, 1993), 54, 56.

[16] Melissa P. Collie, "The Legislature and Distributive Policy Making in Formal Perspective," *Legislative Studies Quarterly* 13 (November 1988): 427-58; Morris P. Fiorina, "Legislative Choice of Regulatory Reforms: Legal Process or Administrative Process?" *Public Choice* 39 (January 1982): 33-66; Matthew C. McCubbins, Roger G. Noll, and Barry R. Weingast, "Structure and Process, Politics and Policy: Administrative Arrangements and the Political Control of Agencies," *Virginia Law Review* 75 (March 1989): 431-82; Elizabeth Sanders, "The Contributions of Theodore Lowi to Political Analysis and Democratic Theory," *PS: Political Science & Politics* 23 (December 1990): 574-76.

[17] Frank Goodnow, *Politics and Administration* (New York: MacMillan, 1900); Frank Goodnow, *The Principles of the Administrative Law of the United States* (New York: G. P. Putnam's Sons, 1905); *Papers on the Science of Administration*, Luther Gulick and Lyndall Urwick, eds. (New York: Augustus M. Kelley, 1937); Leonard D. White, *Introduction to the Study of Public Administration* (New York: MacMillan, 1926).

[18] Richard W. Waterman and Kenneth J. Meier, "Principal-Agent Models: An Expansion?" *Journal of Public Administration Research and Theory* 8 (April 1998): 173-202.

[19] Charles Perrow, *Complex Organizations: A Critical Essay*, 3d. ed. (New York: Random House, 1986); Charles Perrow, "Economic Theories of Organization," *Theory and Society* 15 (January 1986): 11-45.

[20] See, for example, Gerald Benjamin, "Reform in New York: The Budget, the Legislature, and the Governance Process," *Albany Law Review* 67 (2004): 1021-69; Sidney A. Shapiro, "Symposium on the 50th Anniversary of the APA: A Delegation Theory of the APA," *The American University Administrative Law Journal 10* (Spring 1996): 89-109.

[21] Terry M. Moe, "The New Economics of Organization," *American Journal of Political Science* 28 (November 1984): 739-77.

[22] Herbert Kaufman, "Administrative Decentralization and Political Power," *Public Administration Review* 29 (January/February 1969): 3-15; Milakovich and Gordon, *Public Administration in America*, 293-94.

[23] Joseph White, "Making 'Common Sense' of Federal Budgeting," *Public Administration Review* 58 (March/April 1998): 101-8.

[24] Jeffrey L. Pressman and Aaron Wildavsky, *Implementation* (Berkeley: University of California Press, 1973).

[25] Stephen H. Linder and B. Guy Peters, "A Design Perspective on Policy Implementation: The Fallacies of Misplaced Perception," *Policy Studies Review* 6 (February 1987): 459-67; Daniel A. Mazmanian and Paul A. Sabatier, *Implementation and Public Policy* (Lanham, Md.: University Press of America, 1989).

[26] Benny Hjern, "Implementation Research—The Link Gone Missing," *Journal of Public Policy* 2 (August 1982): 301-08; Michael Lipsky, "Standing the Study of Public Policy Implementation on Its Head," in *American Politics and Public Policy*, Walter Dean Burnham and Martha Weinberg, eds. (Cambridge, Mass.: MIT Press, 1978), 391-402.

[27] Herman Finer, "Administrative Responsibility in Democratic Government," in *Combating Corruption/ Encouraging Ethics: A Sourcebook for Public Service Ethics*, edited by William L. Richter, Francis Burke, and Jameson W. Doig (Washington, D.C.: The American Society for Public Administration), 44; Carl J. Friedrich, "Public Policy and the Nature of Administrative Responsibility," in *Combating Corruption/ Encouraging Ethics: A Sourcebook for Public Service Ethics*, edited by William L. Richter, Francis Burke, and Jameson W. Doig (Washington, D.C.: The American Society for Public Administration), 43.

[28] Terry L. Cooper, The Responsible Administrator: An Approach to Ethics for the Administrative Role, 3d. ed. (San Francisco: Jossey-Bass, 1990), 128-32.

[29] See, for example, Paul H. Appleby, *Big Democracy* (New York: Alfred A. Knopf, 1945); Martha Derthick, "American Federalism: Madison's 'Middle Ground' in the 1980s," *Public Administration Review* 47 (January-February 1987): 66-74; William D. Richardson and Lloyd G. Nigro, "Administrative Ethics and Founding Thought: Constitutional Correctives, Honor, and Education," *Public Administration Review* 47 (September/October 1987), 367-76; Martinez, "Law Versus Ethics," 712-18; John A. Rohr, *Ethics for Bureaucrats: An Essay on Law and Values*, 2d. ed. (New York: Marcel Dekker, 1989), 285-91.

[30] See, for example, Vernon Greene, Sally Coleman Selden, and Gene Brewer, "Measuring Power and Presence: Bureaucratic Representation in the American State," *Journal of Public Administration Research and Theory* 11 (July 2001): 379-402; Kenneth J. Meier and John Bohte, "Structure and Discretion: Missing Links in Representative Bureaucracy," *Journal of Public Administration Research and Theory* 11 (October 2001): 455-70; Kenneth J. Meier and Lloyd G. Nigro, "Representative Bureaucracy and Policy Preferences: A Study in the Attitudes of Federal Executives," *Public Administration Review* 36 (July-August 1976): 458-69.

[31] Rohr, *Ethics for Bureaucrats: An Essay on Law and Values*, 2d. ed. (New York: Marcel Dekker, 1989).

Index